River Cafe Cook Book Green

River Cafe Cook Book Green Rose Gray and Ruth Rogers

Ebury Press London   Design the Senate   Photography Martin Gray

contents

by month

contents

by recipe

White truffle risotto 382

Celery and dried porcini risotto 393

Rosemary and borlotti bean risotto 414

Radicchio and bresaola risotto 448

Trevise and gorgonzola risotto 453

polenta

Fried polenta with cime di rapa 18

Polenta with sprouting broccoli and pancetta 105

Polenta with hot olive sauce 360

Polenta with borlotti beans and rocket 361

Cavolo nero polenta and sausages 427

frittatas

Frittata with wild leaves 123

Sorrel frittata 124

Spinach and prosciutto frittata 130

New potato and black truffle frittata 221

Trompettes de mort and chanterelle frittata 304

bruschettas

Broad beans braised in milk 198

Bruschetta of tomatoes and peppers 254

Zucchini and prosciutto bruschetta 270

Bruschetta of puffball and field mushrooms with tomato and thyme 326

Chanterelle and prosciutto bruschetta 306

Rosemary bruschetta 416

pizza

Pizza with artichokes and breadcrumbs 54

Pizza with rocket and goat's cheese 130

Spring onion and thyme pizza 193

Focaccia stuffed with gorgonzola and marjoram 282

Pizza with olives, radicchio and thyme 404

salads

Savoy cabbage and bresaola salad 42

Salad of bitter greens, lemon and capers 62

Cedro lemon and celery salad 68

Mint and lentil salad 113

Mixed wild leaf salad 122

Salad of potatoes, celery and bottarga 142

Asparagus and gulls' egg salad 170

Summer herb salad 238

Borlotti beans with langoustines and rocket 244

Baked aubergines with oregano 316

Figs, buffalo mozzarella and basil 332

Celery and puntarelle roman style 394

Pomegranate and pheasant salad 408

Jerusalem artichokes with barolo bagna cauda 444

vegetable dishes

Chickpeas, potatoes and anchovies 23

Braised porcini and spinach 28

Baked porcini and potatoes 30

Deep-fried artichokes and radicchio 58

Braised wild greens 64

Potatoes, leeks and anchovy gratin 144

Braised spring carrots and artichokes 188

Carrots marsala 189

Peas braised with spring onions 192

Grilled and marinated red and yellow tomatoes 260

Green beans stewed with yellow tomatoes [265]
Peppers stewed with red wine [288]
Braised swiss chard with chilli and garlic [300]
Swiss chard with lentils and herbs [301]
Braised potatoes and trompettes de mort [309]
Braised aubergines with potatoes [315]
Wood-roasted summer squash [338]
Braised summer squash [340]
Porcini baked over potatoes [374]
Porcini and bean stew [376]
Smashed celeriac and potatoes [431]
Braised radicchio and leeks [449]

puddings
Vanilla risotto ice-cream [46]
Vanilla and chocolate sorbet [48]
Vernazza cake [49]
Marmalade ice-cream [77]
Chocolate and ginger cake [118]
Almond biscotti [152]
Sweet ricotta [153]
Baked nespole [154]
Apricot, lemon and almond tart [160]
Apricot jam ice-cream [163]
Melon and lemon sorbet [182]
Melon marinated in valpolicella with vanilla [184]
Cherry focaccia [204]
Cherry sorbet [206]
Red wine sorbet with crushed strawberries [224]
Almond meringue with strawberries [226]
Peaches marinated in moscadello [250]

Peach ice-cream [251]
Raspberry and lemon sorbet [297]
Figs baked with crème fraîche [335]
Pear, honey and polenta cake [356]
Walnut and almond cake [421]
Hazelnut praline semifreddo [435]
Hazelnut meringue and chocolate cake [436]
Candied hazelnut and clementine cake [440]

jam
Marmalade [76]
Apricot jam [162]
Roasted raspberry jam [296]

drinks
Milanino [78]
Grappa with cherry juice [208]
Verbena tea [344]
Pomegranate campari [410]

sauces
Artichoke pesto [55]
Etruscan sauce [100]
Anchovy and milk [167]
Parmesan fonduta [173]
Green pesto [236]
Ricotta pesto [241]
Green chilli sauce [322]
Hot olive sauce [360]
Hazelnut sauce [434]
Bagna cauda [444]

Word spread. People started arriving at our door. A woman from our local allotment began to bring her surplus sorrel in the early spring. In April, a friend would pick stinging nettles by the bag-full from his farm in Hampshire. Other enthusiasts appeared with sea kale from the south coast beaches. Later in the year our builder exchanged the huge puffball mushrooms that grow near his house for bottles of Chianti Classico. When people realised we at the River Cafe were interested in fresh, unusual, wild produce they wanted to participate.

Our passion for vegetables and fruit in season has been at the heart of the River Cafe since we first opened in 1987. Every day, outside the kitchen, we pick from our organic garden many varieties of basil, marjoram and mint, and interesting leaves such as purslane, cicoria, and trevise to use in our recipes. And the simple pleasure of all this, of fresh, seasonal eating, is behind River Cafe Cook Book Green, our third cookbook.

Like the others, it is heavily influenced by our love of Italy, our many visits over many years, and our growing appreciation of the glorious variety of Italian food. All cooking starts in the market, the market reflects where you are, and the season around you. There is the joy in April when the first delicate broad beans arrive; that rich day in October when every stall is loaded with wild mushrooms gathered only that morning; the gentle sadness of biting into that last fresh cherry knowing that soon the brief season is over.

Over the years we have worked with our suppliers from New Covent Garden, encouraging them to bring Italian market produce to London. Now lorries arrive laden with trevise from Verona, artichokes from Rome, borlotti beans from Puglia. These wonderful vegetables are slowly spreading throughout Britain and more and more greengrocers and supermarkets are selling them. If you have a garden you should experiment with growing your own. If not, try farmers' markets, pick-your-own farms and organic box schemes. But above all develop a relationship with your greengrocer, urging him to supply interesting varieties.

We thought the moment was ripe for a book of this kind, in which we have divided the year not simply into seasons but into months. We wanted to show how specific vegetables are used in specific months for specific recipes – romanesco artichokes for deep-frying whole, the violettas for slicing finely to be eaten raw in salads; how to choose different varieties of tomatoes – cherry vines for fresh pasta sauces, plums for slow-cooked ones and the huge yellow tomatoes for rubbing on to bruschetta. There are recipes using wild ingredients, stinging nettles, sorrel and thistles – for flavouring pastas or simply combining to make a delicious insalata di campo.

Our cooking has become increasingly focused on the garden and its produce. In the summer we make fresh pasta with olives and tomatoes and a risotto of summer squash; in October when the chestnuts appear we put them in soup with celeriac; in the winter we eat salads of puntarelle with anchovies and vin santo, and for Christmas we make a cake with crystallised clementines; in the spring we make a raw artichoke pesto to go with homemade tagliarini.

These are not complicated recipes, and our message is simple too: good cooking is about fresh seasonal ingredients, organic whenever possible, used thoughtfully. It is something the Italians have always known and we hope that with this book you will share our pleasure in rediscovering this simple truth.

Rose Gray and Ruth Rogers London 2000

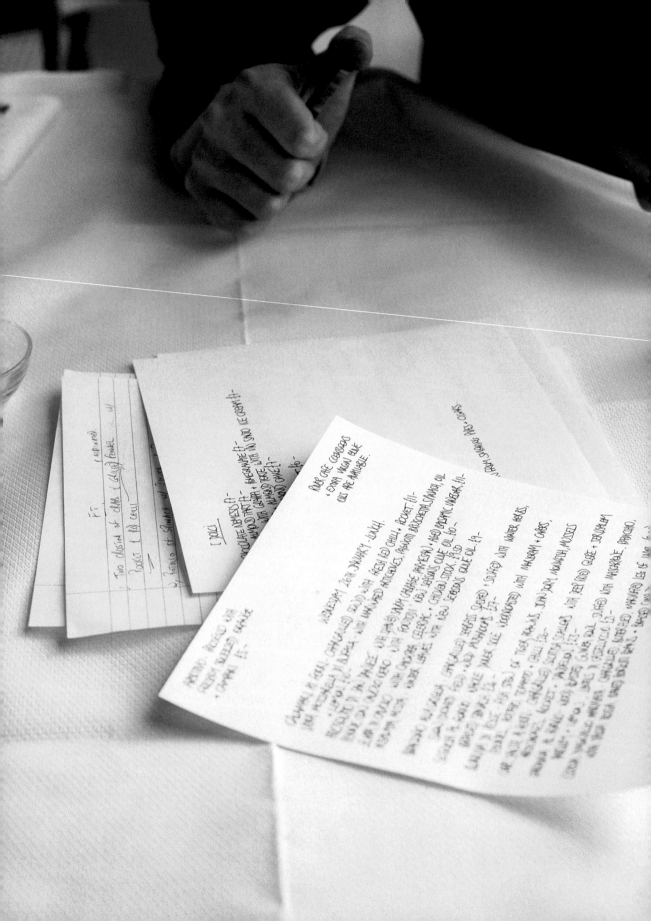

january

cime di rapa [14] *pasta* penne with cime di rapa and pancetta. ravioli with cime di rapa and ricotta. *polenta* fried polenta with cime di rapa. **chickpeas** [20] *antipasto* deep-fried chickpea slices. *vegetable* chickpeas, potatoes and anchovies. *antipasto* chickpea pancake with rosemary. **dried porcini mushrooms** [26] *antipasto* braised porcini and spinach. *risotto* porcini and tomato risotto. *vegetable* baked porcini and potatoes. *soup* porcini and clam soup. **parsley** [34] *pasta* spaghetti with parsley, pancetta and parmesan. *antipasto* parsley, squid and cannellini bean stew. **savoy cabbage** [38] *soup* savoy cabbage soup with anchovy and ricotta crostini. *salad* savoy cabbage and bresaola salad. *risotto* savoy cabbage, pancetta and fontina risotto. **vanilla** [44] *pudding* vanilla risotto ice-cream. vanilla and chocolate sorbet. vernazza cake.

cime di rapa

Cime di rapa, broccoletti di rapa and rapini are the Italian names for this delicious green winter vegetable, part of the turnip and cabbage, or Brassica, family. It is grown for its greens, which form like sprouting broccoli. It tastes bitter and peppery, a little like turnip. Cime di rapa should be picked before the shoots have started to flower, and when the leaves are still green and tender.

Even in Italy this vegetable was only found in particular regions ten years ago. Now it is found in shops and markets all over the country. In Britain it is still hardly known, and is only available in a few speciality vegetable shops. We are starting to grow it on a small scale from Italian seed, and hope that in a few years it will become established as the market widens.

Look for bright green, tender leaves on crisp strong stalks, with tightly closed flower heads. Discard the tough or blemished outer leaves and cut the younger leaves and flower stems from the main stalk.

The leaves of cime are fine and cook very quickly, like spinach. Drain them well and season with extra virgin olive oil, salt and pepper. In Rome, plates of cime di rapa cooked in this simple way are always part of antipasti di verdura.

penne with cime di rapa and pancetta
penne con cime di rapa e pancetta

for 6
2 kg cime di rapa
400 g penne rigate
150 g pancetta, finely sliced, then cut into
    matchsticks
3 tablespoons olive oil
3 garlic cloves, peeled and finely chopped
1 x 800 g tin peeled plum tomatoes
Maldon salt and freshly ground black pepper
zest of 1 washed lemon
2 tablespoons chopped fresh flat-leaf parsley
extra virgin olive oil
150 g Pecorino staginata cheese, freshly grated

Heat the olive oil in a thick-bottomed frying pan and fry the garlic with the pancetta until lightly browned. Add the tomatoes, half their juices and a little salt, and cook over a moderate heat, stirring to prevent sticking, for 20-30 minutes.

Prepare the cime by discarding the tough stalks and outer leaves. Keep the budding flower shoots and the smaller tender leaves. Wash well and roughly chop. Cook the cime in a large saucepan of boiling salted water for 5 minutes, then drain well. Put in a bowl, add the lemon zest, parsley and plenty of extra virgin olive oil. Season with salt and pepper.

Separately bring a large saucepan of salted water to the boil, and cook the penne for the stated time, usually about 8 minutes. Drain and mix into the tomato sauce. Test for seasoning. Toss around to allow the penne to be coated, then stir in the cime. Serve with the freshly grated Pecorino.

ravioli with cime di rapa and ricotta
ravioli di cime di rapa e ricotta

for 6
1.5 kg cime di rapa
Ligurian Basic Pasta (see page 454)
Maldon salt and freshly ground black pepper
3 tablespoons olive oil
2 garlic cloves, peeled and finely chopped
1 dried red chilli, crumbled
250 g buffalo ricotta
150 g Pecorino staginata cheese, freshly grated
plain flour for dusting
extra virgin olive oil

For the filling, remove the tough stalks and outer tough leaves from the cime. Bring a large saucepan of salted water to the boil, and cook the cime for 5-8 minutes. It should be tender but still bright green. Drain, cool and chop quite finely. Heat the olive oil in a thick-bottomed saucepan, and soften the garlic. Add the chilli, cime, salt and pepper, stir briefly to combine the flavours, then remove from the heat and cool.

Beat the ricotta lightly with a fork, and season. Mix in the cime and 3 tablespoons grated Pecorino. Cover and place in the fridge.

Dust your work surface with flour. Roll the pasta dough in the machine as outlined on page 454. Make long thin strips the width of your pasta machine, then cut into manageable lengths. Place half dessertspoons of filling at 7 cm intervals down the middle of each strip. Fold the pasta over the filling and gently press around each mound to seal the pasta. Cut into ravioli of about 4 cm square, using a serrated pasta cutter that seals as it cuts. Place the ravioli on to floured trays until ready for cooking.

Bring a large saucepan of salted water to the boil. Cook the ravioli, uncovered, in batches. They will take about 5 minutes. Drain well, and serve with freshly grated Pecorino and a drizzle of extra virgin olive oil.

fried polenta with cime di rapa
polenta fritta con cime di rapa

for 6
1.5 kg cime di rapa, washed, tough leaves and
    stalks removed
4 tablespoons olive oil
3 garlic cloves, peeled and sliced
2 dried red chillies, crumbled
Maldon salt and freshly ground black pepper
anchovy and polenta fritters
450 g Polenta (see page 360), made without
    butter and Parmesan
10 g (1 sachet) granular dried yeast, dissolved in
    80 ml warm milk
300 g plain flour, plus extra for dusting
sunflower oil for deep-frying
12 salted anchovies, prepared (see page 458)

Pull away any skin from the top of the polenta and discard. Mash the polenta in a bowl, then add the yeast and milk. Sieve in the flour and mix together to form a soft dough. Cover and leave in a warm place to rise for 1 hour.

Heat the olive oil in a thick-bottomed saucepan, add the garlic and fry until beginning to brown. Add the chilli and washed cime, season generously with salt and pepper, cover and cook until tender, about 8-10 minutes.

Preheat the sunflower oil to 180°C/350°F.

Scoop up tablespoon-sized pieces of the dough, and push an anchovy fillet into the centre of each. Roll around in plain flour to form golfballs. Place in the preheated oil and deep-fry, turning to allow the balls to brown on all sides. Serve the cime with the polenta fritters.

chickpeas

Chickpeas are one of the most important pulses in the world. They grow in southern Italy, or anywhere without frost. An ancient pulse that originated in the Near East, the chickpea is easy to grow, high in protein, and has become part of the 'cibo di povero' of many countries.

Chickpeas are harvested in the late summer and dried for use from autumn through to spring. The best chickpeas to buy are always the new season's. In Italy, they sell two or three different sizes of chickpea. We choose the largest, to cook whole, to include in soups or to eat on their own with extra virgin olive oil and fresh chilli. The smaller chickpeas are ground into flour and used to make Farinata and Panisse, the Ligurian street food specialities.

Soak chickpeas for 48 hours before cooking. Add a large peeled potato, a whole tomato, a couple of fresh chillies, some garlic cloves and a green celery stalk to the cooking water. Never add salt. The starch from the potato will help soften the skins of the chickpeas as they cook. New season's will take up to 1 1/2 hours; older chickpeas can take up to 4 hours, and may not be worth it even then! If the skins seem to be tough, allow the chickpeas to cool in their cooking liquid, then rub them within the palms of your hand. The skins should flake off and float. Skim and discard. Only add salt after cooking. Keep in their cooking liquid when storing.

Tinned chickpeas are usually good, but we always rinse off the liquid before use.

deep-fried chickpea slices
panisse

Serve these fried chickpea slices from Liguria with drinks or as part of an antipasti.

for 6-8
300 g new season chickpea flour
1 litre warm water
Maldon salt
sunflower oil for deep-frying

Sieve the chickpea flour into a large bowl and slowly pour in the warm water, whisking all the time to make sure that no lumps form. Add 1 tablespoon salt.

Pour into a medium, thick-bottomed saucepan, and heat, stirring, until the mixture comes to the boil. Reduce the heat and continue to cook, stirring as much as you can, as it will become very thick. Cook for 40-50 minutes or until the mixture comes away from the sides of the pan, just like polenta. Spoon on to a flat plate, to a thickness of about 1-2 cm, and leave to cool and set firm.

Preheat the oil to 190°C/375°F. Cut the panisse into finger-like slices and deep-fry in the hot oil until golden. Drain on kitchen paper and serve sprinkled with salt.

chickpeas, potatoes and anchovies
ceci e patate con acciughe

for 6
200 g dried chickpeas, soaked for 48 hours
500 g medium potatoes (Roseval), peeled
2 large fresh red chillies, kept whole
10 garlic cloves, peeled and kept whole
1 whole head celery, with leaves
3 tomatoes
Maldon salt and freshly ground black pepper
8 salted anchovies, prepared (see page 458)
1 branch of fresh rosemary
juice of 2 lemons
extra virgin olive oil

Wash the chickpeas, put them into a large saucepan, cover with cold water and bring to the boil, skimming the surface. Add 2 potatoes to the pot, the chillies, garlic, 3 green outside celery stalks, and the tomatoes. Turn the heat down and simmer gently for 1½-2 hours or until the chickpeas are soft. Make sure they are covered with water at all times. Remove the tough celery stalks. Remove and discard the skin from the chillies and tomatoes, and return the flesh and seeds to the pot.

Cut the remaining potatoes into quarters. Put in a separate saucepan with the celery heart, cut into quarters, and half the chickpeas. Pour in the chickpea liquor, add salt and bring to the boil. Lower the heat and simmer gently until the potatoes are cooked. Roughly mash the potato and chickpeas together in the pan, allowing them to take up the liquid, so that the dish becomes thick and soupy in consistency. Add to this the whole chickpeas, and stir to combine. Test for seasoning.

Chop the anchovies finely, and put in a small bowl. Strip the rosemary leaves from the stalks and chop finely – you need about 2 tablespoons. Immediately stir the rosemary into the anchovies, with enough lemon juice to liquefy. Then slowly stir in enough extra virgin olive oil to make a thick sauce. Season with pepper. Pour over the chickpeas.

chickpea pancake with rosemary
farinata al rosmarino

The standard Ligurian farinata pans are thick, round, flat copper pans, lined with zinc. They are roughly 40 cm in diameter. You can use a thick-bottomed, stainless-steel frying pan, but it must have an ovenproof handle. If using a frying pan, you can make the farinata in batches.

for 6
300 g chickpea flour
1 litre tepid water
1 teaspoon freshly ground black pepper
1 tablespoon Maldon salt
extra virgin olive oil
2 sprigs fresh rosemary, leaves picked from the
   stalks

Put the water into a large bowl. Gently pour in the chickpea flour, whisking to avoid lumps. Add the pepper and salt, stir, and allow to sit in a warm place for at least 2 hours.

Preheat the oven to 230°C/450°F/Gas 8.

Remove the foam from the top of the batter and stir in 110 ml olive oil. Pour a further tablespoon of oil into the farinata pan, or frying pan, and put into the oven until the oil is just smoking. Quickly remove and pour in the chickpea batter. The farinata should be very thin – no more than 1 cm deep. Sprinkle the rosemary leaves over the top, and return to the oven. Bake for about 10 minutes until the top is brown and crisp and the middle is still soft.

dried porcini mushrooms

Porcini mushrooms dry very effectively, and in their dried form are very important in the Italian larder. They are used throughout the year, not as a substitute for the fresh mushroom, but as a separate valid ingredient in recipes as a seasoning. Dried porcini have a more intense flavour than fresh, and a little goes a long way.

The quality of dried porcini depends on the state of the fresh porcini when picked. Large firm mushrooms with their caps still partially enclosing the stem are best. Sliced finely through the cap and stem, the pieces are laid out, often on newspaper, to dry in the sun. Dehydration concentrates the earthy fragrance.

Dried porcini are usually sold in transparent packets: look for pale cream-coloured stems and light brown caps. Thickly sliced, darker coloured porcini are oven-dried, which seems to affect the flavour. These are usually much cheaper, but not really worth it. If you cannot distinguish the shape of the slice, and there are lots of small pieces and crumbs, they may not be porcini.

Ideally, buy your dried porcini when you are in Italy. Many shops sell them loose, they are cheaper, and you will have a selection.

braised porcini and spinach
porcini brasati con spinaci

for 6
50 g dried porcini, soaked in 200 ml hot water for
   20 minutes
1.5 kg spinach, washed
Maldon salt and freshly ground black pepper
olive oil
3 garlic cloves, peeled and finely sliced
2 dried red chillies, crumbled
500 g large flat field mushrooms, peeled and
   sliced 1 cm thick
juice of 1 lemon
extra virgin olive oil

Drain the porcini, keeping the liquid. Strain this through a fine sieve.
Rinse the porcini under running cold water to get rid of any remaining
grit, and roughly chop.

Bring a large saucepan of salted water to the boil, add the spinach and
cook for 3 minutes. Drain.

Heat 4 tablespoons of olive oil in a large, thick-bottomed frying pan. Add
the garlic and just let it soften, then add the porcini and dried chilli.
Gently fry for 10 minutes, adding a couple of spoons of the porcini liquid
to keep the porcini moist. When the porcini have become soft, let the
liquid evaporate, leaving just the oil, then add the mushroom slices. Fry
them with the porcini for 5 minutes; they will become very dark. Add a
little more liquid to the pan, just to moisten the mushrooms. Season
generously with salt and pepper, turn down the heat and simmer until
the mushrooms are cooked.

Stir in the spinach and adjust the seasoning. Serve with a little lemon
juice and extra virgin olive oil.

porcini and tomato risotto
risotto ai porcini e pomodoro

for 6

100 g dried porcini, soaked in 250 ml hot water for
    20 minutes
600 g tinned peeled plum tomatoes, drained
1.2 litres chicken stock (see page 455)
Maldon salt and freshly ground black pepper
100 g butter
3 tablespoons olive oil
2 small red onions, peeled and finely chopped
inner white heart of 1 head celery, finely chopped
3 garlic cloves, peeled and chopped
2 dried red chillies, crumbled
300 g carnaroli rice
2 tablespoons chopped fresh flat-leaf parsley
freshly grated Parmesan

Drain the porcini, keeping the liquid. Strain this through a fine sieve.
Rinse the porcini under running cold water to get rid of any grit, dry well,
and roughly chop. Heat the stock and check the seasoning.

Heat half the butter and the olive oil in a large thick-bottomed saucepan.
Gently fry the onion and celery until soft and beginning to colour. Add
the porcini pieces, garlic and chilli, and continue to fry to combine and
soften for 5-6 minutes. Stir in the rice and push around to coat each
grain with the vegetables. When the rice becomes opaque, add the
tomatoes and 2 teaspoons salt. Stir and cook for a few minutes to allow
the liquid to evaporate. Turn the heat down, and start adding the stock
ladle by ladle, interspersed with the porcini liquid, not adding the next
ladleful until the last has been absorbed by the rice. Stir constantly, and
continue to cook until the rice is al dente, about 15 minutes. This risotto
is very dark in colour and intensely flavoured.

Stir in the parsley, the remainder of the butter, and a handful of
Parmesan. Serve with more Parmesan.

baked porcini and potatoes
patate e porcini al forno

for 6
150 g dried porcini, soaked (see below)
1.5 kg Roseval or similar waxy yellow potatoes,
    peeled
1 tablespoon olive oil
150 g unsalted butter
6 garlic cloves, peeled and sliced
Maldon salt and freshly ground black pepper
1 bunch of fresh thyme, leaves picked from their
    stalks and washed

Preheat the oven to 200°C/400°F/Gas 6.

Cut the potatoes in half lengthways, wash and pat dry. Soak the porcini in 1 litre boiled water for 20 minutes then strain, retaining the soaking water. Strain this through a fine sieve. Rinse the porcini under running cold water to get rid of any remaining grit. Dry well.

In a thick-bottomed saucepan, heat the olive oil with the butter. When the butter begins to foam, add the garlic and soften for a minute or two before adding the porcini. Cook, stirring to prevent sticking, for a few minutes before adding the porcini liquor. There will be a lot of liquor, which needs to reduce and thicken for about 7-8 minutes.

Now add the potatoes. Coat them in the juices then gently stir and cook for around 15-20 minutes. The potatoes should begin to take on the colour of the porcini juices.

Remove from the pan and tip into roasting trays. Season with salt and pepper and the fresh thyme, and bake in the preheated oven for 30 minutes.

porcini and clam soup
zuppa di porcini e vongole

for 6
80 g dried porcini, soaked in 225 ml hot water for 20
    minutes
2.5 kg vongole (small clams), washed
6 tablespoons olive oil
6 garlic cloves, peeled, 5 of them chopped
1 tablespoon dried oregano
2 small dried red chillies, crumbled
600 g tinned peeled plum tomatoes
Maldon salt and freshly ground black pepper
250 ml white wine
6 slices sourdough bread, 1 cm thick
3 tablespoons chopped fresh flat-leaf parsley
extra virgin olive oil
2 lemons, cut into wedges

Prepare the porcini as on page 30 and roughly chop. Heat half the olive oil in a thick-bottomed saucepan, fry the porcini for a few minutes, then add half the chopped garlic, the oregano and chilli. Fry to combine and cook the garlic. Stir in the tomatoes with half their juices, breaking them up. Add salt and cook for 20 minutes to reduce to a thickish sauce. Season with pepper.

In a separate large saucepan with a lid heat the remaining olive oil, add the remaining chopped garlic and let it colour for a minute, then add the vongole and the wine. Cover and cook, shaking the pan to open the vongole, about 3-5 minutes. You may have to do this in batches. Drain the liquid from the vongole and pass through a fine sieve. Allow the vongole to cool, then remove two-thirds of them from their shells. Add the vongole liquid to the tomato sauce. Stir to combine and keep hot.

Toast the bread on both sides. Rub one side with the remaining whole garlic, and place in the bowls. Add the vongole, shelled and unshelled, to the soup. Test for seasoning. Bring to simmering point, remove and stir in the parsley. Ladle over the bruschetta, drizzle with extra virgin oil and serve with lemon.

parsley

Flat-leaf parsley is the variety mainly cultivated in Italy. The herb originated in Greece and is used in cooking all over the Mediterranean. This parsley is stronger and sweeter than the curly-leaf variety. It is easy to grow in pots or in the garden, and is available most of the year. It tends to become a bit too tough in midsummer when the flower heads form.

We use lots of parsley every day, picking the leaves from the stalks before chopping, and discarding any yellowing leaves. The stalks we use to flavour chicken and fish stocks. A mezzaluna is the best utensil for chopping parsley as you can easily control the texture – not too fine, not too coarse.

Chopped parsley is the essential ingredient for salsa verde. Gremolata, an Italian flavouring added to soups and stews, is primarily chopped parsley combined with grated lemon peel and chopped garlic. Parsley is often part of the soffritto when making soups and sauces.

A handful of parsley in a bowl of water will prevent prepared artichokes from blackening. The young leaves from the tips of the stems are delicious in salads.

spaghetti with parsley, pancetta and parmesan

spaghetti con prezzemolo, pancetta e parmigiano

for 6
8 tablespoons finely chopped fresh flat-leaf
   parsley
3 medium red onions, peeled and finely chopped
200 g pancetta, finely sliced, then cut into 5 mm
   pieces, plus 6 thin slices
400 g spaghetti
150 g butter
2 garlic cloves, peeled and finely chopped
Maldon salt and freshly ground black pepper
1 dried red chilli, crumbled
olive oil
120 g Parmesan, freshly grated

Gently heat the butter in a thick-bottomed saucepan. Add the onion and cook steadily for 15-20 minutes, then add the chopped pancetta and garlic. Turn the heat down, stir and continue to cook to blend the flavours for a further 10 minutes. Season generously with salt, pepper and dried chilli. The mixture should become quite dark. Add the parsley and stir.

Heat a small frying pan, brush with oil, and fry the slices of pancetta to crisp them. Drain.

Cook the spaghetti in a large saucepan of boiling salted water until al dente. Drain, keeping back 2-3 tablespoons of cooking water. Mix the spaghetti into the warm parsley mixture, and toss together, adding a little pasta water to help the sauce coat the spaghetti. Serve with plenty of grated Parmesan and a slice of pancetta on each portion.

parsley, squid and cannellini bean stew

stufato di prezzemolo, calamari e cannellini

for 6

5 tablespoons chopped fresh flat-leaf parsley
150 g dried cannellini beans, cooked (see page
    376), or 2 x 400 g tins, drained and rinsed
1.5 kg squid, the smallest you can find
olive oil and extra virgin olive oil
3 garlic cloves, peeled and finely chopped
600 g tinned peeled plum tomatoes, drained of
    half their juices
Maldon salt and freshly ground black pepper
2 dried red chillies, crumbled
1 teaspoon fennel seeds, crushed
80 ml white wine
3 large fresh red chillies, seeded and chopped,
    marinated in extra virgin olive oil
2 lemons

Clean the squid. Remove the beak from the tentacles, and the soft blade
from inside the body. If the squid are very small, keep the bodies and
legs whole. If they are larger than plums, slice each body into two or
three, and the tentacles in half. Heat 3 tablespoons of olive oil, and add
half the garlic. Allow it to colour, then add the tomatoes and 2 teaspoons
salt. Reduce over a moderate heat for 30 minutes until you have a thick
sauce. Stir occasionally.

Heat the beans in their liquor. Heat 2 tablespoons olive oil in a large,
thick-bottomed frying pan, and add the remaining garlic, dried chilli and
fennel seeds. Cook until the garlic begins to brown, then add the squid,
salt and pepper. Fry to colour the squid, then add half the parsley, the
wine and the tomato sauce. Finally add the hot beans and the remainder
of the parsley. Test for seasoning. Serve with the fresh chilli and extra
virgin olive oil drizzled over, and a segment of lemon.

savoy cabbage

Savoy cabbage is harvested after the first frosts. It is very hardy, with a delicious nutty flavour and is a favourite of the Milanese. The large outer, bright blue-green, crinkled leaves have a mild flavour and strong texture when cooked. The inner paler leaves taste more strongly of cabbage, delicious when eaten raw. In restaurants around Modena, Savoy cabbage is often served shaved very finely, seasoned with balsamic vinegar and extra virgin olive oil, and mixed with shavings of Parmesan cheese.

To prepare, discard any damaged outer leaves. The dark green leaves should snap off easily, a sign of freshness. Cut away the thick centre spine and wash thoroughly in cold water. Keep the pale centre of the cabbage whole, and slice or shave according to the recipe.

Cook the leaves in boiling salted water for a few minutes until al dente. Do not refresh in cold water as the leaves will absorb the water, become soggy and lose their texture.

savoy cabbage soup with anchovy and ricotta crostini

zuppa di verza con crostini alla acciughe e ricotta

for 6
1 firm fresh Savoy cabbage, about 1 kg in weight
2 tablespoons olive oil
2 garlic cloves, peeled and finely chopped
1 tablespoon chopped fresh flat-leaf parsley
200 g tinned peeled plum tomatoes, drained of
   their juices
Maldon salt and freshly ground black pepper
1 litre chicken stock (see page 455)
to serve
6 slices ciabatta bread
Anchovy and Milk Sauce (see page 167)
1 x 250 g pack of buffalo ricotta, sliced
extra virgin olive oil

Remove any tough or damaged outer leaves from the cabbage and discard. Cut the cabbage in half and remove the core. Cut into fine slices.

In a thick-bottomed saucepan, heat the oil, add the garlic and parsley, and cook until soft. Add the tomatoes and stir, breaking them up with the spoon. Season with salt and pepper, and cook for 5 minutes. Add the cabbage, stir to combine, then cook for a further 5 minutes. Add the chicken stock and bring to the boil. Lower the heat to a simmer and cook until the cabbage is completely tender, about 20 minutes. Test for seasoning.

Grill the ciabatta slices, and place one in each soup bowl. Spread with a thin layer of anchovy sauce, then place a slice of ricotta on top. Spoon the cabbage and broth over, and finish with a drizzle of extra virgin olive oil.

savoy cabbage and bresaola salad
insalata di verza e bresaola

for 6
1 firm fresh Savoy cabbage, about 1 kg in weight
500 g bresaola, finely sliced
Maldon salt and freshly ground black pepper
3 tablespoons aged balsamic vinegar
extra virgin olive oil
juice of 1 lemon
200 g Parmesan, for shaving

Remove the outer leaves of the cabbage. Cut the firm pale heart of the cabbage in half. Using a wide-bladed knife, shave the cabbage as finely as you can. Place in a bowl and season with salt and pepper. Shake over the balsamic vinegar and drizzle with extra virgin olive oil.

The proportion of bresaola to Savoy cabbage should be almost equal. Cut the bresaola slices into 1 cm shreds and toss into the cabbage. Squeeze over the lemon juice. Shave the Parmesan into similar width pieces, and mix with the salad.

savoy cabbage, pancetta and fontina risotto
risotto alla verza, pancetta e fontina

for 6

1 small Savoy cabbage, about 600 g in weight
150 g pancetta, finely sliced and cut into 2 cm
    pieces
150 g Fontina cheese, cut into 2 cm cubes
1.5 litres chicken stock (see page 455)
Maldon salt and freshly ground black pepper
100 g butter
1 large red onion, peeled and chopped
inner white heart of 1 head celery, chopped
2 garlic cloves, peeled and chopped
1 teaspoon fennel seeds, lightly ground
300 g carnaroli rice
100 g Parmesan, freshly grated

Wash the cabbage and remove the thick stalks. Cut the cabbage into very fine shreds. Heat the stock and check for seasoning.

Melt the butter in a large, thick-bottomed pan, add the onion and celery, and cook slowly to soften for 10 minutes. Add the pancetta, garlic and fennel seeds, and cook for a further 5 minutes or until the pancetta starts to brown. Stir in 3 tablespoons of the shredded cabbage and let it cook into the buttery vegetables for a few minutes. Add the rice, stir to coat with the vegetables, then when it becomes opaque, start to add the hot stock, ladle by ladle, only adding the next when the rice has absorbed the last. Continue to cook until the rice becomes al dente, about 15-20 minutes. Meanwhile, cook the remaining cabbage in a large saucepan of boiling salted water for 3-5 minutes until tender. Drain well.

Finally, stir the Fontina cheese cubes into the risotto, just allowing them to melt. Add the cooked cabbage, and stir to combine. Serve with the freshly grated Parmesan.

vanilla

Vanilla comes from a climbing plant, native to the tropics, which is a member of the orchid family. Vanilla pods, which can be up to 30 cm in length, are gathered before completely ripe; they are not perfumed at this stage. The pods are plunged into boiling water, then packed, still damp, into airtight containers, where they develop their extraordinary pungent sweet aroma.

The best vanilla pods are those that have a smooth black skin and a white surface bloom. The latter consists of vanilla crystals, which are strongly aromatic. Keep vanilla pods in an airtight tin. Pods kept in caster sugar in a sealed jar will make a mild-flavoured vanilla sugar. Chop whole pods with caster sugar in the food processor to make a more intensely flavoured sugar.

We like to use whole vanilla pods split open when baking apricots, peaches and plums. When flavouring cream and milk for ice-creams, split open the pods, scrape out all the vanilla seeds into the mixture, and add the pods as well.

vanilla risotto ice-cream
gelato al riso e vaniglia

for 6-8
ice-cream
4 fresh vanilla pods
400 ml milk
1 litre double cream
9 large, organic free-range egg yolks
175 g caster sugar
risotto
3 fresh vanilla pods
2 litres milk
500 g vialone nano rice
100 g vanilla sugar (see page 48)
1/2 nutmeg, freshly grated
grated rind of 2 washed organic lemons

For the 'risotto', heat the milk in a large saucepan. Scrape the vanilla seeds from the pods, and add to the milk with the pods. Bring to the boil, then add the rice, sugar, nutmeg and lemon rind. Lower the heat and simmer, stirring frequently, until the rice is very soft and the milk absorbed, about 45 minutes. Remove the pods, pour the mixture into a bowl, and cool.

For the vanilla ice-cream, scrape the vanilla seeds out into a mixture of milk and double cream in a thick-bottomed saucepan. Add the pods as well, and gently heat until just below boiling point. Meanwhile, beat the egg yolks and sugar together until pale and thick. Add the hot milk and cream mixture to the egg yolks very slowly, stirring. Return to the pan and cook, stirring constantly, over a very low heat until the custard thickens. When just below boiling point, pour into a bowl and cool.

Place half the rice mixture into the food processor and pulse-chop to a coarse purée. Combine this and the remaining rice with the custard. Put in an ice-cream machine and churn until frozen, or freeze in a suitable container in the usual way.

vanilla and chocolate sorbet
sorbetto alla vaniglia e cioccolato

for 6
2 fresh vanilla pods
250 g caster sugar
750 ml water
150 g cocoa powder
100 ml Amaretto (an apricot and almond liqueur)
2 teaspoons vanilla essence

To make vanilla sugar, cut the vanilla pods into 2 cm lengths, place in a food processor, and process to a fine powder. Mix with the sugar.

Gently dissolve the vanilla sugar in the water over a medium heat. Very slowly bring to the boil, then add the cocoa powder, stirring all the time. Turn the heat down and gently simmer for 25 minutes, or until the cocoa has completely dissolved and become smooth. Cool, and then stir in the Amaretto and vanilla essence.

Put the mixture into an ice-cream machine and churn until frozen. Alternatively, freeze in flat freezer trays, stirring every now and again to break up the crystals.

vernazza cake
torta di vernazza

This is delicious with a cappuccino or a glass of Vin Santo. It comes from Trattoria Franzi in Vernazza, Liguria.

for 6
3 vanilla pods, seeds scraped out
250 g unsalted butter, softened, plus extra for the
　　tin
200 g plain flour, plus extra for the tin
225 g caster sugar
4 large, organic free-range eggs, at room
　　temperature
1 large, organic free-range egg yolk, at room
　　temperature
1 tablespoon potato flour
1 tablespoon polenta

Preheat the oven to 180°C/350°F/Gas 4. Line the base of a 500 g loaf tin with parchment paper. Butter and flour this generously.

Cream the butter in an electric mixer, then add the sugar and beat for 5 minutes. The mixture should be very light. With the mixer on its slowest speeds, add the whole eggs, one at a time, making sure each egg is mixed in before adding the next. Mix the vanilla seeds with the egg yolk, and whisk in.

Sift together the plain flour and potato flour, and fold into the mixture. Fold in the polenta. Pour the batter into the prepared tin and bake in the preheated oven for an hour, or until a skewer inserted in the middle comes out clean. Cool on a wire rack.

february

globe artichokes [52] *pizza* pizza with artichokes and breadcrumbs. *pasta* spaghetti with artichoke pesto. *antipasto* artichokes with salt cod. *vegetable* deep-fried artichokes and radicchio.

chicories [60] *salad* salad of bitter greens, lemon and capers.

vegetable braised wild greens. *soup* chicory and canellini bean soup.

citrus [66] *salad* cedro lemon and celery salad. *pasta* tagliatelle with lemon cream and parsley. tortelloni with ricotta, lemon and pine kernels.

jam marmalade. *pudding* marmalade ice-cream. *drink* milanino.

leeks [80] *risotto* leek, clam and prawn risotto. *pasta* leek and porcini pappardelle. **bay leaves** [86] *pasta* bay and red mullet tagliarini.

globe artichokes

Globe artichokes are one of the most traditional vegetables in Italian cooking, and have been grown in Italian vegetable gardens since the Renaissance. Particular varieties reflect their regions, as do the recipes – Carciofi Spinosi from Sicily, Romanesco from Rome and Violetta di Chioggia from the north. The season stretches from December through to early summer. In Italy the large and smaller heads are harvested together, then separated by size for use in different recipes.

When choosing globe artichokes, the stalks should be stiff and snap when broken, and the buds should be tightly closed, indicating that they will not have developed chokes.

In Italian markets, you can find artichokes pared down to their hearts, stored in water acidulated with parsley stalks and leaves to prevent them from browning, an alternative to lemon juice.

Violetta di Chioggia, the purple-leafed variety with yellowish hearts, are easy to peel, and are the best to use in the recipe for pesto on page 55.

pizza with artichokes and breadcrumbs
pizza con carciofi e pangrattato

for 6, making 3 pizzas
3 x Pizza Dough Bases (see page 454), 30 cm in
  diameter
topping
12 young, small artichokes, prepared (see page 101)
a handful of parsley stalks
1 ciabatta loaf, made into coarse breadcrumbs
120 ml extra virgin olive oil
4 garlic cloves, peeled and finely chopped
Maldon salt and freshly ground black pepper
2 small dried red chillies, crushed
3 tablespoons fresh thyme leaves

Preheat the oven to 230°C/450°F/Gas 8 for 30 minutes, with a pizza stone if you have one. Prepare the pizza dough bases.

Cut the artichokes lengthways into thin slices and, as you complete each one, drop into a bowl of water acidulated with the parsley stalks. Set aside until needed, then drain well.

Place the breadcrumbs on an oven tray and bake until golden, shaking occasionally, for about 5 minutes, and then set aside.

In a large, thick-bottomed frying pan, heat 100 ml of the oil and add the garlic. When the garlic begins to colour, add the artichoke slices. Cook until soft and tender, about 10 minutes. Season generously with salt, pepper and dried chilli, and then add the breadcrumbs. Stir together.

Evenly distribute the artichoke mixture over the rolled-out pizza dough bases. Sprinkle with the thyme leaves, pepper and some extra virgin olive oil. If using a pizza stone, slide the pizzas from the baking sheets on to the preheated stone. Otherwise, place the baking sheets in the oven and bake until the pizza crust starts to brown, about 8-10 minutes.

spaghetti with artichoke pesto
spaghetti al pesto di carciofi

for 6
400 g spaghetti
Maldon salt and freshly ground black pepper
freshly grated Parmesan or Pecorino
artichoke pesto
6 small globe artichokes
lemon juice or parsley stalks
100 g pine kernels
4 garlic cloves, peeled and halved
250 ml milk
2 handfuls of fresh flat-leaf parsley leaves
150 g Parmesan, freshly grated
150 ml olive oil
75 g unsalted butter

To make the pesto, prepare the artichokes as on page 58.

It's easier to make the pesto in two batches. Drain half the artichokes, put into a food processor with half the pine kernels and garlic, and blend to a rough pulp. Add half the milk, parsley and Parmesan, and blend again very briefly. Slowly add half of the olive oil to the mixture, to form a cream. Season and put into a small saucepan. Repeat with the remaining ingredients, and mix together.

Cook the spaghetti in boiling salted water until al dente. Drain and reserve the cooking water. Return the pasta to the pan with 1 ladleful of water. Gently heat the pesto with the butter and another ladleful of the pasta cooking water. Stir into the pasta and, if it still seems too thick, add a little of the remaining water. It should be wet and creamy. Serve with freshly grated Parmesan or Pecorino.

artichokes with salt cod
baccalà con carciofi

for 6
12 small globe artichokes, prepared (see page 58)
    and cut into eighths
600 g salt cod, prepared (see page 458)
7 tablespoons olive oil
Maldon salt and freshly ground black pepper
2 medium red onions, peeled and chopped
4 large garlic cloves, peeled and cut into slivers
a handful of fresh flat-leaf parsley, finely chopped
2 dried red chillies, crumbled
extra virgin olive oil
4 lemons
125 ml white wine or water

In a large thick-bottomed saucepan heat 2 tablespoons of the olive oil, and fry the artichokes until they begin to colour. Season generously with salt and pepper, and cook, stirring occasionally. When the artichokes start to stick to the bottom of the pan, add 150 ml warm water and scrape the juices from the bottom of the pan. Cover with the lid askew, and cook for a further 30 minutes, adding small amounts of water, just enough to keep the artichokes moist. Set aside.

Heat 2 tablespoons olive oil in a large frying pan, and cook the onion, half the garlic and half the parsley until the onion softens. Season with pepper. Add the artichokes, stir and cook, covered, for about 3-4 minutes.

Heat 3 tablespoons olive oil in a large, thick-bottomed flat pan with a lid. Add the remaining garlic and fry briefly. Place the cod in, skin side down, and sprinkle over the chilli, pepper, juice of 1 lemon and the wine or water. Cover, reduce the heat, and simmer for 4-5 minutes or until the cod is cooked. Allow to cool a little, then carefully flake the flesh from the skin. Add the cod to the artichokes and test for seasoning. Drizzle over some extra virgin olive oil, a squeeze of lemon juice and then stir in the remaining parsley. Heat through briefly and serve with lemon.

deep-fried artichokes and radicchio
carciofi fritti con radicchio

for 6
12 globe artichokes
2 heads round radicchio
lemon juice or parsley stalks
sunflower oil for deep-frying
500 g plain flour
Maldon salt and freshly ground black pepper
3 lemons, cut into wedges

Prepare the artichokes by carefully pulling away the tough outer leaves. Cut off the tips and peel the stalks, removing the outer layer of fibres. Cut each heart into quarters through the stalk. Remove the choke if any, and put the artichoke pieces into water acidulated with lemon juice or parsley stalks.

Pull off the outside leaves of the radicchio. Cut each head in half and then into eighths through the stalk.

Meanwhile, heat the sunflower oil to 180°C/350°F.

Mix together the flour, 2 tablespoons salt and 1 tablespoon pepper. Remove the artichoke pieces from the water in batches, shake dry, and toss in the flour. Add the radicchio pieces. Remove to a sieve, and shake off the excess flour. Carefully place each piece in the preheated oil and fry until cooked, about 4-5 minutes. Remove and drain well on kitchen paper. Sprinkle with salt and serve with lemon.

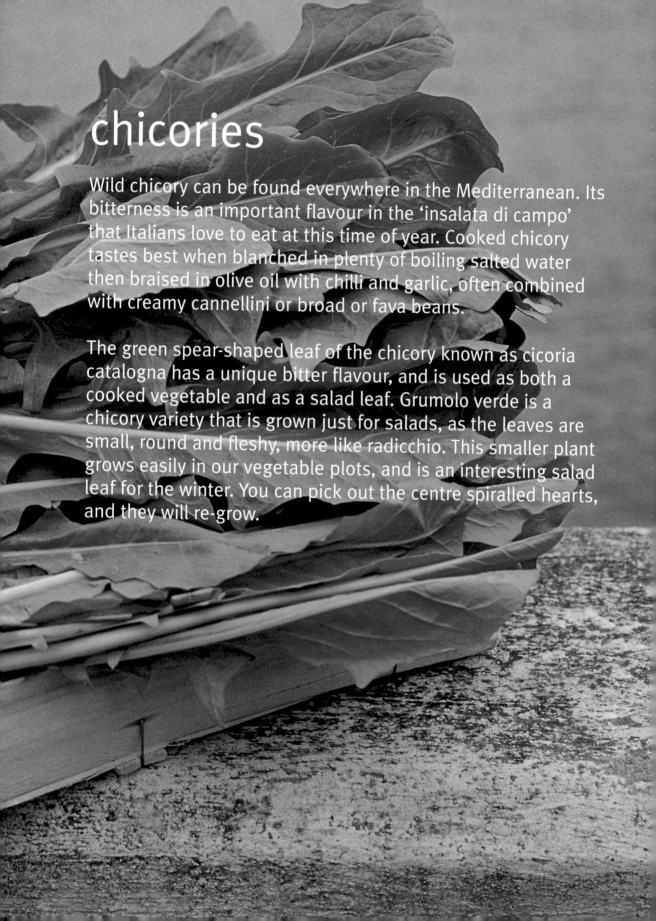

chicories

Wild chicory can be found everywhere in the Mediterranean. Its bitterness is an important flavour in the 'insalata di campo' that Italians love to eat at this time of year. Cooked chicory tastes best when blanched in plenty of boiling salted water then braised in olive oil with chilli and garlic, often combined with creamy cannellini or broad or fava beans.

The green spear-shaped leaf of the chicory known as cicoria catalogna has a unique bitter flavour, and is used as both a cooked vegetable and as a salad leaf. Grumolo verde is a chicory variety that is grown just for salads, as the leaves are small, round and fleshy, more like radicchio. This smaller plant grows easily in our vegetable plots, and is an interesting salad leaf for the winter. You can pick out the centre spiralled hearts, and they will re-grow.

salad of bitter greens, lemon and capers

cicorie con limone e capperi

We use the unusual grumolo verde variety of chicory, which appears in the vegetable markets in Italy in January and February. You could use dandelion leaves or radicchio instead.

for 6

500 g catalogna chicory or trevise, grumolo verde,
   dandelion or radicchio
3 large thick-skinned lemons, washed
50 g salted capers, prepared (see page 458)
Maldon salt and freshly ground black pepper
extra virgin olive oil
1 small dried red chilli
1 small bunch of fresh thyme, leaves picked from
   the stalks
juice of 2 Seville oranges

Slice across the lemons as finely as you can. Cut away only the yellow peel, leaving a little white pith, and remove any pips. Lay the slices out on a flat plate, season with salt and pepper, and drizzle with olive oil. Crumble the dried chilli into the capers, and add the thyme leaves and 3 tablespoons olive oil. Scatter over the lemon slices on the plate.

Remove any damaged outer leaves from the grumolo verde, and break open the hearts. Use only the tender hearts of chicory, dandelion and trevise. Wash and dry well.

Mix the Seville orange juice with an equal amount of olive oil. Season. Toss the leaves with this dressing, and then place the leaves over the lemon slices. Serve.

braised wild greens
erbette saltate

This recipe is suitable for any early spring greens. We use cime di rapa, especially when the flowering heads have barely begun to form; the large pointed-leaf catalogna chicory that looks like lush dandelion leaves; white and purple sprouting broccoli when the shoots are small and tender; Swiss chard leaves when first sprouting and the stalks are still small; the thin-leafed wild rocket, kale or mustard greens. Monk's beard, which is an oddity here in the UK (called *agritti* in Italian), has thin spaghetti-like leaves with a salty earthy taste, and is delicious when combined with the bitter-sweet cime di rapa and peppery rocket.

for 6
250 g bitter chicory
250 g rocket
250 g Swiss chard
250 g cime di rapa or purple sprouting broccoli
Maldon salt and freshly ground black pepper
4 tablespoons extra virgin olive oil
6 garlic cloves, peeled and finely sliced
4 dried red chillies, crushed
3 lemons, halved

Blanch the greens separately in boiling salted water, then taste for doneness. The rocket takes least time, about 3 minutes; the bitter chicory up to 8 minutes; the cime takes less than 5 minutes; and the chard will take up to 10 minutes. Drain the greens thoroughly. Roughly chop the larger leaves.

Heat a large thick-bottomed frying pan and add the oil, garlic and chillies. Allow the garlic to colour, then add the greens and toss together until all the leaves are coated with oil. This takes seconds. Generously season with salt and pepper, and serve at room temperature with lemon halves to squeeze over.

chicory and cannellini bean soup
zuppa di cicorie e cannellini

for 6
1.5 kg catalogna chicory
250 g dried cannellini beans, cooked (see page
   376), cooking water retained
Maldon salt and freshly ground black pepper
5 tablespoons olive oil
4 garlic cloves, peeled and chopped
extra virgin olive oil
6 thick-fleshed, fresh red chillies
juice of 1 lemon

Remove the tough outer leaves from the chicory. Pull the leaves away from the heart, cutting away any rib base of the leaf that seems tough. Blanch the chicory leaves in a large pot of boiling salted water until tender, about 5 minutes. Drain well and roughly chop.

In a thick-bottomed saucepan heat 3 tablespoons of the olive oil, and cook the garlic until soft. Add the chicory and cook for another 5 minutes, seasoning with salt and pepper.

In a food processor briefly pulse three-quarters of the cannellini beans, adding some of the reserved cooking liquid. Combine with the chicory and stir, adding more liquid, keeping in mind that this soup should be very thick. Add the remaining whole beans, season with salt and pepper, and add a few tablespoons of extra virgin olive oil.

Cut the chillies open lengthways, leaving the stalk on, so they remain whole, and remove the seeds. Heat the remaining olive oil, and gently fry the chillies until they are soft. Squeeze a little lemon juice over them.

Reheat the soup and pour into serving bowls. Place a chilli on top of each portion of soup and drizzle with more extra virgin olive oil.

citrus

Citrus plays an important role in Italian cooking. The finely chopped rind is used for flavouring meat broths, and, combined with garlic and parsley, forms the classic gremolata. The juice is used for dressing salads, seasoning fish and flavouring sorbets, and the whole fruits and rinds are crystallised for use in cakes and ice-creams. Because of the frequent use of the skins in cooking, always try to buy organic lemons.

• Sicilian lemons These are thick-skinned, and are often sold with their leaves attached.

• Cedro lemons Large and sweet, these lemons have more in common with grapefruit in terms of size and skin. Inside is mostly white pith, which is the edible part, with very little flesh. This pith is sliced finely and eaten raw in salads. Whole fruits can be crystallised to be used in cassatas, panettone and panforte.

• Seville oranges Traditionally used for making marmalade, their juice is a delicious alternative to lemon juice for salad dressings. The lemon tart recipe in the first *River Cafe Cook Book* can be made using Seville oranges.

cedro lemon and celery salad
insalata di cedro e sedano

for 6
1 large cedro lemon
inner white hearts and leaves of 2 heads celery
150 g rocket leaves
2 large, fresh red chillies
Maldon salt and freshly ground black pepper
juice of 1 lemon
spicy new season extra virgin olive oil

Peel off any discoloured or rough parts of the lemon skin. Wash the lemon and slice across very finely like leaves. Wash the celery hearts and slice at an angle. Wash the celery leaves and finely chop. Wash the rocket leaves and spin dry. Cut the chillies in half lengthways, and remove the seeds. Finely slice.

Mix the sliced lemon and celery together in a bowl. Add the chopped celery leaves and the chilli, and season generously with salt and pepper. Pour over the lemon juice and drizzle with olive oil. Serve with the undressed rocket leaves.

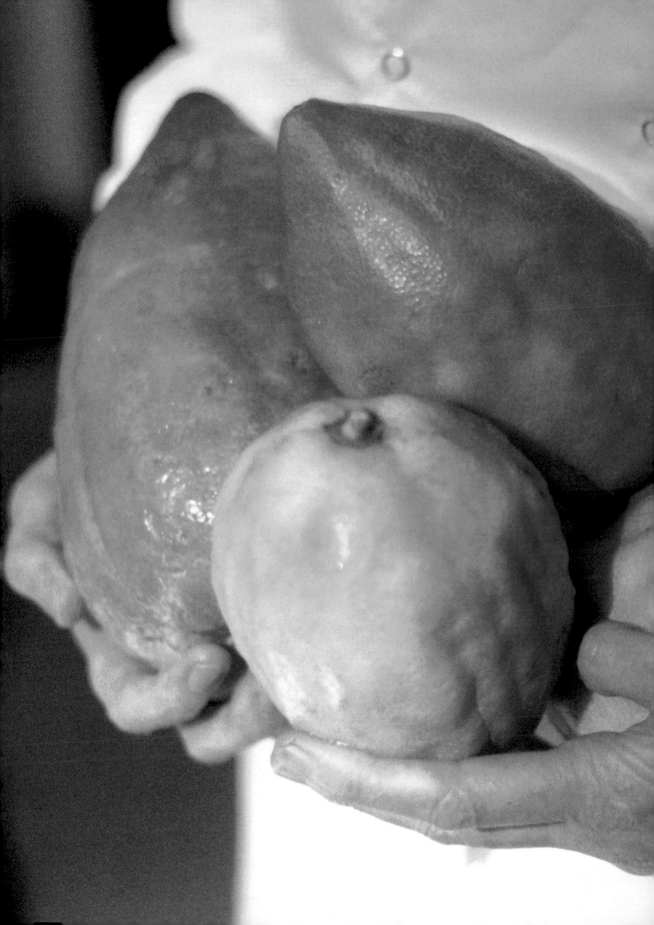

tagliatelle with lemon cream and parsley

tagliatelle con limone e prezzemolo

for 6
Rich Egg Pasta (see page 454), made into
    tagliatelle
Maldon salt and coarsely ground black pepper
lemon cream sauce
300 ml double cream
120 g unsalted butter, softened
zest and juice of 4 large and juicy organic lemons
to serve
6 tablespoons roughly chopped fresh flat-leaf
    parsley
150 g Parmesan, freshly grated

In a large thick-bottomed saucepan, gently heat the cream. When warm, add the soft butter, lemon juice and zest. Stir briefly together until the butter is completely melted, then remove from the heat.

Cook the tagliatelle in a generous amount of boiling salted water until al dente, and then drain. Stir into the warm cream, and season with salt and pepper. Add half the parsley and toss together. Serve immediately on warm plates with the remainder of the parsley and the Parmesan.

tortelloni with ricotta, lemon and pine kernels
tortelloni di ricotta, limone e pinoli

for 6
Fresh Pasta (see page 454)
semolina flour for dusting
Maldon salt and freshly ground black pepper
filling
400 g buffalo ricotta cheese
1/3 nutmeg, freshly grated
150 g Parmesan, freshly grated
2 small dried red chillies, crushed
75 g pine kernels, lightly toasted
peel of 1 lemon, white pith removed
sauce
juice of 2 large lemons
200 ml double cream
75 g softened butter
100 g Parmesan, freshly grated

To make the filling, break up the ricotta with a fork, and add the nutmeg, Parmesan, chilli and generous salt and pepper. Crush the pine kernels and carefully stir into the mixture. Finely chop the lemon peel and add to the ricotta. Stir in a little double cream if the mixture seems very stiff.

Dust your work surface with semolina flour. Divide the pasta dough into quarters. Roll the pieces out one at a time to the finest setting on your pasta machine, to form long strips the width of your machine. Cut into 8 cm squares. Place a teaspoon of the filling in the centre of each square and fold in half to form a triangle. Gently press to seal the dough around the filling. Bend each triangle around your finger, joining the folded ends to slightly overlap, and press to seal, leaving the third point sticking up – rather like tying a headscarf around your head (see overleaf).

To make the sauce, heat the cream gently, then add the softened butter, lemon juice, Parmesan and salt and pepper. Keep warm over the gentlest possible heat.

Bring a large saucepan of water to the boil, season with 1 tablespoon of salt, and add the tortelloni. Simmer gently until the tortelloni are tender but firm to the bite, about 8-10 minutes. Drain, keeping a little of the pasta water. Place the tortelloni carefully into the thickened sauce. Add a little of the hot pasta water to liquefy, and serve with extra grated Parmesan.

marmalade
marmellata di arance siviglia

We have given no quantities, as the recipe works in proportion of fruit to sugar.

Seville oranges, washed
caster sugar

Soak the oranges for 24-48 hours in cold water, then drain and rinse. This soaking allows the skin of the oranges to soften up and expand.

Fill a large, thick-bottomed saucepan with oranges, cover with cold water and slowly bring to the boil. Reduce the heat, cover the saucepan with the lid askew, and simmer very gently for 3-4 hours or until the oranges are completely soft, stirring from time to time. Make sure that the liquid does not totally evaporate during the cooking; add a drop more water if it does. Remove from the heat and cool.

Take the soft oranges out of the pan, and put the pan and any remaining juices to one side. Cut each orange in half, and remove the seeds and any tough fibres. Roughly cut the flesh and skin into 1 cm pieces. Weigh this orange pulp, then return to the saucepan.

Measure out two-thirds of the orange pulp weight in caster sugar. Add the sugar to the saucepan, return to the heat, and gently bring to the boil, stirring to prevent sticking and to help the sugar dissolve. Turn the heat down a little and simmer for about 30 minutes. The jam should be very dense and dark in colour. Cool for 5 minutes and then spoon into sterilised jars.

marmalade ice-cream
gelato di marmellata di arance

for 6
1 litre double cream
275 ml milk
9 large, organic free-range egg yolks
200 g caster sugar
500 g Marmalade (see left)

In a thick-bottomed saucepan combine the cream and milk. Heat gently until just below boiling point.

Beat the egg yolks and sugar together quite slowly until pale and thick.

Pour a ladleful of the hot cream into the egg mixture to loosen it, then add this mixture back to the hot cream. Cook gently on a very low heat to 72°C/161°F, stirring constantly to prevent curdling, until thick. Pour into a bowl and cool.

Pour the cold custard into an ice-cream machine and churn for 6 minutes or until the cream begins to freeze. Add half the marmalade and churn for a further 6-8 minutes to thoroughly incorporate the marmalade into the custard. Finally add the remaining marmalade, and churn briefly just to combine and to solidify the ice-cream. If you do not have a machine, freeze the mixture until on the point of setting, then stir in all the marmalade, and return to the freezer until solid.

milanino

per person

25 ml amaro rabarbaro

50 ml Campari

juice of 1 blood orange

soda water

1 twist of lemon peel

Put the two amari – the amaro rabarbaro and Campari – into a highball glass, add the orange juice, and stir together. Top up with soda water. Pinch the lemon peel over the drink to squeeze out the essential oil, then stick over the edge of the glass to make the rim bitter. This is a delicious aperitif.

leeks

We choose to cook with small leeks, in particular a fast-growing variety called Pancho. This has long white stems when young, and its green tips are also very tender.

Try to buy leeks with their roots attached as this keeps them fresh. The leaves should be dark green and firm, the stalks white and stiff. Never use leeks that have begun to shoot as they will have lost their sweet taste and have tough centres.

Leeks always have sand or dirt stuck between their leaves. To clean, fill a sink with cold water and push the leeks up and down in it, leafy side down, to help release the dirt.

We use the white part of larger leeks instead of, or combined with, red onions in the base of fish risottos.

leek, clam and prawn risotto
risotto ai porri, vongole e gamberetti

You could use large brown shrimps, live langoustines or small tiger prawns in this risotto.

for 6

1 kg small leeks, tough green part removed,
   washed thoroughly
2 kg fresh clams, scrubbed
1 kg raw prawns
3 tablespoons olive oil
4 garlic cloves, peeled and finely chopped
250 ml fruity, un-oaked, Italian white wine
150 g unsalted butter
1.75 litres fish stock (see page 455)
Maldon salt and freshly ground black pepper
2 medium white onions, peeled and finely
   chopped
inner white heart and leaves of 1 head celery (use
   outer leaves in the stock)
1 teaspoon fennel seeds
3 salted anchovies, prepared (see page 458) and
   roughly chopped
3 tablespoons roughly chopped fresh flat-leaf
   parsley
400 g vialone nano rice
juice of 2 lemons
250 g crème fraîche

Heat the olive oil in a large thick-bottomed saucepan with a tight-fitting lid. Add half the garlic and, as soon as it begins to colour, add the clams and half the wine. Cover the pan and cook just until the clams open. Strain using a colander set over a bowl to collect the liquid. Leave to cool. Meanwhile strain the liquid through muslin or paper towels to remove any sand or grit. Take the clams from their shells and return to the liquid.

Slice the white parts and green parts of the leeks finely, keeping them separate. Heat half the butter in a small pan, add the green leek, cover and cook for 2 minutes.

Bring the stock to a simmer and taste for seasoning. Add the prawns, and cook for 1 minute. Remove with a slotted spoon and allow to cool. Shell and devein the prawns, and add to the clams. Add a few of the prawn shells to the stock and allow to simmer gently. When ready to use, strain out the shells and again taste for seasoning.

Heat a large thick-bottomed saucepan over a medium heat, and melt the remaining butter. Add the onion and celery, and cook gently, stirring to prevent sticking. When soft, add the white of leek, the remaining garlic, the fennel seeds, anchovies, 2 tablespoons of the parsley and cook together, stirring. Add the rice, and stir to coat each grain, then pour in the remainder of the wine. Cook until almost reduced, then start to stir in the stock, ladle by ladle, stirring continuously, and not adding any more stock until the previous ladleful has been absorbed. Continue stirring and adding stock until the rice is almost cooked, about 15 minutes.

At the last minute, stir in the green leeks and their butter, and the clams and prawns along with their liquid. Stir to combine and allow the clam liquid to be absorbed. Quickly stir in the remaining parsley, the lemon juice and crème fraîche. The risotto should be quite wet and creamy in consistency. Serve immediately.

leek and porcini pappardelle
pappardelle con porri e porcini

for 6
polenta pappardelle
375 g Tipo 'oo' pasta flour
50 g bramata polenta, plus 50 g for dusting
Maldon salt
2 large, organic free-range eggs
6 large, organic free-range egg yolks
sauce
1.4 kg thin leeks, no thicker than 2 cm
100 g dried porcini
4 tablespoons olive oil
50 g butter, softened
2 garlic cloves, peeled and chopped
Maldon salt and freshly ground black pepper
1 large bunch of fresh thyme, leaves picked from
    the stalks
to serve
100 g Parmesan, freshly grated

To make the pappardelle, put the flours and salt in an electric mixer fitted with a dough hook, and add the eggs and egg yolks. Slowly knead together for 10 minutes. Remove, wrap in clingfilm and allow to rest in the fridge for 2 hours.

To prepare the dough for cutting, remove from the fridge, unwrap and divide into cricket ball-sized pieces. Dust the surface with polenta.

Pass each ball through the pasta machine on the thickest setting ten times. Fold the sheet into three each time to form a short strip, then turn it by a quarter and put through the machine again. After ten such folds the pasta will feel silky. Only then start to reduce the machine setting, gradually bringing it down to the thinnest setting. Fold the pasta loosely and cut into 2.5 cm thick ribbons. Shake out the pappardelle and leave to dry.

Soak the porcini in hot water for 20 minutes. Remove the porcini, keeping the liquid, and rinse thoroughly to get rid of any grit. Pass the liquid through fine muslin or a sieve lined with kitchen paper, and reserve.

To prepare the leeks, trim off and discard the tough top dark green leaves and the roots. Wash thoroughly and dry. Cut the leeks into diagonal slices about 1 cm thick.

In a frying pan, heat 1 tablespoon of the olive oil and half the butter, then add half the chopped garlic. Add the porcini and cook for a few minutes over a gentle heat. Add a little of the porcini liquid to keep the porcini moist as they cook, about 20 minutes. The time it takes will depend on the quality of the porcini. Season with salt and pepper, cool and then roughly chop.

In a thick-bottomed saucepan heat the remaining olive oil, then add the rest of the garlic and the thyme. Cook together to combine the flavours. Then add the leeks, and cook until the leeks are soft and lightly browned. Add the chopped porcini and a little of the porcini juices, and cook together briefly. Finally, stir in the remaining butter. The sauce should be quite liquid.

Cook the pappardelle until al dente, drain, then add to the leeks and gently stir to combine. Add the Parmesan and serve.

bay leaves

Bay trees grow wild everywhere in the Mediterranean. The aromatic leaves have been essential in marinating, pickling, roasting, stocks and soups since the time of the Romans.

Bay grows well in large pots. It likes a sunny position and must be watered frequently. The glossy green leaves always need to be washed before using. Dried bay leaves last well in airtight containers.

We buy fresh bay from our British gardeners, but have noticed that bay brought back from Italy has a more powerful, pungent flavour and perfume. If hung in an airy place, this will keep for up to a year.

Bay and lemon combined are often used to flavour fish and meat when roasting.

bay and red mullet tagliarini
tagliarini con triglie e alloro

for 6
8 fresh bay leaves, centre stems discarded,
   pounded in a pestle and mortar
500 g Rich Egg Pasta (see page 454), made into
   tagliarini
3 large red mullet, each about 500 g in weight,
   scaled, filleted and pinboned
80 g unsalted butter
3 garlic cloves, peeled and chopped
1 x 800 g tin peeled plum tomatoes, put through a
   mouli with their juices
Maldon salt and freshly ground black pepper
30-40 ml red wine vinegar (depending on strength)
1 large lemon, washed
3 tablespoons chopped fresh flat-leaf parsley
extra virgin olive oil

Melt the butter in a thick-bottomed saucepan, add the garlic and bay,
and allow the garlic to colour a little. Add the tomato pulp and season.
Add the vinegar and simmer gently for 30 minutes, stirring from time to
time. The sauce should stay liquid, but become amalgamated.

Carefully cut the peel from the lemon, remove any white pith, and chop
the peel finely. Mix with the parsley. Squeeze the juice from the lemon.
Finely cut across the mullet fillets into 5 mm widths. Add the mullet
slices to the tomato sauce, pour in the lemon juice, and stir gently to
allow the mullet to 'melt' in the sauce, about 2-3 minutes.

Meanwhile bring a large saucepan of boiling salted water to the boil,
add the tagliarini and cook for 3 minutes or until al dente. Drain well.

Adjust the seasoning of the tomato sauce. Stir in the lemon zest and
parsley. Combine the sauce and fish with the tagliarini and serve with
extra virgin olive oil drizzled over.

march

globe artichokes [92] *antipasto* chickpea pancake with artichokes. *pasta* tagliarini with artichokes and cream. *antipasto* artichokes piperno style. artichokes in oil. *pasta* linguine with etruscan salsa. *antipasto* roast artichoke hearts. sprouting broccoli [102] *soup* sprouting broccoli and farro soup. *polenta* polenta with sprouting broccoli and pancetta. sea kale [106] *antipasto* sea kale, lemon and bottarga. sea kale with pecorino romano and lemon. mint [110] *risotto* mint and prosciutto risotto. *salad* mint and lentil salad. ginger [114] *pasta* spaghetti with ginger and tomato. *pudding* chocolate and ginger cake. wild salad leaves [120] *salad* mixed wild leaf salad. *frittata* frittata with wild leaves. sorrel frittata.

globe artichokes

Romanesco artichokes have much thicker edible stalks and leaves than other varieties. The loosely packed heads, which are the size of cricket balls, are purplish green in colour. The inner chokes are small, and the leaves have rounded tips, without thorns.

When prised open, the leaves easily part like a flower to reveal the centre choke. This is the way this particular artichoke is prepared for the famous Roman dish, Carciofi alla Giudea, in which the artichokes are deep-fried and then flattened, resulting in crisp, creamy discs that are eaten whole.

The Romanesco's large stems and yellowish inner leaves at the base are delicious eaten raw. They have a sweet nutty taste and only need lemon juice and extra virgin olive oil.

chickpea pancake with artichokes
farinata con carciofi

This is served in Liguria as street food, like pizza, and is delicious with drinks or with a plate of prosciutto.

for 6
2 fresh, medium globe artichokes
250 g chickpea flour, sieved
750 ml warm water
Maldon salt
lemon juice or parsley stalks
extra virgin olive oil
2 tablespoons fresh thyme leaves

To make the farinata, add the sieved flour to the warm water in a bowl, whisking all the time to prevent any lumps from forming. Add 1 tablespoon salt, cover the bowl, and leave in a warm place for at least 2 hours.

Remove the dark green outer leaves from the artichokes, until you get to the tender pale leaves. Cut off the tough tops of the hearts, and use a teaspoon to scrape out the chokes, if any. Slice the hearts and tender leaves very finely, and cover with water acidulated with lemon juice or parsley stalks.

Preheat the oven to 230°C/450°F/Gas 8.

Remove the foam from the top of the batter and stir in 75 ml olive oil. Pour a further tablespoon of oil into the farinata pan (see page 24) and put into the oven until the oil is just smoking. Quickly remove and pour in the chickpea batter. The farinata should be very thin – no more than 1 cm deep. Scatter over the artichoke slices, salt and thyme, and dribble on some olive oil. Place in the preheated oven and bake for 10-15 minutes. The surface should bubble slightly, and the edges will have become crisp. Serve immediately.

tagliarini with artichokes and cream
tagliarini con carciofi

for 6
8 small young artichokes on their stalks
Rich Egg Pasta (see page 454), cut into tagliarini
1/2 bunch fresh flat-leaf parsley, leaves picked from
    the stalks (keep the stalks)
3 garlic cloves, peeled
50 g butter
2 tablespoons olive oil
Maldon salt and freshly ground black pepper
4 tablespoons double cream
50 g Parmesan, freshly grated

To prepare the artichokes, break off the dark green outer leaves until
you get to the tender pale leaves. Cut off the tough tops of the hearts
and peel the fibres from the stalks. Halve the artichokes lengthways and
remove the chokes, if any, with a teaspoon. Cut off the stalks from the
heads. Very finely slice the heads and put in a bowl of water acidulated
with the parsley stalks.

Chop the garlic together with the peeled artichoke stalks and a handful
of the parsley leaves.

Melt the butter with the olive oil in a large thick-bottomed frying pan.
Add the artichoke stalks, garlic and parsley, and gently push around the
pan until softened, about 2 minutes. Add 100 ml boiling water, season,
then after a few minutes add the drained sliced artichokes. Stir together,
adding a little more hot water if too dry. Cover and simmer for 5-8
minutes or until the artichokes are cooked. Stir in the cream.

Cook the tagliarini in a generous amount of boiling salted water, about
2-3 minutes. Drain, keeping back a little of the pasta water. Add the
pasta to the sauce and mix well together over a gentle heat, adding the
retained pasta water if too dry. Test for seasoning. Serve with grated
Parmesan over each portion.

artichokes piperno style
carciofi alla piperno

Piperno is a restaurant in the old Jewish quarter of Rome, which is famous for artichokes cooked in this way. They use Romanesco artichokes and taught us to reject artichokes that have opened out, as the chokes will be too developed for this recipe.

for 6
12 Romanesco artichokes
sunflower oil for deep-frying
Maldon sea salt and freshly ground black pepper
3 large lemons

Heat the oil to 100°C/212°F in your deep-fryer.

Peel away one layer of the outside leaves of the artichokes. Don't peel the stalks yet. Cut the stalks 2 cm from the heads.

Fry the artichokes in batches, depending on the size of your fryer. The artichokes are to be fried twice, so first fry each artichoke for 15 minutes until the leaves are beginning to crisp and the heart beginning to soften. Lift out of the fat and drain on kitchen paper. When cool, peel off the outside leaves, trim the tops of the artichokes and peel the stalks. Increase the temperature of the oil to 170°C/340°F.

To fry the second time, check your oil has reached the desired temperature. Place the artichokes two or three at a time in the hot oil and fry until completely crisp, about 2-3 minutes.

To flatten out the artichokes, set each artichoke on a board and gently separate the leaves of the head out to expose the heart. Squeeze between two plates so that the oil drips out. Season the flattened artichokes, and serve two per portion with a half lemon.

artichokes in oil
carciofi sott'olio

For this recipe, you need the smallest artichokes you can find, that are in tight buds, and have no choke. The ones we use are about the size of a golf ball.

for 6

20 small artichokes, any damaged outer leaves
   removed
250 ml red wine vinegar
500 ml olive oil
peel of 1 lemon
4 bay leaves, crushed
Maldon salt and freshly ground black pepper
4 garlic cloves, peeled
3 tablespoons fresh flat-leaf parsley leaves
3 tablespoons fresh marjoram leaves

Put the artichokes into a large saucepan so that they fit tightly, and add enough water to come halfway up the artichokes. Add the vinegar, and then pour in enough olive oil to cover. Add the lemon peel, crushed bay leaves and 2 tablespoons salt. Cover and very slowly bring to a gentle simmer. Cook for 15-20 minutes or until the artichokes are tender. Remove from the heat and cool in their liquid.

Remove the arcichokes, cut off the tips and peel off the outer tough leaves. Trim the stems of any fibres. Return to the liquid.

Chop the garlic together with the parsley and marjoram. Stir into the artichokes and their liquid. Taste for seasoning. Serve on bruschetta or as part of an antipasti.

linguine with etruscan salsa
linguine con carciofi sott'olio

for 6
18 artichokes in oil (see previous recipe)
400 g linguine or other flat dried pasta
2 garlic cloves, peeled and finely chopped
3 tablespoons chopped fresh flat-leaf parsley
Maldon salt and freshly ground black pepper
finely grated zest of 1 lemon
etruscan salsa
¼ stale sourdough loaf, about 250 g in weight, crusts
   removed
1 garlic clove, peeled and finely sliced
100 ml red wine vinegar
1 tablespoon each of fresh rosemary, sage, mint, thyme
   and marjoram leaves, finely chopped
75 g pine kernels
150 ml olive oil
1 dried red chilli, crumbled

For the sauce, break up the bread, and put in a bowl with the garlic slices, vinegar and 300 ml water. Leave for 30 minutes. Chop the herbs together with the pine kernels. Squeeze out excess water and vinegar from the bread and mix with the herbs. Pass through a mouli. Slowly add the olive oil and season with salt and pepper and the chilli.

Slice the artichokes across the hearts as finely as possible. Heat a large thick-bottomed saucepan with 3 tablespoons of the artichoke liquid, then add the garlic and soften for a few minutes. Add the artichokes, stir and cook briefly, to heat up. Add the parsley and check the seasoning.

Bring a large saucepan of water to the boil, add salt and the linguini, and cook until al dente. Drain and add to the warm artichokes. Over a very low heat, cook and stir to combine the pasta with the sauce, adding 6 tablespoons of the Etruscan sauce until totally mixed and hot. Serve on warm plates with a little of the lemon zest scattered over.

roast artichoke hearts
carciofi ripieni al forno

for 6
12 small artichokes
2 thick-skinned organic lemons
4 tablespoons chopped fresh flat-leaf parsley
3 tablespoons chopped fresh mint leaves
200 g pancetta, cut into small pieces
3 garlic cloves, peeled and roughly chopped
1/2 stale sourdough loaf, crust removed, made into
   coarse breadcrumbs
Maldon salt and freshly ground black pepper
extra virgin olive oil
150 ml white wine

Preheat the oven to 220°C/425°F/Gas 7.

To prepare the artichokes, cut off the stems about 3 cm from the base of each head. Pull off the tough outer leaves, removing two to three layers until you reach the leaves that are mostly pale green or yellow except for the tips. With a sharp knife cut off the tip of each artichoke. Trim the end of the stem of any fibres and use a peeler to remove any green leaf bases that may surround the top of the stem.

Grate the rind from the lemons, and put to one side. Cut each lemon in half. Cut the prepared artichokes in half lengthways through the stalk. Use the lemon halves to rub round the artichoke cut surfaces. Mix the parsley, mint, pancetta, garlic and lemon rind in a bowl, then add the breadcrumbs. Season and stir in 3 tablespoons of the olive oil.

Oil a shallow baking dish and arrange in it the artichokes, cut side up, side by side. Season, then push the stuffing into the centre of each artichoke where the bud leaves are soft. Press a little stuffing between each leaf, and drizzle with oil. Add 150 ml of hot water and the wine, and bake for 35 minutes or until the artichokes are tender, the liquid has been absorbed, and the stuffing has browned and become crisp.

sprouting broccoli

Sprouting broccoli is the hardy variety of broccoli that we choose to cook with. Planted in the spring it grows throughout the summer, producing delicious flowering shoots in the early part of the following year. Both white and purple, early and late, varieties are very good, and grow successfully, playing an important role in the serious vegetable garden, as they can be harvested at a time when there are few other green vegetables.

Sprouting broccoli is sold by the branching stem, often with lots of large leaves still attached. Choose stems that have many tightly closed flower shoots. Discard the large leaves and the main stem. It is these shoots with their smaller, paler leaves enclosing the flower heads that are tender and delicious. Broccoli is available from organic growers, and it is important that you buy it freshly picked.

Fresh broccoli shoots, cooked in boiling salted water and seasoned with extra virgin olive oil, are often found in vegetable antipasti in Rome, served at room temperature alongside other seasonal vegetables. Equally delicious, broccoli cooked in this way is used as the base of pasta sauces and soups.

Calabrese broccoli is a different vegetable, with a less interesting flavour and texture.

sprouting broccoli and farro soup
zuppa di broccoli e farro

for 6
1.5 kg purple sprouting broccoli
inner white heart of 1 head celery, with leaves
2 small red onions, peeled
1 handful of fresh flat-leaf parsley leaves
2 garlic cloves, peeled
olive oil and extra virgin olive oil
5 salted anchovies, prepared (see page 458)
1 fresh red chilli, seeded and finely chopped
Maldon salt and freshly ground black pepper
250 g cooked Farro (see page 458)
1 large sprig fresh rosemary
juice of 1 lemon
6 thin slices ciabatta bread, grilled

Finely chop the celery, onion, parsley and garlic. Heat 2 tablespoons of the olive oil in a heavy saucepan and fry the vegetable mixture until soft, about 20 minutes. Add half of the anchovies and mash with a spoon until they disappear into the vegetables. Add the chilli and season.

Remove the smaller leaves from the thick stalks of the broccoli. Cut the flower heads from the stems, and discard the stems and stalks. Wash well, then stir the heads and leaves into the mixture, coating them with the oil. Season, then add 150 ml hot water and stir. Bring to the boil, then cook, adding more hot water as necessary, until the broccoli is completely soft – about half an hour over a low to moderate heat.

Add the farro, stir, and add hot water just to cover the soup. Bring to the boil, and cook for a few minutes. The soup should be very thick. Season.

Put the remaining anchovies in a pestle and mortar and pound coarsely. Add the rosemary, lemon juice and 3 tablespoons extra virgin olive oil. Spread the ciabatta with the anchovy sauce, and place in soup bowls. Cover with soup, and drizzle with more extra virgin olive oil.

polenta with sprouting broccoli and pancetta

polenta con broccoli e pancetta

for 6
Polenta (see page 360)
1.5 kg purple sprouting broccoli
Maldon salt and freshly ground black pepper
4 tablespoons olive oil
300 g smoked pancetta, finely sliced, then cut into
   1 cm pieces
6 garlic cloves, peeled and finely sliced
3-4 small dried red chillies, crumbled
175 g unsalted butter
150 g Parmesan, freshly grated
extra virgin olive oil

Make the polenta as described on page 360. While the polenta is cooking, bring to the boil a separate pan of salted water and prepare the broccoli. Remove the smaller leaves from the thick stalks. Cut the flower heads from the stems and discard the thick stems and stalks. Wash the leaves and flower heads and blanch them in the salted water for 5 minutes until tender. Drain well.

Heat the olive oil in a large frying pan, add the pancetta and cook for a minute or two until beginning to colour. Add the garlic and crumbled chilli. As soon as the garlic becomes golden, add the broccoli leaves and flowers and mix together to combine the flavour of the pancetta with the broccoli. Season with salt and pepper.

When the polenta is ready, stir in the butter and 100 g of the grated Parmesan. Taste for seasoning, adding black pepper.

To serve, divide the polenta between serving plates and spoon the broccoli over each mound. Drizzle with a little extra virgin olive oil and sprinkle with the remaining freshly grated Parmesan.

sea kale

Wild sea kale grows on shingle beaches in northern Europe. This variety has thick stems, fleshy green leaves and dark purplish flower stems. When young, these leaf stems and flower heads are all good to eat. We cook them in boiling salted water like broccoli, and season them with lemon juice and extra virgin olive oil.

Cultivated sea kale is grown for its crisp long shoots that have been blanched under pots or cloches during February to make them whiter, more delicate and more tender. These young shoots are creamy white with small curly leaves tinged purple and pale green. They are sold in bundles like asparagus and need very little preparation. Choose stems that are crisp and firm, not flabby and soft. There is very little waste, just trim the ends and tie in bundles. Blanch as for wild kale above.

Sauces that complement asparagus go equally well with sea kale. The sea kale season, like that of asparagus, is very short.

sea kale, lemon and bottarga
cavolo marino con limone e bottarga

Bottarga is the sun-dried roe of the grey mullet, a speciality of Sardinia.

for 6
2 kg sea kale
extra virgin olive oil
juice of 3 lemons
Maldon salt and freshly ground black pepper
100 g bottarga
3 lemons, halved

Trim away the tough split ends from the sea kale stalks and wash the stalks thoroughly. Blanch in boiling salted water until tender, about 3-5 minutes.

Drain carefully and place in a warmed bowl. Drizzle with olive oil and squeeze over the fresh lemon juice. Season with salt and black pepper and toss gently.

Divide the sea kale between six warm plates. Shave the bottarga over each plate equally, and serve still warm with a fresh cut lemon half.

sea kale with pecorino romano and lemon

cavolo marino con pecorino romano e limone

This recipe also works well with cime di rapa and purple sprouting broccoli.

for 6
2 kg sea kale
150 g Pecorino Romano cheese, freshly grated
peel of 1 thick-skinned lemon, washed and finely
    chopped
1 x 800 g tin peeled plum tomatoes, drained of
    their juices
3 garlic cloves, peeled and finely chopped
3 tablespoons finely chopped fresh flat-leaf parsley
Maldon salt and freshly ground black pepper
2 small dried red chillies, crumbled
85 ml extra virgin olive oil

Remove the tough part of the sea kale stalks and the larger outside leaves. Wash thoroughly.

Put the tomatoes into a thick-bottomed pan and gently heat, stirring to prevent sticking and to help break them up into a sauce. Cook for 10 minutes, then add half the garlic and parsley. Add salt, pepper and dried chilli and cook very briefly, about 2 minutes.

Bring a large saucepan of water to the boil, add salt and blanch the kale for 5-8 minutes or until tender. Drain.

Mix together the remaining garlic and parsley and half the lemon peel. Add the extra virgin olive oil. Toss the sea kale with this mixture and put on to a warm serving plate. Top with the tomato sauce and sprinkle with the remaining lemon zest and the Pecorino.

mint

Mint is one of the best-known and most used herbs in Italian cooking. There are many wild and cultivated varieties. All have powerful and refreshing perfumes, and are consequently used for their individual flavours in different dishes. We like to include mints such as ginger mint, lemon mint, apple mint and peppermint in herb salads, but it is normally spearmint that we use in risottos, soups and sauces.

Nepitella or wild mint is a favourite for flavour. This grows everywhere in central and northern Italy, and it is gathered in bunches, strung up and dried. Its strong flavour is a cross between mint and oregano, and it is traditionally used when cooking fresh porcini mushrooms. We also use nepitella as a sweet complement to artichokes.

Although mint grows throughout the year, the plants become dormant in the winter, and the first young, fragrant and tender leaves in the early spring are particularly good. The flavour is delicate and the texture fine. Mint leaves taste better before the plants start to flower. Use the smaller leaves from the top of the stems.

We use mint nearly every day in the kitchen. In the winter months, only mint and parsley are used in a salsa verde, and that same mint, parsley and garlic combination is used for stuffing artichokes. We put whole branches of mint into the water when cooking peas and broad beans.

mint and prosciutto risotto
risotto alla menta e prosciutto

for 6
1 large handful of fresh mint leaves
10 prosciutto slices, not too thin, about 500 g
1.5 litres chicken stock (see page 455)
Maldon salt and freshly ground black pepper
100 g unsalted butter
1 medium onion, peeled and finely chopped
inner white heart of 1 head celery, finely chopped
300 g carnaroli rice
100 ml vermouth
100 g Parmesan, freshly grated

Wash the mint, and drain well. Heat the chicken stock to a simmer and check for seasoning.

Finely slice four of the prosciutto slices into 2-3 cm pieces.

Melt half the butter in a large, thick-bottomed saucepan over a medium heat. Gently fry the onion and celery until soft and beginning to colour. Add the prosciutto pieces, and then the rice, and stir quickly until each grain is well coated with the butter and vegetable mixture. Add the vermouth, cook and stir until almost absorbed, then start to add the hot stock ladleful by ladleful. Turn the heat to low and stir constantly, only adding more stock when the risotto has absorbed the previous ladleful. Continue to cook the risotto until the rice has become al dente. Carnaroli rice takes about 20 minutes to cook.

Finally chop the mint leaves and add to the risotto, stirring in the remainder of the butter and the Parmesan. Mix together. The rice should have a creamy consistency. Serve with the remaining prosciutto slices on top.

mint and lentil salad
insalata di lenticchie e menta

for 6

6 tablespoons fresh mint leaves, torn into small
  pieces
300 g Castelluccio or Puy lentils, rinsed
1 dried red chilli, crumbled
3 whole garlic cloves, peeled
4 tablespoons extra virgin olive oil
juice of 1/2 lemon
Maldon salt and freshly ground black pepper

Place the lentils in a thick-bottomed saucepan with the garlic, and cover generously with cold water. Bring to the boil and then lower to a simmer. Add a few mint stalks and cook, covered, for 30 minutes, or until the lentils are al dente. Drain and discard the mint stalks and garlic.

Return the lentils to the saucepan and, while still warm, stir in the extra virgin olive oil and lemon juice, dried chilli and torn mint. Season well with salt and pepper, and serve warm, not hot, with a salad or green vegetable dressed with oil and lemon.

ginger

Ginger comes from a reed-like plant native to India and warm parts of Asia. It has never been found growing wild and is always cultivated. The edible part of the plant is the underground tuberous stem. This knobbly stem or rhizome is used fresh and dried as a spice.

We have discovered that fresh 'green' ginger, as it is called, has been used in Italian cooking since the time of the Romans. It has a strong, distinctive peppery flavour and is sometimes used as a substitute for chilli, usually combined with garlic, in pasta sauces.

Buy whole, hard fresh tubers. The skin should be pale brown and quite smooth. Best-quality fresh ginger should be juicy when cut. Peel off the thin skin, and grate, using a Parmesan grater. Freshly cut ginger will discolour very quickly, so use it immediately. Instead of grating you could cut the peeled ginger into very fine slices, discarding the fibrous parts, then into very fine cubes.

We have only found ginger used in recipes from the south of Italy.

spaghetti with ginger and tomato
spaghetti con zenzero e pomodoro

Ricotta salata is a hard sheep's milk ricotta that comes from Sardinia. It is a lighter cheese than Pecorino.

for 6
150 g fresh root ginger, peeled and finely chopped
1 x 800 g tin peeled plum tomatoes, drained of
   their juices
400 g spaghetti
150 ml olive oil
4 garlic cloves, peeled and chopped
3 small dried red chillies, crumbled
Maldon salt and freshly ground black pepper
juice of 2 lemons
300 g ricotta salata cheese, freshly grated
2 large handfuls of fresh marjoram leaves, roughly
   chopped

In a large, thick-bottomed saucepan heat 3 tablespoons of the olive oil. Add the garlic and just allow to soften and begin to colour. Add the ginger and chilli and stir together, then add the drained tomatoes and season with salt and pepper. Cook over a medium heat, stirring from time to time, for 35 minutes so that the tomatoes break up. Remove from the heat and pass through a mouli.

Cook the spaghetti in a large saucepan of boiling salted water until al dente. Drain, and return to the pasta saucepan. Add the remaining olive oil and the lemon juice and toss. Stir in half the grated ricotta, then the tomato sauce and marjoram. Taste for seasoning. Serve with the remaining ricotta.

chocolate and ginger cake
torta al cioccolato e zenzero

for 12
200 g fresh root ginger
500 g unsalted butter, plus extra for greasing
500 g bitter-sweet Callebaut chocolate, with a
   minimum of 70% cocoa solids
70 g fine polenta flour
2 tablespoons cocoa powder
10 medium, organic free-range eggs
400 g caster sugar
a pinch of baking powder

Preheat the oven to 150°C/300°F/Gas 2. Butter and line a 30 cm cake tin with parchment paper.

Melt the chocolate and butter together in a bowl over a pan of simmering water. Do not let the bowl touch the water. Peel and finely chop the ginger, and add to the chocolate mixture once it has melted, along with the flour and cocoa powder. Allow to cool a little.

In a mixer combine the eggs and sugar and whisk until they have trebled in volume. Slowly fold the whisked eggs, sugar and baking powder into the chocolate mixture. Pour into the prepared tin and bake in the preheated oven for 45 minutes.

When the cake is cooked, place a plate on the top for 5 minutes. This will give the cake a good dense texture.

wild dandelion

sour thistle

mixed wild leaf salad
insalata di campo

You can make a salad from many varieties of leaves: young sorrel leaves when they first shoot out of the ground; small, soft thistle leaves that grow in rosettes in short grass; and wild garlic leaves which start to appear at the end of March. Dandelion leaves are delicious, and slightly bitter: pick small leaves only, and from plants that have not yet produced flowers. Mix these with watercress, land cress and rocket. If you have a vegetable garden, you can add to this salad small leaves from any chicory plants or cavolo nero, mint leaves, young borage leaves, and spinach and beet leaves.

for 6
1 large bowl of mixed leaves (see above)
100 ml new season extra virgin olive oil
juice of 1 large lemon
Maldon salt and freshly ground black pepper
2 teaspoons aged thick balsamic vinegar

Mix the oil with the lemon juice, season, and pour over the leaves. Toss to coat each leaf, then drizzle over the balsamic vinegar. Serve immediately.

frittata with wild leaves
frittata di preboggion

'Preboggion' is the Ligurian name for wild greens. Use a mixture of wild and cultivated greens - dandelion, borage, sorrel, wild chicory, wild rocket, cultivated rocket, small beet leaves and/or Swiss chard leaves, mint and marjoram leaves.

for 4
1.5 kg leaves (see above), washed
½ ciabatta loaf, bottom crust removed, torn into
   3-4 pieces
300 ml milk
Maldon salt and freshly ground black pepper
150 g Parmesan, freshly grated
8 large, organic free-range eggs
2 garlic cloves, peeled
olive oil

Preheat the oven to 230°C/450°F/Gas 8. Soak the ciabatta in the milk for 20 minutes until soft, then squeeze out excess milk and chop finely.

Bring a large saucepan of water to boiling point, add some salt, the garlic and then the leaves. Cook for 5 minutes, then drain well and squeeze out all the water. Chop finely, using a mezzaluna. Mix well with the chopped bread, and season with salt, pepper and half the Parmesan.

Break the eggs into a large bowl, season generously, and beat. Mix in the greens mixture and stir to combine.

Use two 20-25 cm frying pans with ovenproof handles. Heat 2 tablespoons olive oil in each pan, and when hot, pour half the mixture into each pan. Reduce the heat and cook for a few minutes until just set, but still quite runny. Scatter with the remaining Parmesan, drizzle with olive oil, and place in the hot oven. Leave until the frittata becomes crisp at the edges and slightly brown on top, a minute or two only. Remove from the oven, loosen with a long spatula, and place on warm serving plates. Cut into wedges to serve.

sorrel frittata
frittata di acetosa

for 2
1 large handful of sorrel leaves, washed, tough
   stalks removed
4 large, organic free-range eggs
Maldon salt and freshly ground black pepper
olive oil
20 g butter
150 g mascarpone cheese
50 g Parmesan, freshly grated

Preheat the oven to 230°C/450°F/Gas 8.

Roughly chop the sorrel. Break the eggs into a bowl and lightly beat.
Season with salt and pepper. Add half the sorrel.

Heat 4 tablespoons of the olive oil and the butter in a medium ovenproof
frying pan, tilting the pan to coat the surface. Add the egg mixture and
almost immediately half the mascarpone. Push the mascarpone into the
egg mixture with a wooden spoon as it begins to thicken. When the
frittata is almost set, add the remaining sorrel leaves and spoon over the
rest of the mascarpone. Scatter with 1 tablespoon of the Parmesan and
drizzle with a little olive oil. Season with salt and pepper and place in the
preheated oven for a minute or two.

Remove from the oven. The frittata will be crisp on the edges and slightly
runny in the centre. Loosen the frittata from the pan with a spatula and
serve on a warm plate. Scatter over the remaining Parmesan.

april

rocket [128] *pizza* pizza with rocket and goat's cheese. *soup* rocket and pasta soup. *pasta* tagliatelle with rocket. **spinach** [134] *soup* spinach and lentil soup with pancetta. *frittata* spinach and prosciutto frittata. *antipasto* spinach with olive oil. **potatoes** [140] *salad* salad of potatoes, celery and bottarga. *vegetable* potato, leek and anchovy gratin. *antipasto* potatoes, salt cod and olives. **nettles** [146] *pasta* fresh tagliatelle with nettles. **nespole** [150] *pudding* almond biscotti. sweet ricotta. baked nespole.

rocket

We put rocket – or rucola in Italian – into salads in both winter and summer. In April the hardier autumn-planted rocket begins to grow well, and the flavour is particularly strong. It is these stronger-flavoured rockets that are best for blanching.

We grow three kinds in the herb box at the restaurant.

• Wild rocket is a perennial that we started to grow ten years ago from seeds gathered from wild roadside plants in Turkey. It is a small shrubby plant with small blade-like, pointed leaves. Pick the shoots from the woody stems, and fresh succulent leaves re-grow quite quickly. This is the strongest, most peppery rocket, and we use it more like a herb, to flavour beans etc.

• We grow Capri rocket too, which has similar small leaves, though they are more jagged in shape and coarser in texture. It is an annual, and can always be found in the Rome markets.

• Large-leaf rocket, particularly the young first cuttings, is quite mild, usually paler in colour, and does not last at all. The larger mature leaves are more robust and less likely to bruise.

Rocket is very easy to grow: it makes edible leaves within six weeks; it grows successfully in tubs; and it is hardy. It is probably our first choice when it comes to space in the garden. In summer it must be watered frequently or it will shoot into spindly stalks and flower heads.

pizza with rocket and goat's cheese
pizza con caprino e rucola

for 6, making 3 pizzas
300 g large-leafed rocket, washed and dried
3 x 30 cm Pizza Dough Bases (see page 454)
9 small individual goat's cheeses, about 120 g each
extra virgin olive oil
300 g black olives, pitted
3 tablespoons finely chopped fresh flat-leaf
    parsley
3 dried red chillies, crumbled
3 teaspoons red wine herb vinegar
1 ciabatta loaf, crusts removed
3 tablespoons fresh thyme leaves
Maldon salt and freshly ground black pepper
lemon juice

Preheat the oven to 230°C/450°F/Gas 8 for 30 minutes, and put in a pizza stone if you have one. Prepare the pizza dough base.

Cut the cheeses in half horizontally, place in one layer in a shallow dish, and cover with olive oil. Place the olives in a bowl, add the parsley, chilli and herb vinegar, cover with olive oil and stir to combine. Leave to marinate.

Place the bread in a processor and grate into coarse crumbs. Add the thyme and pulse-chop to combine. Place in a bowl. Gently roll the cheese in the breadcrumbs to coat completely. Place the cheese on the pizza base, and sprinkle with the remaining thyme and breadcrumb mixture and the marinated olives. Drizzle over some of the marinating olive oil, season with salt and pepper, and bake in the preheated oven until the cheese has melted and the crust is crisp, about 6-8 minutes.

Dress the rocket leaves with a tablespoon of olive oil and a squeeze of lemon juice. Season with salt and pepper, and place on top of the hot pizza.

rocket and pasta soup
zuppa di rucola e pasta

for 6
1 kg rocket leaves, washed
100 g pasta shells, broken up
100 g dried cannellini beans, cooked (see
    page 376)
Maldon salt and freshly ground black pepper
3 tablespoons olive oil
3 garlic cloves, peeled and chopped
2 small dried red chillies, crumbled
5 salted anchovies, prepared (see page 458)
extra virgin olive oil
freshly grated Parmesan

Blanch three-quarters of the rocket in boiling salted water for 2 minutes, then drain. Cool a little then roughly chop. Cook the pasta in a large saucepan of boiling salted water until al dente, then drain.

Using a large, thick-bottomed saucepan, heat the olive oil over a medium heat and add the garlic and cook until soft and brown. Add the chilli and anchovy fillets, breaking up the anchovies by pushing them around the pan. As soon as they have 'melted', about 2 minutes, stir in the chopped blanched rocket. Stir to combine the flavours, then add 5 tablespoons of cannellini beans and enough of their cooking water to lubricate the soup. Cook for a few minutes and season. Add the pasta and the remaining fresh rocket leaves. Cook just until the rocket has wilted. Serve with extra virgin olive oil and grated Parmesan.

tagliatelle with rocket
tagliatelle con la rucola

for 6

1 kg large-leafed rocket, washed and roughly
    chopped
600 g Fresh Pasta (see page 454), made into
    tagliatelle
3 tablespoons olive oil
3 garlic cloves, peeled, sliced and chopped
4 salted anchovies, prepared (see page 458)
1 teaspoon fennel seeds, crushed
2 dried red chillies, crumbled
1 x 800 g tin peeled plum tomatoes, drained of
    their juices
Maldon salt and freshly ground black pepper
extra virgin olive oil
200 g ricotta salata, freshly grated

Gently heat the olive oil in a thick-bottomed saucepan. Add the garlic
and fry until golden. Add the anchovies, fennel seeds and chilli, and
push around the pan to melt and combine them. Add the tomatoes and 1
tablespoon salt. Stir with a spoon to break the tomatoes up, and simmer
gently until they have reduced to a thick sauce, about 20-25 minutes.

Bring a large saucepan of salted water to the boil and cook the
tagliatelle for 2 minutes, then add the rocket. Cook together for 2-3
minutes until the pasta is al dente. Drain and return to the saucepan.
Pour over extra virgin olive oil and season with salt and pepper. Finally
stir in the tomato sauce and half the grated ricotta. Serve with more
olive oil and the remaining ricotta.

spinach

Spinach is traditionally served in Italy at room temperature, after having been lightly blanched in boiling salted water, drained and gently squeezed dry. It is then dressed with the best-quality extra virgin olive oil, salt and pepper, and a piece of lemon. Some prefer their spinach with more lemon or less. On a trip to Rome, a chef told us that the only way to eat cold spinach is with just olive oil, salt and pepper, never lemon.

The Italian spinach variety we like most produces very broad round leaves, which are thick and fleshy, and a glossy green in colour. They are harvested and sold in clumps. When preparing spinach, reject any leaves that are yellow or limp. The stems of larger leaves must be removed before cooking. Spinach is often full of grit, and so needs to be washed carefully. Fill the sink with water and plunge in the spinach to release the dirt, which will settle on the bottom. Continue plunging, with clean water, until there is no more dirt at the bottom of the sink.

spinach and lentil soup with pancetta
zuppa di spinaci e lenticchie con pancetta

for 8
500 g fresh spinach, weighed after removing tough
    stalks
250 g Puy or Castelluccio lentils
16 slices pancetta
2 onions, peeled
2 carrots, peeled and trimmed
inner white heart of 1 head celery
3 garlic cloves, peeled
2 tablespoons olive oil
1.5 litres chicken stock (see page 455)
Maldon salt and freshly ground black pepper
4 tablespoons crème fraîche
extra virgin olive oil

Chop the onions, carrots, celery and garlic very finely. In a thick-bottomed saucepan, heat the olive oil and fry the vegetables until very soft, about 10 minutes. Add the lentils and stock and boil until the lentils are soft, about 20 minutes. Drain the lentils, reserving the stock. Put the lentils and vegetables through a mouli, then return to the saucepan. Season.

Meanwhile, blanch the spinach briefly in boiling salted water, then drain and pulse-chop in a food processor. Stir into the lentils. Add enough of the reserved chicken/lentil stock to make a thick soup consistency, and cook until hot. Stir in the crème fraîche, and season again.

Just before serving, grill the pancetta until crisp. Place two slices of pancetta in each bowl of soup. Drizzle with extra virgin olive oil, and serve.

spinach and prosciutto frittata
frittata di spinaci e prosciutto

for 4
1kg fresh spinach, tough stalks removed, leaves
    washed
6 large slices prosciutto
Maldon salt and freshly ground black pepper
100 g unsalted butter
8 large, organic free-range eggs
100 g Parmesan, freshly grated
4 tablespoons olive oil

Preheat the oven to 230°C/450°F/Gas 8.

Blanch the spinach briefly in boiling salted water. Drain, and then season
and add 50 g of the butter.

Break the eggs into a bowl and beat lightly. Add the spinach and half the
Parmesan, then season with salt and pepper. Stir to combine.

Use two 20-30 cm frying pans with ovenproof handles. Heat 2
tablespoons of the olive oil in each pan. When hot, pour half the mixture
into each pan. Reduce the heat and cook for a few minutes until just set,
still a bit runny. Scatter over the remaning Parmesan, and place knobs of
the remaining butter over the surface. Put into the hot oven for a minute
or two or until the frittata begins to rise and become crisp at the edges.

Remove from the oven, loosen the edges with a spatula, and place on
warm serving plates. Divide each frittata into three, and serve with the
prosciutto draped over.

spinach with olive oil
spinaci con olio

for 6
2 kg spinach
Maldon salt and freshly ground black pepper
extra virgin olive oil

Carefully pick through the spinach, leaving the stalks. just trim off any tough parts. Soak in cold water to wash off grit and mud. Rinse well.

Bring a large saucepan of water to the boil. Add 2 tablespoons of salt and the spinach. Cover and cook for 2 minutes. Drain and allow to cool until you can handle it. Squeeze out excess water gently with your hands.

Spread the spinach out on a serving plate and liberally season with freshly ground black pepper and Maldon salt. Pour over extra virgin olive oil and toss so that the spinach is coated. Serve as part of an antipasti.

potatoes

The maincrop potatoes that we use are the varieties Linska and Roseval. They remain thin-skinned during storage, and retain their yellow waxy texture. Desirée is another potato that we use in April, and it is our first choice when making gnocchi.

There are a number of Italian varieties that taste different from each other, some nutty, some sweet. Spunta, Primura and Sistema are all potatoes that you should try if you ever see them in the shops.

Italians appreciate potatoes as a vegetable in their own right, not just as an accompaniment to other vegetables. They are eaten much more in the north, where they have been grown since the eighteenth century. They are not used every day as a starch, though, in contrast to the rest of Europe.

Potatoes in Italian cooking are mostly cooked with other ingredients and vegetables, in recipes for soups, risottos and salads, as well as accompaniments for fish and meat.

salad of potatoes, celery and bottarga
insalata di patate, sedano e bottarga

for 6
1.5 kg red Roseval potatoes, peeled
300 g bottarga
Maldon salt and freshly ground black pepper
4 tablespoons red wine herb vinegar
extra virgin olive oil
2 heads celery, leaves intact, washed
3 large fresh red chillies, washed
juice of 1 lemon

Bring a large saucepan of salted water to the boil, add the potatoes and cook until al dente. Drain and cut into finger lengths. Put in a bowl, and season with salt and pepper. Shake over the vinegar and drizzle in 6 tablespoons extra virgin olive oil.

Pick the freshest pale leaves from the inside celery stalks, about a large handful. Chop roughly and add to the potatoes. Remove and discard the tough outer stalks from the celery heads, and trim the tops. Cut the remaining stalks at an angle into fine slices across the whole head. Add the slices to the potatoes, and toss together.

Finely slice the whole chillies across at an angle. As you cut, some of the seeds should drop out.

Divide the potato mixture between serving plates, and dot the chilli slices over. Use a catapult-shaped potato peeler to finely shave the bottarga over each plate, and then squeeze lemon juice over the bottarga. Finally drizzle with a little more extra virgin olive oil.

potato, leek and anchovy gratin
patate, porri e acciughe gratinati

for 6
1 kg small red Roseval potatoes, peeled and cut in
    half lengthwise
1 kg spring leeks, no thicker than a thumb, white
    and pale green parts cut diagonally 1 cm thick
5 salted anchovies, prepared (see page 458),
    roughly chopped
Maldon salt and freshly ground black pepper
30 g butter
4 garlic cloves, peeled and finely chopped
200 ml milk
100 ml double cream
1 handful of fresh flat-leaf parsley, chopped
1 ciabatta loaf, crust discarded, made into coarse
    breadcrumbs
olive oil

Preheat the oven to 200°C/400°F/Gas 6.

Soak the leeks in a bowl of cold water for 30 minutes, then drain. Rinse a
second time so that they are completely free of earth and sand. Boil the
potatoes in salted water for 8 minutes, then drain, keeping the water.
Return the water to the boil, and boil the leeks for 5 minutes. Drain and
run cold water through them so they remain al dente.

In a thick-bottomed pan, heat 15 g of the butter, add the garlic and
anchovies, and mash together. Add the milk and cream, then slowly
bring to the boil. Remove from the heat, and test for seasoning.

Butter an ovenproof china dish, and add the potatoes and leeks mixed
together. Season and pour over the anchovy mixture. Scatter with
parsley and breadcrumbs, drizzle with a little olive oil, and bake for 30
minutes. The top should be crisp and the leeks and potatoes cooked
through.

potatoes, salt cod and olives
patate con baccalà e olive

for 6
500 g Roseval potatoes, peeled, halved lengthwise
650 g salt cod, prepared (see page 458)
150 g black olives, pitted, kept whole
80 g pine kernels, briefly toasted
Maldon salt and freshly ground black pepper
85 ml red wine vinegar
extra virgin olive oil
olive oil
3 garlic cloves, peeled and finely chopped
1 x 800 g tin peeled plum tomatoes, drained
3 large fresh red chillies, seeded and finely sliced
4 lemons
125 ml white wine or water
4 tablespoons chopped fresh flat-leaf parsley

Cook the potatoes in boiling salted water until al dente. Drain, put in a bowl, and add the vinegar, salt, pepper and 4 tablespoons extra virgin olive oil. Keep warm. Heat 2 tablespoons olive oil in a large, thick-bottomed frying pan, add half the garlic and cook for a few minutes. Add the tomatoes and some salt, then cook for 30 minutes.

Heat 3 tablespoons olive oil in a large, thick-bottomed flat pan with a lid. Add the remaining garlic and fry briefly. Place the cod in, skin side down, and sprinkle over the chilli, pepper, juice of 1 lemon and the wine or water. Cover, reduce the heat, and simmer for 4-5 minutes or until the cod is cooked. Remove from the heat, allow to cool a little, then carefully flake the flesh from the skin. Place in a warm serving bowl. Pour over any pan juices. Combine the tomato sauce with the cod.

Mix the warm potatoes with the olives and most of the parsley. Place on a large serving plate, and all but cover with the cod and tomatoes. Scatter over the pine kernels, and sprinkle with the remaining parsley. Drizzle over some extra virgin olive oil, and serve with lemon wedges.

nettles

Young, bright green nettle leaves are delicious when cooked.
Pick them from plants that have not made flowers and avoid
larger leaves, which have a coarse texture and bitter taste.
Wear gloves and use scissors to snip off the leaves.

Look for nettles in gardens and fields away from roadsides.
Remove leaves from stalks, if any, and wash in two or three
changes of water. Nettles cook quickly like spinach; they
completely lose their sting when cooked.

In Italy, nettle leaves are often used as a substitute for spinach
when making fresh pasta.

fresh tagliatelle with nettles
tagliatelle con le ortiche

for 6
nettle pasta
at least 2 kg young nettle leaves
Maldon salt and freshly ground black pepper
350 g fine semolina flour
300 g Tipo 'oo' pasta flour, plus 100 g for dusting
3 large, organic free-range eggs
10 large, organic free-range egg yolks
to serve
150 g unsalted butter, softened
freshly grated Parmesan

Wash the nettle leaves carefully in cold water. Blanch them in boiling salted water until soft and beginning to break up, about 1 minute. Drain gently, squeezing out the excess liquid. Shape some into 3-4 balls, roughly the same size as an egg. Put the rest of the nettles to one side. Allow to cool.

Sieve the flours into the bowl of a food processor and add the eggs, egg yolks and the 3-4 nettle balls. Using a dough hook, knead slowly, allowing the mixture to come together until the dough is consistently bright green and smooth. If it is too sticky, add a little extra pasta flour. Dust the work surface with the dusting flour, halve the dough, and knead each half by hand for 3-4 minutes, until completely pliable and smooth. Wrap each ball in clingfilm and chill for at least 1 hour.

Roll the pasta in the machine as described on page 454, then cut into tagliatelle. Cook the tagliatelle in a generous amount of boiling salted water for 1 minute, then add the remaining nettle leaves, which will take less than a minute to become tender. Test the tagliatelle and nettles, then drain, keeping 3-4 tablespoons of the pasta water. Put the retained water into a warm pasta bowl, add the softened butter, some salt and pepper, and then add the cooked nettles and tagliatelle. Toss gently and serve immediately, making sure that each portion is quite wet with an equal amount of nettle leaves. Serve in bowls with Parmesan.

nespole

Nespola giapponese is the fruit known in Britain as the loquat, or Japanese medlar, which is native to China and Japan. The beautiful evergreen tree is often used as a decorative feature in many gardens in the Mediterranean.

Nespole ripen in the early spring and we usually have them in the River Cafe in April. Their skin is orange in colour, and there are distinctive curved stones inside. When ripe, the white to yellow flesh is soft and pear-like in texture, with an acid-sweet, pleasant flavour. However, nespole are not traditionally eaten raw, but cooked for jams. The way we bake them is rather like making jam, as we use lemon juice, vanilla and sugar.

almond biscotti
biscotti alla mandorle

makes about 30 biscuits
150 g whole blanched almonds, coarsely chopped
100 pine kernels
2 vanilla pods, chopped into 2 cm lengths
250 g caster sugar
250 g plain flour
1/4 teaspoon baking powder
a pinch of fine salt
2 large, organic free-range eggs
finely grated zest of 2 oranges
finely grated zest of 1 lemon
unsalted butter for greasing

Preheat the oven to 190°C/375°C/Gas 5. On a baking tray toast the almonds and pine kernels until light brown. Allow to cool.

Process the vanilla pods to a fine powder in a food processor, or pound in a pestle and mortar. Add to the sugar and mix. Put all the dry ingredients – the vanilla sugar, the flour, baking powder and salt – on to a clean work surface and form into a mound. Make a well in the centre.

Whisk together the eggs and the zest of the oranges and lemon, then pour into the well. Use your hands to combine to a dough. Gradually knead in the almonds and pine kernels. Divide into two, and roll each piece out into oval log shapes about 7-8 cm in diameter. Place these on a buttered baking tray and bake for about 15 minutes. Remove from the oven and slice the logs diagonally into biscuits about 1 cm thick. Place the slices back on the baking tray and return to the oven for another 5 minutes, turning them once, or until just brown.

sweet ricotta
ricotta dolce

for 6

600g fresh ricotta cheese, drained
   of any liquid

5 tablespoons icing sugar

4 tablespoons dark rum

3 teaspoons finely ground espresso
   coffee beans

Beat the ricotta with a fork to lighten it and then add the sugar, rum and coffee. Mix well. Put in the fridge to cool. Ricotta dolce can be served with tart fruit such as the Baked Nespole overleaf, or with biscotti (see left).

baked nespole
nespole al forno

for 6
1 kg nespole
2 vanilla pods
4 tablespoons caster sugar
120 ml brandy
juice of 1 lemon
crème fraîche to serve

Preheat the oven to 160°C/325°F/Gas 3.

Cut the nespole in half and take out the centre stones. These are encased in a tough skin which needs to be pulled away from the flesh of the fruit.

Slit the vanilla pods lengthways and scrape out the seeds. Mix these with the caster sugar.

Place the nespole, cut side up, in an ovenproof dish. Spoon a little of the vanilla sugar mixture on to each fruit. Sprinkle a few spoonfuls of brandy over, squeeze over the lemon juice, and bake in the preheated oven for 45 minutes.

Serve with crème fraîche and a little more brandy over the fruit.

may

apricots [158] *pudding* apricot, lemon and almond tart. *jam* apricot jam. apricot jam ice-cream. asparagus [164] *risotto* white asparagus risotto. *antipasto* asparagus with anchovy and milk sauce. *pasta* penne with asparagus carbonara. *salad* asparagus and gulls' egg salad. *pasta* pasta with asparagus, peas, prosciutto and cream. tagliatelle with asparagus and parmesan. broad beans [174] *soup* minestrone of broad beans. *pasta* broad bean and pecorino tagliatelle. *risotto* risotto of peas and small broad beans. melons [180] *pudding* melon and lemon sorbet. melon marinated in valpolicella with vanilla. spring carrots [186] *vegetable* braised spring carrots and artichokes. carrots marsala. spring onions [190] *vegetable* peas braised with spring onions. *pizza* spring onion and thyme pizza.

apricots

Apricots arrive early in the summer, after the almond and before the peach and cherry. Choose apricots that look ripe and have a lovely fruity smell. The stronger their colour, the sweeter the taste. Avoid apricots that are green and hard.

Apricots that are less ripe may be used for cooking, best roasted with vanilla sugar, which brings out their juices and creates a dense texture. If not cooked, apricots should be eaten at room temperature, never chilled. The apricot and almond tart is the summer version of our pear and almond tart, as apricots are the only summer fruit that cooks so well.

It is almost impossible to peel an apricot, and in any case much of the flavour is in the skin.

apricot, lemon and almond tart
torta di albicocche, limone e mandorle

for 6

pastry
350 g plain flour
225 g unsalted butter
100 g caster sugar
a pinch of salt
3 large, organic free-range egg yolks
filling
450 g fresh, ripe, small to medium apricots
300 g unsalted butter
300 g caster sugar
300 g blanched whole almonds, finely ground
juice and finely grated peel of 1 lemon
3 large, organic free-range eggs

For the pastry, pulse the flour and butter together in a food processor until the mixture resembles coarse breadcrumbs. Add the sugar, salt and egg yolks, and pulse until the mixture just leaves the sides of the bowl. Form into a ball, wrap in clingfilm, and chill for at least an hour.

Using the largest holes on the side of a cheese grater, coarsely grate the pastry into a 30 cm fluted, loose-bottomed tart tin. Working very quickly to keep the pastry cold, press it evenly into the sides and base of the tin. Return to the fridge for half an hour. Preheat the oven to 180°C/350°F/ Gas 4. Blind-bake the pastry case for 20 minutes. Let cool completely.

For the filling, cut the apricots in half and remove the stones. Place them cut side down in the tart case. In a food processor, cream the butter and sugar together until pale and light. Add the almonds, pulse to combine, then slowly add the grated lemon peel and lemon juice, pulsing again. Stir in the eggs one by one. Pour the filling over the apricots and smooth over just to surround the apricots. Bake for 40 minutes. Leave to cool.

apricot jam
marmellata di albicocche

fills 4 x 250 g jars
1 kg very ripe, dark-coloured apricots, stoned
   weight (keep the stones)
4 ripe nectarines, peeled and stones discarded
500 g caster sugar
120 ml water

Crack the apricot stones open and remove the kernels. Blanch these for 30 seconds in boiling water, then cool a little and peel. Keep the peeled kernels to one side.

Put the apricots, sugar and measured water into a large thick-bottomed, low-sided saucepan. Heat very gently, stirring all the time, until the sugar dissolves, and the juices begin to flow from the apricots. Raise the heat slightly, add the nectarines and boil, stirring to prevent the fruit sticking. The fruit should break down, and the liquid should evaporate. The jam is ready when the steam rising from the pan is less dense and the surface begins to seethe rather than bubble. This will take about 25-30 minutes, depending on how ripe the apricots are.

Test for setting by placing a spoon of the jam on a cold plate. If the jam runs very slowly, it is ready. Finally, stir in the apricot kernels. Spoon the jam into clean glass jars and seal well. Store in a cool dark place.

apricot jam ice-cream
gelato alla marmellata di albicocche

for 6
500 g apricot jam
1 litre double cream
275 ml milk
9 large, organic free-range egg yolks
200 g caster sugar
125 ml Vecchio Romagna brandy

In a thick-bottomed saucepan combine the cream and milk. Heat gently until just below boiling point.

Beat the egg yolks and sugar together quite slowly until pale and thick.

Pour a ladleful of the hot cream into the egg mixture to loosen it, then add this mixture back to the hot cream. Cook gently on a very low heat to 72°C/161°F, stirring constantly to prevent curdling, until thick. Pour into a bowl and cool.

Pour the cold custard into an ice-cream machine and churn for 6 minutes or until the cream begins to freeze. Stir the brandy into the apricot jam and add half of this to the cream. Churn for a further 6-8 minutes to thoroughly incorporate the jam into the custard. Finally add the remaining jam, and churn briefly just to combine and solidify the ice-cream.

asparagus

The asparagus season starts at the end of April and lasts through June. This is when asparagus should be eaten and appreciated, for when the season ends it should not be bought until the following year.

Asparagus is best eaten soon after picking as it quickly loses its sweetness. When buying asparagus look for firm, bright green spears, with tightly closed heads. Don't buy spears that look dry, wrinkled or yellow.

White asparagus is grown in the northern regions of Italy, in Friuli and the Veneto where it is paired with risotto. The spears are banked up with soil as they grow to deprive them of light. They are much more delicate in flavour than green asparagus, which grows in the sun. As the season progresses, the spears get larger. When they are thin – known as sprue - we like to roast or grill them, delicious with anchovies.

The larger spears must be peeled. Use a potato peeler, and work from the bottom of the tip to the cut end.

white asparagus risotto
risotto agli asparagi bianchi

for 6
1.5 kg white asparagus
1.25 litres chicken stock (see page 455)
Maldon salt and freshly ground black pepper
150 g unsalted butter, softened
4 large round spring onions, roughly chopped
2 medium leeks, white part only, finely sliced
400 g carnaroli rice
100 ml vermouth
4 tablespoons fresh basil leaves
150 g Parmesan, freshly grated

Heat the chicken stock and check for seasoning.

Cut the tips off the asparagus. Peel and chop the tender part of the stalks into 2 cm lengths. Heat a small saucepan of water to boiling, and add 1 tablespoon salt. Add the asparagus tips and cook for 2 minutes. Drain, season, and add 25 g of the butter.

In a heavy, thick-bottomed saucepan, melt half the remaining butter, then add the spring onion, leek and asparagus stalks, and gently soften and cook to combine the flavours. When the onion begins to colour, add the rice and stir to coat each grain for 2-3 minutes. Add half the vermouth and let it be absorbed by the rice, then start to add the hot stock, ladle by ladle, stirring constantly, allowing each ladleful to be absorbed before adding the next. Continue until the rice is al dente, about 20 minutes. Finally stir in the asparagus tips, the basil, the remaining vermouth and butter. Stir just to wilt the basil, and combine to make a wet creamy risotto.

Taste for seasoning, and serve immediately on warm plates with freshly grated Parmesan.

asparagus with anchovy and milk sauce

asparagi al latte e acciughe

This sauce is also good with potatoes cooked with chickpeas, or other green vegetables such as spinach and sea kale.

for 6

3 kg thin to medium asparagus, tough
   stalk ends removed
Maldon salt

sauce

8 salted anchovies, prepared (see page 458)
peel of 1 thick-skinned lemon, washed, white pith
   discarded, chopped
3 small dried red chillies
3 garlic cloves, peeled and crushed
150 ml milk
about 4 tablespoons extra virgin olive oil

To make the sauce, put the anchovies, lemon peel, chillies and garlic into the food processor and chop briefly. Add the milk and pulse to a smooth sauce. Pour into a bowl, and slowly stir in the olive oil.

Boil the asparagus in salted water until al dente. Drain well. Serve on warm plates with the sauce.

penne with asparagus carbonara
penne alla carbonara con asparagi

for 6
1.5 kg sprue asparagus, freshly picked
400 g dried penne rigate
Maldon salt and freshly ground black pepper
8 large, organic free-range egg yolks
150 g Parmesan, freshly grated
100 g butter
3 tablespoons fresh thyme leaves, picked from
    their stalks

Snap off the tough ends of each asparagus spear. Cut off the tips and put to one side. Slice the remainder of the spears at an angle, about 2 cm long.

Bring two saucepans of water to the boil and add salt to both. Put the penne into one pan of boiling water: the pasta will take 9 minutes to become al dente. Meanwhile, put the asparagus stalks into the other pan of boiling water and begin to blanch. After 2 minutes add the tips, and blanch together for 4 minutes. Drain well.

Lightly beat the egg yolks with a fork, and season. Add about 2 tablespoons of the grated Parmesan.

Melt the butter in a small thick-bottomed pan. When beginning to foam, add the thyme and, almost immediately, the drained asparagus. Season and toss for a few seconds.

Drain the penne, and immediately add the hot asparagus and butter. Stir briefly together, then pour in the egg mixture. Toss a little to allow the egg yolks to coat the pasta. Serve immediately, with the remaining Parmesan.

asparagus and gulls' egg salad
insalata di nizza

for 6
1.5 kg sprue asparagus, or as thin as you can find
Maldon salt and freshly ground black pepper
extra virgin olive oil
12 gulls' eggs, or 18 quails' eggs
80 g Niçoise or other black olives, pitted
3 tablespoons roughly chopped fresh flat-leaf
    parsley
2 small dried red chillies, crumbled
6 salted anchovies, prepared (see page 458)
juice of 1 lemon
150 g Parmesan, in shavings

Break off the tough ends of the asparagus spears and tie the spears together into two bunches. Bring a large saucepan of water to the boil, add 2 tablespoons salt, and blanch the asparagus for 5 minutes. Drain and cool. Remove the strings. Season with salt and pepper, and drizzle with extra virgin olive oil.

Put the gulls' eggs into a small saucepan, cover with cold water, and gently bring to the boil. Simmer for 3 minutes, drain, cool a little and then peel off the shells. Cut the eggs in half lengthways; they should be soft in the centre. (Quails' eggs will take only 1 minute from coming to the boil.)

Add the olives and parsley to the asparagus, and very gently toss together. Place the asparagus on to a large serving dish, and put the gulls' eggs on top. Sprinkle each egg with a tiny bit of chilli, salt and pepper. Arrange the anchovy fillets on top as well. Squeeze the juice of the lemon over each fillet, and finally add the Parmesan shavings.

pasta with asparagus, peas, prosciutto and cream
pasta con asparagi, piselli e prosciutto

for 6
1.5 kg sprue asparagus, freshly picked
1 kg fresh young peas (podded weight 500g)
Maldon salt and freshly ground black pepper
25 g unsalted butter
200 g prosciutto slices, cut into strips
250 ml chicken stock (see page 455)
500 ml double cream
400 g dried conchiglie (pasta shells)
3 tablespoons finely chopped fresh mint
freshly grated Parmesan

Prepare the asparagus by snapping off the tough ends of the stems, keeping only the most tender parts. Slice the stems and tips on the diagonal.

In a pot of boiling salted water, blanch the peas until tender but still firm, about 2 minutes. Remove with a slotted spoon and set aside. Return the water to the boil and blanch the asparagus for about 2 minutes, depending on size. The pieces should be slightly firm still. Drain and add to the peas.

In a large frying pan heat the butter and fry the prosciutto until it is just soft and translucent. Add the peas and asparagus. In a separate pan bring the stock and cream to the boil. Season with salt and pepper, and cook gently for 3 minutes. Pour over the asparagus, peas and prosciutto.

In a large saucepan cook the pasta shells in a generous amount of salted boiling water until al dente. Drain, leaving a small amount of cooking water in the bottom of the pot. Return the pasta to the pot and add the sauce and the mint, tossing well over a very low heat until all the pasta is coated with the sauce. Season well, and serve with grated Parmesan.

tagliatelle with asparagus and parmesan
tagliatelle con fonduta agli asparagi

for 6
1.5 kg sprue asparagus, freshly picked
600 g Fresh Pasta (see page 454), made into
   tagliatelle
200 g Parmesan, freshly grated, plus extra for
   sprinkling
1 garlic clove, peeled and crushed
400 ml crème fraîche
2 large, organic free-range egg yolks
Maldon salt and freshly ground black pepper

Use a medium saucepan that will fit inside another larger saucepan with enough room to half fill with water. Put on to heat.

Rub the crushed garlic round the surface of the smaller pan. Add the crème fraîche, Parmesan and egg yolks. Place the pan on top of the hot water and, stirring gently all the time, cook until the sauce thickens, about 15-20 minutes. Season with salt and pepper. Keep warm.

Prepare the asparagus. Snap off the tough ends of the stems, keeping only the most tender parts. Slice the stems and tips thinly on the diagonal. Bring a very large saucepan of water to the boil, season with 2 tablespoons salt, and add the tagliatelle. Stir into the water and cook for 1 minute, then add the asparagus and continue to cook for a further 3-4 minutes, or until the pasta and asparagus are al dente. Drain and place in a warm serving bowl.

Pour the fondue over the pasta and asparagus, and serve immediately with freshly grated Parmesan on warm plates.

broad beans

In Italy the first broad beans signal the beginning of spring. In Sicily this occurs as early as March, when they have special 'festas' to celebrate their arrival. The new beans – known in Tuscany as baccello and in Sicily as prima fave – are so delicate they are eaten raw. Here broad beans appear in May, coming to a finish in June.

Broad beans should be eaten as soon as possible after picking. They are best if left on the stem, for the beans stay softer and more moist. We always look for pods that appear young and green, without blackened marks, for we prefer not to shell the beans once out of the pods, enjoying the texture and taste of the young skins.

minestrone of broad beans
zuppa di fave fresche

for 6
3 kg fresh broad beans (podded weight 1.5 kg)
3 tablespoons olive oil
2 red onions, peeled and finely chopped
3 spring carrots, scrubbed and finely chopped
inner white heart of 1 head celery, finely chopped
2 young leeks, white parts only, finely sliced
2 garlic cloves, peeled and finely chopped
3 new potatoes, peeled and finely chopped
150 g pancetta, finely chopped
Maldon salt and freshly ground black pepper
500 ml chicken stock (see page 455)
extra virgin olive oil
freshly grated Parmesan

Heat the olive oil in a thick-bottomed saucepan and add the onion, carrot, celery and leek. Cook together until very soft, then add the garlic, potato and pancetta. When the garlic is soft and the pancetta translucent, add the broad beans and salt and pepper, and stir to combine. Bring the chicken stock to the boil and add just enough to cover the vegetables. Simmer for 20 minutes or more, depending on the size of the broad beans, adding more stock as necessary. The broad beans must be very tender. Check the seasoning.

Put half of the soup into a food processor and pulse-chop to a thick purée. Return to the bulk of the soup and stir, adding more chicken stock if necessary. The consistency should be very thick. Drizzle with extra virgin olive oil, and serve with a generous amount of grated Parmesan.

broad bean and pecorino tagliatelle
tagliatelle con fave fresche e pecorino

for 6

2 kg fresh broad beans (podded weight 1 kg)
200 g Pecorino Staginata from Tuscany, or similar
   cheese
500 g dried tagliatelle, or 800 g Fresh Pasta (see
   page 454), made into tagliatelle
2 medium bunches fresh basil, leaves picked from
   their stalks
2 spring garlic cloves, peeled
Maldon salt and freshly ground black pepper
150 ml extra virgin olive oil
juice of 1 lemon

Pod the broad beans and divide them into three batches. Tear the basil leaves roughly. Grate the Pecorino quite coarsely.

Pound a third of the beans in a pestle and mortar (alternatively you can use a food processor and pulse-chop) with 1 garlic clove, 3 tablespoons basil and a little salt until you have a coarsely broken-up pulp. Add a little extra virgin olive oil to lubricate, and remove to a large bowl. Repeat, pounding the second third of the beans with the other garlic clove, a handful of basil and a little salt. Lubricate with oil as before, and add to the first mixture. Finally stir together with the remaining whole beans, and the rest of the oil and basil. Season with pepper and the lemon juice.

Bring a large saucepan of water to the boil and add some salt. Cook the pasta until al dente, then drain, keeping the pasta quite wet. Immediately combine with the broad bean sauce, and stir together with the Pecorino and some more extra virgin olive oil if needed. Serve immediately on warm plates.

risi e bisi con baccelli
risotto of peas and small broad beans

for 6
2 kg fresh broad beans (podded weight 1 kg)
1 kg fresh young peas (podded weight 500 g)
Maldon salt and freshly ground black pepper
200 g unsalted butter, softened
3 tablespoons chopped fresh flat-leaf parsley
1.75 litres chicken stock (see page 455)
200 g spring onions, chopped
300 g vialone nano rice
100 g Parmesan, freshly grated

Pod the broad beans and the peas. Keep the pea pods. Bring a large saucepan of water to the boil and add 2 tablespoons salt. Add the pea pods and cook for 5 minutes. Remove with a slotted spoon. Put through a mouli, then add 2-3 tablespoons of the cooking water. Blanch the peas in the boiling salted water, drain and add to the pea-pod pulp. Season and add 25 g of the butter.

Add the broad beans to a clean pan of boiling unsalted water, and cook for 2-4 minutes. Drain and add 25 g of the butter, the parsley and salt and pepper. Put half of this into the food processor and pulse-chop. Return to the whole beans. Heat the stock and check for seasoning.

Melt half the remaining butter in a large, thick-bottomed saucepan. Gently fry the onion until soft and beginning to colour. Add the rice, stir to coat each grain with butter, and cook for 2-3 minutes. When the rice is opaque, start adding the hot stock ladle by ladle, adding the next only when the rice has absorbed the last. Stir continuously. Continue to cook until the rice is al dente, about 15 minutes.

Finally, stir in the peas and their pea-pod liquor and the broad beans. Add the remaining butter, and stir in the Parmesan. Serve immediately.

melons

Melons are the first of the summer fruits to arrive, beginning in the warmth of May and continuing through July. On the Italian menu they are classically paired with prosciutto as an antipasto. For dessert, we like to combine them with Valpolicella or, when they are very ripe, make them into a sorbet.

The melons we use are melone di Apricena, or cantaloupe, the latter known as charentais in France. Charentais melons, although developed in Charentes, are mostly now grown in Cavaillon, thus the alternative name. These are the most readily available in Britain. The flesh is sweet, highly scented and deep orange in colour.

When choosing a melon, first smell it. If the aroma is too strong it will be over-ripe; no smell, and it is not ready. It should also give a little if pressed at the stalk end. The melon should be firm, with no soft spots. To be sure of one in its prime, weigh several in your hand and choose the heaviest.

melon and lemon sorbet

sorbetto al melone e limone

for 6

5 very ripe Cavaillon melons

200 g caster sugar

120 ml lemon juice

Remove the seeds from the melons and scoop out the flesh. Pulse-chop the flesh to a coarse texture in the food processor, and place in a bowl. Make a syrup with the sugar and 125 ml water. When cool, add to the melon along with the lemon juice. Pour into an ice-cream machine and churn until frozen, or freeze in a suitable container. Eat on the same day.

melon marinated in valpolicella with vanilla
melone al valpolicella con vaniglia

for 6
4 large, ripe Cavaillon melons, or 6 small
3 whole vanilla pods
150 g caster sugar
1 bottle Valpolicella Classico
juice of 1 lemon
crème fraîche to serve

Split the vanilla pods, and pull some of the seeds away from the pods.

In a small saucepan over a gentle heat, dissolve the caster sugar in a third of the wine, then add the vanilla pods and their seeds. Simmer to thicken the wine syrup over a gentle heat. Allow to cool.

Cut the melons in half and scoop out the seeds. Scrape out the flesh in big pieces, and place in a large serving bowl. Pour over the lemon juice and the Valpolicella syrup, then finally the remainder of the Valpolicella. Cover and leave in a cool place for an hour. Serve with crème fraîche.

spring carrots

The first spring carrots in May have a uniquely sweet flavour. They should be eaten as soon as possible as that flavour soon dissipates. Carrots, like other root vegetables that stay in the soil, have a far superior flavour if grown organically. When choosing carrots, look for those with bright leafy tops, which indicate how fresh the carrots are. Spring carrots should be cleaned but not peeled as most of their flavour is in the skin. Cut the greens off, leaving about a centimetre of stalk, and trim off the hairy tip.

braised spring carrots and artichokes
carote e carciofi trifolati

for 6
1.5 kg spring carrots
1.5 kg small artichokes
lemon juice or parsley stalks and leaves
3 tablespoons fresh fennel herb
2 tablespoons fresh thyme leaves
4 garlic cloves, peeled
3 tablespoons olive oil
Maldon salt and freshly ground black pepper
extra virgin olive oil

Scrub the carrots and roughly slice horizontally. Peel the artichokes down to their hearts. Remove the chokes if any. Cut the artichokes in half and put into water acidulated with lemon or parsley. Chop the fennel herb and thyme together, and the garlic. Cut the drained artichoke hearts into fine slices just before cooking.

Heat the olive oil in a large, thick-bottomed saucepan with a tight-fitting lid. Add the garlic and as soon as it begins to colour, add the carrots. Stir to combine, then add salt and put on the lid. Cook on a medium heat for 5 minutes, then add the artichokes and half the chopped herbs. Stir together and cook for 1 minute. Pour in 100 ml hot water, cover with the lid, lower the heat, and simmer for 30-45 minutes. Stir from time to time.

Finally stir in the remainder of the herbs and season generously. Stir in a little extra virgin olive oil. Serve with grilled fish or with other vegetables as part of an antipasti.

carrots marsala

carote al marsala

for 6
2 kg spring carrots, scrubbed
3 tablespoons olive oil
400 g spring garlic, outer skins removed, cloves
    kept whole, peeled
Maldon salt and freshly ground black pepper
2 branches fresh rosemary
150 ml dried grape wine such as Vin Santo

Slice the carrots diagonally across into elongated discs 5 mm thick.

Use a large flat thick-bottomed frying pan. Heat the olive oil gently, and place half the carrot discs flat into the oil. Add half the garlic. Sprinkle with salt and pepper, place half the rosemary on top, and cook for 15 minutes until the carrots are brown. Turn the carrots and garlic over and brown the other side.

Remove from the pan and repeat with the remainder of the carrots, garlic and rosemary. Add some more oil if necessary. When all the carrots are cooked, put together in the pan. Pour over the sweet wine and heat gently to allow it to reduce and thicken. Serve the carrots with the rosemary.

spring onions

Spring onions from Italy are a different vegetable from the finger-sized spring onions known and used in Britain. There, the spring onions are white, red and purple, the size of golf balls. They are juicy and fresh with a delicate sweet flavour, and are known as cipolline verde.

When cooking with these luscious onions, choose to match them with other spring vegetables and herbs. Their size and crisp texture means that they retain their identity when cooked with other vegetables. Spring onions are best simply and quickly pan-fried or char-grilled, but as their arrival coincides with the new peas, we cook them together.

As the season gets warmer, these sweet onions develop dry, papery skins, and become suitable to store.

peas braised with spring onions
piselli con cipolline verdi

for 6
500 g spring onions
3 kg fresh young peas (podded weight 1.5 kg)
350 ml chicken stock (see page 455)
4 tablespoons olive oil
Maldon salt and freshly ground black pepper
1 head curly endive
extra virgin olive oil

Trim the spring onions, removing the green leafy stalks and the roots.
Pod the peas.

Bring the chicken stock to the boil.

In a large, thick-bottomed saucepan, heat the olive oil and gently cook
the spring onions until they become translucent but not brown. Add the
peas, season with salt and pepper, and stir to coat all the peas with the
olive oil. Add enough stock to cover the peas generously and cover the
mixture with a piece of greaseproof paper. Reduce the heat as low as
possible and cook for 15 minutes or until the spring onions are
completely tender.

Remove all the outer leaves of the curly endive and discard. Tear the
small white leaves into shreds and stir into the peas. Cook for a further
few minutes until the endive is wilted. Drizzle with extra virgin olive oil to
finish. Serve at room temperature.

spring onion and thyme pizza
pizza con cipolline verdi e timo

for 2
200 g spring onions, round if possible, trimmed
1 x 30 cm Pizza Dough base (see page 454)
300 g new potatoes, scrubbed
olive oil
2 tablespoons fresh thyme leaves
Maldon salt and freshly ground black pepper
3 tablespoons red wine herb vinegar
150 g pancetta, very finely sliced

Preheat the oven to 220°C/425°F/Gas 7 for 30 minutes, and put in a pizza stone if you have one. Prepare the pizza dough base.

Slice the potatoes 2-3 mm thick, or as thin as you possibly can, and toss in 3 tablespoons of the olive oil and the thyme leaves. Season generously with salt and pepper. Place on a baking tray and roast for 10-15 minutes until beginning to colour.

Split the onions in half lengthways through the green stalk and bulb. Heat a thick-bottomed frying pan, add 3 tablespoons of the oil, and add the onions. Fry gently until soft and brown. Season and pour over the vinegar.

Roll out the pizza dough base on a floured surface as thinly as you can. Spread over the spring onion mixture, top with the potatoes and then place the slices of pancetta over. Drizzle with a little olive oil and bake in the preheated oven until the crust is crisp and the pancetta is cooked, about 8-10 minutes.

june

broad beans [196]
bruschetta broad beans braised in milk.

antipasto slow-cooked broad beans and prosciutto. broad beans and chicory with marinated anchovies.

cherries [202]
pudding cherry focaccia. cherry sorbet. *drink* grappa with cherry juice.

peas [210]
risotto pea, ricotta and lemon zest risotto. pea and vongole risotto.

antipasto pea and mint torte.

new potatoes [218]
risotto new potato risotto. *frittata* new potato and black truffle frittata.

strawberries [222]
pudding red wine sorbet with crushed strawberries. almond meringue with strawberries.

marsh samphire [228]
antipasto samphire with olive oil and lemon.

broad beans

Later in the season, as broad beans become larger, they need to be prepared and cooked in a different way from the small first beans of the season.

These beans are never served raw, nor are they cooked with their pods. When podding, we separate the large and medium beans, and cook them separately. If they are very large and starchy, we discard them. Unlike the early beans, we often remove the skin from the beans after cooking them, when they are cool enough to handle.

We tend to use the medium beans for slow cooking, combined with peas or prosciutto, in soups and pastas. They are delicious with anchovies in salads.

broad beans braised in milk
fave fresche brasate al latte

for 6
3 kg broad beans (podded weight 1.5 kg)
4 tablespoons olive oil
1 whole head spring garlic, divided into cloves,
    peeled
10 sage leaves, finely sliced
Maldon salt and freshly ground black pepper
150 ml milk
6 slices of sourdough bread
finely grated zest of 1 lemon
extra virgin olive oil

Gently heat the olive oil in a medium, thick-bottomed saucepan with a lid. Add the broad beans and garlic (apart from 1 clove, save it for the bruschetta), and slowly cook together for 10-15 minutes or until they become soft. Add the sage, salt and pepper, and carry on cooking just to allow the sage flavour to penetrate the beans. Pour in the milk, cover the pan and simmer very gently for 20 minutes, or until the beans have absorbed most of the milk. Test for seasoning.

Preheat the grill. Toast the bread on both sides, then rub lightly on one side only with the reserved garlic clove. Spoon the broad beans and some of their juices over each bruschetta. Scatter over the lemon zest, and drizzle over each a generous amount of extra virgin olive oil.

slow-cooked broad beans and prosciutto
fave fresche e prosciutto

for 6
3 kg fresh broad beans (podded weight 1.5 kg)
1/2 head spring garlic, divided into cloves, peeled
6 slices prosciutto (Parma or San Daniele)
extra virgin olive oil
1 tablespoon chopped fresh rosemary leaves
Maldon salt and freshly ground black pepper

Heat 4 tablespoons of the extra virgin olive oil in a large saucepan. Add the rosemary and then the broad beans, and stir to coat the beans with the herbs and oil. Add the garlic cloves, season with salt and pepper, and stir. Pour in just enough water to cover, bring to the boil, then lower the heat and simmer for 15 minutes. If the water evaporates before the broad beans are cooked (they should be soft with the skin shrivelled and a grey colour), add more water in small amounts. As the water evaporates, it is important to stir the beans to prevent them from sticking to the pan.

Tear the prosciutto into 4-5 cm pieces. Lay these over the beans, drizzle with more extra virgin olive oil, cover and remove from the heat; this will merge the flavours of the prosciutto and the beans. Serve at room temperature.

broad beans and chicory with marinated anchovies
fave fresche e cicorie con acciughe marinate

for 6
2 kg broad beans in their pods
2 kg chicory (grumolo verde, dandelion etc) or
  spinach, washed, stalks removed
Maldon salt and freshly ground black pepper
1 bunch fresh mint with small leaves
extra virgin olive oil
2 garlic cloves, peeled and sliced
2 small dried chillies, crumbled
1/2 large, thick-skinned organic lemon
marinated anchovies
12 salted anchovies, prepared (see page 458)
1/2 large, thick-skinned organic lemon
coarsely ground black pepper
extra virgin olive oil

Place the anchovy fillets on a plate, and squeeze the juice of the half lemon over. Sprinkle with black pepper, and grate over the zest from the lemon. Pour over enough olive oil to cover, and leave to marinate for a couple of hours or so.

Bring two saucepans of water to the boil, and add salt to one. Cook the chicory or spinach in this for 5-6 minutes. Drain and cool. Put the broad beans and mint into the unsalted saucepan and cook for 3-4 minutes. Drain, and while still hot, pour over 4 tablespoons oil. Season.

Heat 3 tablespoons olive oil in a medium thick-bottomed saucepan, and fry the garlic until pale gold. Add the chicory, and stir around a bit before seasoning with salt, pepper and the chilli. Remove from the pan. Place in a large serving dish, add the broad beans and their juices, and squeeze over the juice of the half lemon. Place the anchovy fillets among the broad beans and chicory, and serve with bruschetta.

cherries

Cherries have perhaps the briefest season of all fruits. There are two species: the sour and the sweet. The sweet cherries that we use at the River Cafe for our ice-creams and drinks are native to Europe. There are more than 600 varieties of cherry in cultivation, with colours varying from dark red to almost white or yellow. Fresh cherries should have stems that are crisp and green, the fruit firm and glossy.

The best way of testing the quality of a cherry before purchasing is to taste (just) one.

cherry focaccia
focaccia con ciliege

for 10
1 kg cherries
1 teaspoon dried yeast
350 ml warm water
500 g plain flour
extra virgin olive oil
100 g caster sugar
Maldon salt

In a warm bowl mix the yeast with the warm water, and let it rest for 5 minutes. Gently pour in and combine the flour; the dough should be very soft. Now slowly pour in 50 ml of the olive oil along with half the sugar and a pinch of salt. Knead on a floured work surface for about 5 minutes. Return to the bowl, cover with a cloth, and set aside to rise for an hour.

Remove the stones from the cherries, and put the flesh in a bowl.

When the dough has risen, roll it out and place on a lightly oiled pizza pan 30 cm in diameter, or in a shallow cake tin of the same size. Place the cherries over the dough and let it rise again for half an hour.

Preheat the oven to 180°C/350°F/Gas 4.

Sprinkle the remaining sugar over the top of the cake, and drizzle with a small amount of olive oil. Place the cake in the oven and bake for about 30 minutes until brown.

Serve warm or at room temperature.

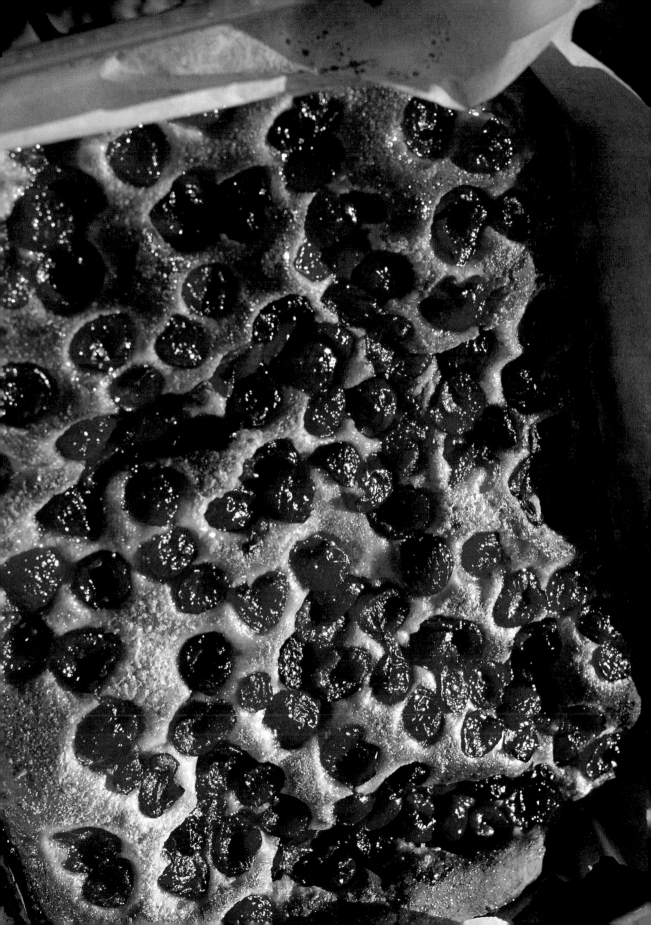

cherry sorbet

sorbetto di ciliege

for 6

1.5 kg cherries

600 g caster sugar

250 ml Vin Ruspo (a rosé wine
   from Tuscany)

Wash and dry the cherries, then remove the stones. Put the flesh in a food processor with the sugar, and pulse-chop to a purée. Add the wine.

Pour into an ice-cream machine and churn until frozen, or freeze in a suitable container.

grappa with cherry juice
aperitivo alle ciliege

for 6

1 kg very ripe, large and juicy cherries

60 ml grappa Nardini or other traditional, unscented clear grappa

1 bottle Prosecco

Wash the cherries and pat dry. Remove the stalks and stones, and pulse-chop the fruit very gently in a food processor. Push through a fruit sieve. Use immediately. In a cocktail shaker, make 2 glasses at a time. Put 60 ml of cherry pulp in the shaker, add 20 ml of grappa, then 200 ml of Prosecco. Carefully pour into champagne flutes. Repeat twice.

peas

As soon as the pea has been picked from the plant, the sugars start turning to starch, so if you want to eat the sweetest peas, they must be extremely fresh. They should also be small, bright green and firm.

In Italy the best peas are the tiny sweet variety that grow on the islands in the lagoon around Venice. Their sweetness makes the traditional risotto of the area – risi e bisi – seem more like a dessert.

Choose peas with bright green pods that are juicy when snapped open. When podding peas, use two containers to separate the large from the small peas. Cook them separately, with a generous handful of fresh mint.

pea, ricotta and lemon zest risotto
risotto con piselli, limone e ricotta

for 6
3 kg fresh young peas (podded weight 1.5 kg)
250 g fresh ricotta cheese, lightly beaten
finely grated rind of 2 washed lemons
1.5 litres chicken stock (see page 455)
Maldon salt and freshly ground black pepper
2 tablespoons fresh mint leaves
3 garlic cloves, peeled, 2 chopped
200 g unsalted butter
500 g spring onions, roughly chopped
400 g carnaroli or arborio rice
2 tablespoons torn fresh basil leaves
150 ml dry vermouth
50 g Parmesan, freshly grated

Heat the chicken stock to boiling and check for seasoning. Bring a medium saucepan of water to the boil, and add 1/2 tablespoon salt, the peas, half the mint and the whole garlic clove. Simmer for 3-4 minutes or until the peas are al dente. Drain, keeping back 150 ml of the water. Return the peas, mint and garlic clove to this water and put aside.

Melt 150 g of the butter in a large, thick-bottomed saucepan, add the onion and soften. Add the chopped garlic, then the rice, stirring to coat each grain for about 2-3 minutes. Add a ladle of hot stock and stir, adding another when the rice has absorbed the first. Continue stirring and adding stock for 10 minutes or until the rice is not quite al dente.

Add half the peas, keeping back the cooked garlic and mint and their liquor. Mash the remainder of the peas, mint and garlic with the liquor in the food processor, then add to the risotto and stir. Stir in the basil. Add the vermouth, about 2 tablespoons of ricotta, and the remaining butter. Cook briefly to wilt the basil and melt the butter. Test for doneness: the rice should be al dente. Serve with the remaining ricotta over each portion, sprinkled with lemon zest, salt and pepper and Parmesan.

pea and mint torte
sformato di piselli e menta

for 6
5 kg fresh young peas (podded weight 3 kg)
100 g unsalted butter
200 g Parmesan, freshly grated
250 g spring onions, finely chopped
2 tablespoons fresh mint leaves
4 tablespoons fresh basil leaves
Maldon salt and freshly ground black pepper
300 g ricotta cheese
4 tablespoons double cream
4 large, organic free-range eggs
extra virgin olive oil

Preheat the oven to 190°C/375°F/Gas 5. Butter a 25 cm spring-release tin generously, then dust equally generously with grated Parmesan.

Melt the remaining butter in a medium saucepan, add the onion, and fry gently until soft. Add the peas, stir to combine, then add half the mint and basil and 150 ml hot water. Season with salt, cover and cook for 5 minutes. Remove from the heat and allow to cool. Put half the pea mixture into a food processor with half the ricotta and half the cream. Blend to mix, quite briefly. Add the rest of the ricotta and cream and, while blending, add the eggs, one at a time.

Remove the mixture from the food processor, and put into a large mixing bowl. Season with salt and pepper, and fold in the remaining peas, about 100 g of the grated Parmesan and the rest of the herbs. Pour into the prepared tin, drizzle over a little olive oil and sprinkle with the remaining Parmesan. Bake in the preheated oven for 30-45 minutes. The sformato will rise and become crisp and brown on top. When it is firm in the centre and pulling away from the sides, it is cooked. Remove from the oven, rest for 5 minutes, then remove from the tin on to a large serving plate. Cut into wedges to serve, warm or at room temperature.

pea and vongole risotto
risotto con piselli e vongole

for 6
3 kg fresh young peas (podded weight 1.5 kg)
2 kg vongole (small clams)
5 tablespoons olive oil
2 garlic cloves, peeled and chopped
150 ml Pinot Grigio (white wine)
Maldon salt and freshly ground black pepper
1.25 litres fish stock (see page 455)
200 g spring onions, finely chopped
inner white heart of 1 head celery, finely chopped
400 g carnaroli or arborio rice
3 tablespoons chopped fresh flat-leaf parsley
extra virgin olive oil
3 lemons

Heat 2 tablespoons of the olive oil in a large, thick-bottomed saucepan with a tight-fitting lid. Add half the garlic and as soon as it colours, add the clams and half the wine. Cover and cook just until the clams open. Strain, using a colander over a bowl to collect the liquid. Leave to cool. Strain the liquid through muslin or paper towels to remove sand or grit. Take the clams from their shells and return to the liquid.

Blanch the peas in boiling salted water for about 4-5 minutes. Bring the stock to a simmer and test for seasoning. Heat the remaining olive oil in a large, thick-bottomed saucepan over a medium heat, add the onion and celery and cook gently, stirring. When soft, add the remaining garlic and the rice. Stir to coat each grain with oil and vegetables, then pour in the remainder of the wine. Cook to reduce then stir in the stock, ladle by ladle, stirring continuously and not adding more stock until the previous ladleful has been absorbed. Continue stirring and adding stock until the rice is almost cooked, about 15 minutes. At the last minute add the peas and vongole, with their liquid, and cook briefly. Season and add the parsley. Serve with extra virgin olive oil and wedges of lemon.

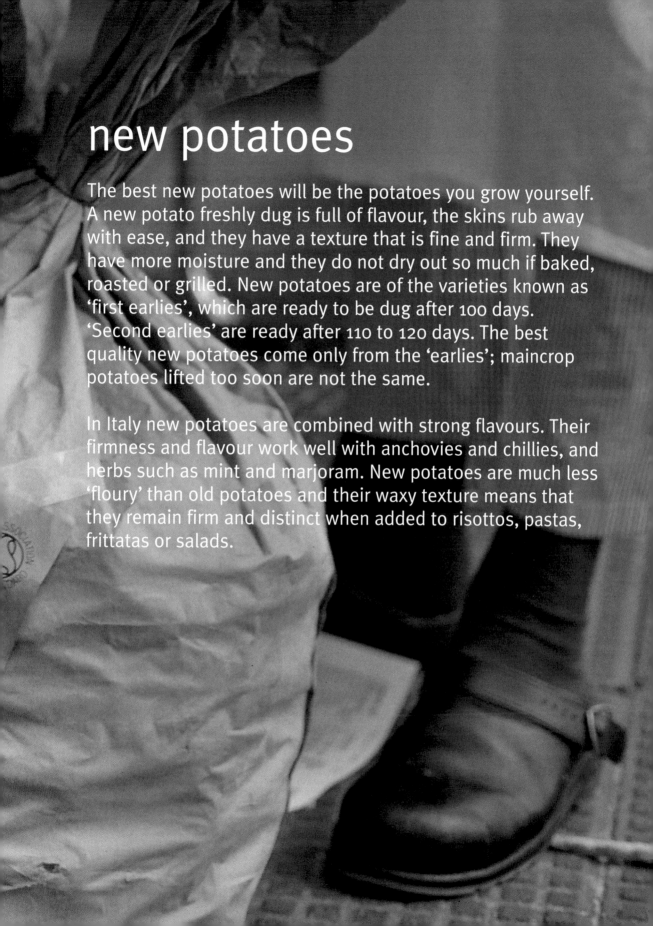

new potatoes

The best new potatoes will be the potatoes you grow yourself. A new potato freshly dug is full of flavour, the skins rub away with ease, and they have a texture that is fine and firm. They have more moisture and they do not dry out so much if baked, roasted or grilled. New potatoes are of the varieties known as 'first earlies', which are ready to be dug after 100 days. 'Second earlies' are ready after 110 to 120 days. The best quality new potatoes come only from the 'earlies'; maincrop potatoes lifted too soon are not the same.

In Italy new potatoes are combined with strong flavours. Their firmness and flavour work well with anchovies and chillies, and herbs such as mint and marjoram. New potatoes are much less 'floury' than old potatoes and their waxy texture means that they remain firm and distinct when added to risottos, pastas, frittatas or salads.

new potato risotto
risotto con patate novelle

for 6

500 g new potatoes, peeled, halved or quartered,
   according to size
1 kg rocket, stalks removed
1.5 litres chicken stock (see page 455)
Maldon salt and freshly ground black pepper
2 tablespoons olive oil
100 g unsalted butter
1 medium red onion, peeled and finely chopped
inner white heart of 1 head celery, finely chopped
1 tablespoon chopped fresh flat-leaf parsley
400 g arborio or carnaroli rice
6 tablespoons torn fresh basil leaves
freshly grated Parmesan

In a thick-bottomed saucepan, heat just enough water to cover the bottom. Bring to the boil and add the rocket. Stir briefly, cover and remove from the heat. This will wilt the rocket. Drain, allow to cool and chop coarsely.

Heat the chicken stock to boiling, and test for seasoning.

In a large thick-bottomed saucepan, heat the olive oil and half the butter. Add the onion and celery and fry until soft and beginning to colour. Add the parsley and potatoes and cook, stirring, for 5 minutes until the potatoes start to soften, but are not browning. Add the rice and stir until each grain of rice is coated with the oil. Add enough hot stock just to cover and then keep adding stock, ladle by ladle, stirring continuously. Allow each ladleful to be absorbed by the rice before adding the next.

Continue until the rice is al dente, about 15-20 minutes, by which time the potatoes should be tender. Stir in the remaining butter, the chopped rocket and the torn basil. Sprinkle with Parmesan and serve immediately.

new potato and black truffle frittata
frittata di patate e tartufo nero

for 4

500 g new potatoes, scrubbed
80 g black truffles
Maldon salt and freshly ground black pepper
3 tablespoons chopped fresh flat-leaf parsley
120 g unsalted butter, softened
8 large, organic free-range eggs
about 2 tablespoons freshly grated Parmesan

Preheat the oven to 200°C/400°F/Gas 6.

Cook the potatoes in boiling salted water until al dente, then drain and cut into 5 mm slices. Add the parsley, half the butter and salt and pepper. Shave a few shavings of truffle into the potatoes.

Break the eggs into a large bowl and beat lightly. Add the potato mixture and season with salt and pepper.

Make one frittata at a time for two people. Use a 26 cm frying pan with an ovenproof handle. Heat 30 g of the butter in the pan, tilting the pan to coat all the sides. Add half of the egg and potato mixture, lower the heat and cook until the frittata is starting to set, loosening the egg at the sides. It should be quite runny. Scatter with Parmesan, and place in the oven for 1 minute only.

Loosen the frittata from the pan with a spatula and put on a warm plate. Shave black truffle all over. Cut in two and serve. Repeat, using the same pan with the remaining ingredients, for the second frittata.

strawberries

The fruit most associated with hot summer months is the strawberry. In fact in its cultivated form it is a rather new fruit – the result of a chance cross between two American wild varieties in the early nineteenth century. It is worth waiting for the prime of the season's strawberries, for eaten too early they will have no taste. Strawberries ripened naturally with lots of sun are the best.

Wild strawberries have a smaller, softer fruit, which are more scented, and have a delicate flavour. They are extremely perishable and should be eaten soon after buying or picking.

It is best to avoid washing strawberries, but if necessary do so before removing the calyx, to prevent water penetration. Strawberries should never be put in the refrigerator.

In Italy, strawberries are served with just lemon juice and sugar, never cream.

red wine sorbet with crushed strawberries
sorbetto al vino rosso con fragole

for 6
500 g strawberries, hulled
4 tablespoons caster sugar
sorbet
1 litre Valpolicella (red wine)
100 g caster sugar
10 whole white peppercorns
6 cloves
grated zest of 2 washed oranges, discarding any
    pith

Put the wine, sugar, white pepper, cloves and orange zest into a non-reactive saucepan and boil to reduce by half. Leave to cool, then strain carefully. Discard the bits and pieces. Put into the ice-cream machine and churn until frozen, or freeze in a suitable container until beginning to harden.

Roughly chop the strawberries and mix with the caster sugar. Place in individual bowls and cover with the sorbet. Serve immediately.

almond meringue with strawberries
meringa alle mandorle con fragole

for 10
meringue
olive oil and butter for greasing the trays
175 g shelled whole blanched almonds
5 large, organic free-range egg whites
225 g caster sugar
110 g unsalted butter, melted
70 g plain flour
strawberries and cream
1.5 kg strawberries, hulled and halved
1 vanilla pod
1 litre double cream
150 g icing sugar
150 ml Vecchio Romagna brandy

Preheat the oven to 120°C/250°F/Gas ½. Rub olive oil over three flat
oven trays. Line each tray with parchment paper. Butter the paper. Put
the almonds into a food processor and pulse-chop to a medium fine
flour. Using an electric mixer, beat the egg whites with half the sugar
until stiff, then add the almond flour and the remaining sugar. Beat
briefly to combine. Fold in the melted butter. Finally sieve the flour into
the bowl, and fold in carefully.

Spoon the mixture on to the three trays and spread it out flat, each the
same shape and diameter, as thin as you can (1 cm thick at most). Bake
for 50 minutes, or until set and nearly crisp. It is essential to peel off the
paper whilst the meringues are still hot. Place on wire racks to cool.

Scrape the seeds from the vanilla pod. Lightly whip the cream with the
vanilla seeds and icing sugar. When stiff, fold in the brandy. Choose a
large flat cake plate. Place the first meringue layer on the plate and
cover it with one-third of the cream. Place one-third of the strawberry
halves on to the cream. Repeat twice.

marsh samphire

There are two varieties of samphire, both of which grow wild. Rock samphire is found on many shorelines and cliffs throughout Europe, and marsh samphire, the one that we use, grows in muddy salt-marshes by the sea. It is mostly sold by fishmongers. The alternative name for samphire is glasswort, which derives from the historic use of the plant in the production of glass.

The samphire season runs from June to September. The stems are soft, small and thin in the early part of the season, and grow more fibrous towards the end. As it grows by the sea, samphire has a salty, woody taste, and is perfect with fish. It is delicious boiled until tender and then dressed with olive oil and lemon juice.

samphire with olive oil and lemon
salicornia all'olio e limone

for 6
2.5 kg samphire
Maldon salt and freshly ground black pepper
extra virgin olive oil
3 organic lemons

Cut off any tough stems or stalks from the samphire. Wash the samphire in two or three changes of water, then drain.

Bring a large saucepan of water to the boil, then add $1/2$ teaspoon salt and the samphire. Cook until tender, about 6-8 minutes. Drain and immediately season with black pepper, salt if necessary and plenty of extra virgin olive oil. Toss and serve with lemon wedges.

july

basil [234] *pasta* silk handkerchiefs with pesto. *salad* summer herb salad. *soup* minestrone alla genovese. *sauce* ricotta pesto. borlotti beans [242] *salad* borlotti beans with langoustines and rocket. *soup* roast ribollita. peaches [248] *pudding* peaches marinated in moscadello. peach ice-cream. tomatoes [252] *bruschetta* bruschetta of tomatoes and peppers. *pasta* fresh pasta pieces with tomato and olives. penne with tomato and nutmeg. *vegetable* grilled and marinated red and yellow tomatoes. *soup* fresh pappa pomodoro. *pasta* penne with capers and tomato. *vegetable* green beans stewed with yellow tomatoes. zucchini [266] *pasta* zucchini and aubergine rigatoni. *soup* zucchini, tomato and bread soup. *bruschetta* zucchini and prosciutto bruschetta.

basil

Basil grows in warm climates, and will flourish here only if planted in sunny places. Basil grown in Italy has more flavour, but is rather fragile. It is sold with the root attached, often wrapped in wet newspaper to prevent it from wilting.

To have a constant supply of fresh basil, try to grow your own in a warm, sunny protected place, picking the leaves before the flowers appear. Cutting off the flower spike will encourage the growth of new side leaves.

There are many varieties of basil, and more seem to appear every day. We grow at least two varieties of purple basil, common basil and lemon basil, and last year we were given seeds of giant basil with its lettuce-like leaves. The tiny-leaf bush basil has a different flavour and grows very easily. We include mixed basil leaves along with other herbs when making summer salads.

Thick leaves from the bottom of the plant stem usually taste too aniseedy and they go black when chopped or pounded. The fragrant smaller leaves which tear or pound easily, will give you the best results, particularly when making pesto.

silk handkerchiefs with pesto
mandilli di sæa con pesto

for 6
Ligurian Basic Pasta (see page 454)
200 g fine green beans, tailed
Maldon salt and freshly ground black pepper
25 g butter
extra virgin olive oil
freshly grated Parmesan
pesto
2 handfuls of fresh basil, washed and dried
2 small garlic cloves, peeled
10 g pine kernels
30 g Pecorino Romano cheese, finely grated
20 g Parmesan, finely grated
60 ml extra virgin olive oil

Make the pesto. Crush 1 teaspoon of salt and some of the basil leaves in a pestle and mortar. Add the garlic and then more basil leaves, a few at a time. Add the pine kernels, and crush until it becomes smooth. Remove to a bowl, and fold in the cheeses. Pour in the extra virgin olive oil slowly, mixing, until the sauce has a thick but creamy consistency.

For the pasta, follow the instructions for rolling out the dough on page 454, but keep rolling the dough until it is as fine as possible, almost transparent! Cut into rectangular shapes about 12 cm long and 5 cm wide.

Cook the beans in boiling salted water until very tender. Drain, retaining some of the water. Return the beans to the pan and stir in the butter. Add a small amount of cooking water to the pesto, then stir 1 tablespoon of pesto into the beans. In a separate large saucepan, bring plenty of salted water to the boil, then cook a few pasta sheets at a time. They will take only 30-60 seconds. To serve, place a small amount of pesto on each plate, arrange the pasta on top, and spread a further tablespoon of pesto over the pasta. Scatter over the beans, drizzle with oil and sprinkle with Parmesan.

summer herb salad
insalata estiva di erbe

for 6
100 g fresh herbs (to include basil, purple basil,
   mint, fennel herb and wild rocket)
200 g fresh vegetable leaves (to include small
   spinach leaves, red and/or green purslane,
   orache, rocket, landcress and small leaves from
   the centre of young beetroot, chard and chicory
   plants)
juice of 2 lemons
extra virgin olive oil
Maldon salt and freshly ground black pepper

Wash and spin dry the herb and vegetable leaves.

Mix the lemon juice with four parts its volume of extra virgin olive oil.
Season with salt and pepper and toss with the salad just seconds before
serving.

minestrone alla genovese

for 6
100 g fresh cannellini beans, cooked (see page 276)
3 tablespoons olive oil
1 medium red onion, peeled and finely chopped
inner white heart of 1 head celery, finely chopped
3 garlic cloves, peeled and finely chopped
2 tablespoons chopped fresh flat-leaf parsley
2 medium potatoes (Roseval), peeled and cubed
2 fresh ripe tomatoes, skinned (see page 265),
    seeded and chopped
2 medium zucchini, trimmed and coarsely chopped
50 g each of podded fresh peas and broad beans
100 g fresh green beans, tailed and chopped
Maldon salt and freshly ground black pepper
1 litre chicken stock (see page 455)
4 Swiss chard leaves, chopped
100 g small pasta such as digitali or gnocchetti
Ricotta Pesto (see opposite)
60 g Parmesan, freshly grated
extra virgin olive oil

In a large, thick-bottomed saucepan heat the olive oil, and cook the onion, celery, garlic and parsley until very soft, about 15 minutes. In a separate saucepan heat the chicken stock. Stir the potatoes and tomatoes into the vegetable mixture, then add half of each of the zucchini, peas, broad beans and green beans. Season, then cover with chicken stock. Bring to the boil, then lower the heat and simmer for 45 minutes. Add the remaining zucchini and other vegetables, the chard leaves and cannellini beans, and bring to the boil. Cook for a further 15 minutes.

Remove a quarter of the soup to a food processor and pulse-chop to a thick purée. Return to the bulk of the soup and stir. In a separate saucepan cook the pasta in boiling salted water until al dente. Drain and add to the soup. Stir in half the pesto and the Parmesan, and drizzle with extra virgin olive oil. Serve the remaining pesto separately.

ricotta pesto
pesto alla ricotta

This is best made with buffalo or sheep's ricotta as they have a creamier texture.

for 6
2 large bunches of fresh basil, washed and dried
2 garlic cloves, peeled
15 g pine kernels
Maldon salt and freshly ground black pepper
1 tablespoon freshly grated Pecorino cheese
1 tablespoon freshly grated Parmesan
100 g ricotta cheese
4 tablespoons extra virgin olive oil

Put the basil, leaves and stalks, into a pestle and mortar with the garlic, pine kernels and a pinch of salt. Pound thoroughly with the pestle to a rough paste. Add the grated cheeses, and continue to pound to a smooth paste. Remove to a bowl and stir in the ricotta and the extra virgin olive oil. Check the seasoning.

The first step may be done in a food processor rather than a pestle and mortar.

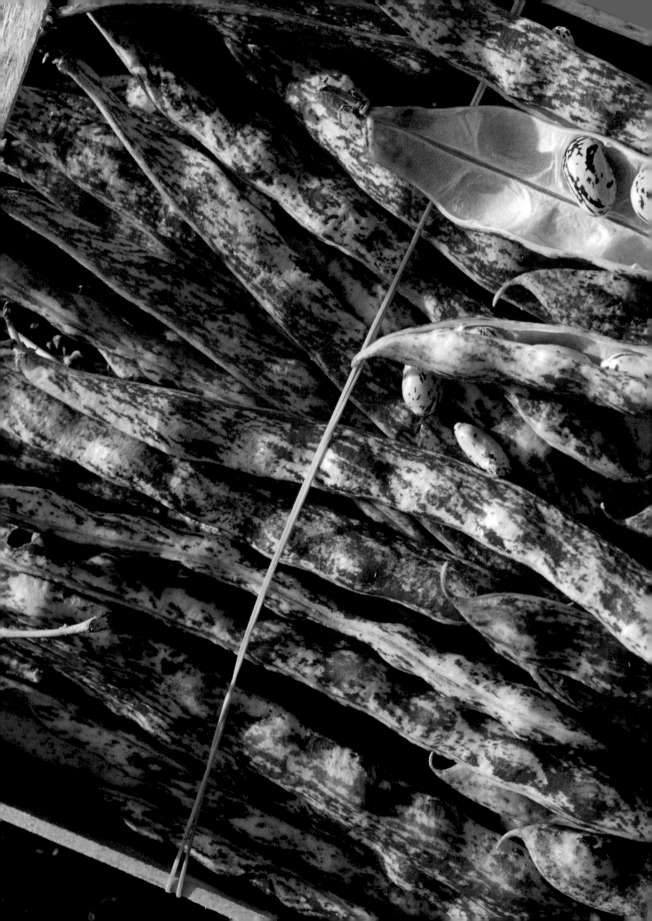

borlotti beans

Fresh borlotti beans, sold in their beautiful mottled pods, are found in all the markets in Italy and increasingly, because of demand, in specialist Italian shops here. Four or five different varieties are grown.

When buying fresh borlotti beans, choose ripe pods that are stiff. The red flecks should be dark rather than pale. The beans are round, and the colour white or cream with red stripes, hence the name 'fagioli scritti', 'written beans'. Unripe pods tend to be flatter in shape, often quite greenish with pale red mottling, and the beans inside will still be green.

Ripe pods split open easily to reveal their plump beans. Discard split beans, shooting beans and green beans. You do not need to wash them. Never cook beans in salted water – the salt toughens the skins - but season them when cooked.

Fresh borlotti beans have a marvellous creamy and nutty flavour, and are delicious just seasoned and served with extra virgin olive oil as they do in Tuscany. In Venice and the Veneto, borlotti beans, fresh and dried, are used in pasta soups and risottos.

Many of the varieties grown dry well. Borlotti di Lamon, found only in an area in the north-east, are considered the best. Recently, frozen fresh borlotti beans have become available. We find them excellent.

borlotti beans with langoustines and rocket
borlotti con mazzancolle e rucola

for 6
30 fresh langoustines
300 g Capri rocket, coarsely chopped
$\frac{1}{2}$ bottle dry white wine
6 fresh parsley stalks
10 black peppercorns
4 dried fennel sticks
Maldon salt and freshly ground black pepper
1 tablespoon chopped fresh flat-leaf parsley
1 fresh red chilli, seeded and finely chopped
juice of 1 lemon
extra virgin olive oil
2 tablespoons olive oil
2 garlic cloves, peeled and finely chopped
fresh borlotti beans
1.5 kg fresh borlotti beans in their pods
1 tomato
a handful of flat-leaf parsley leaves and stalks
$\frac{1}{2}$ head garlic
Maldon salt and freshly ground black pepper

To cook fresh borlotti beans, remove them from their pods, discarding any brown or mouldy ones. Place in a large saucepan, cover with water, and add the tomato, parsley and garlic. Bring to the boil, turn the heat down, and cook gently for about 45 minutes. Make sure the beans are covered with water at all times. Test to see if they are soft. Season with salt and pepper.

For the langoustines, place the wine, parsley stalks, peppercorns and fennel sticks in a large, thick-bottomed saucepan, fill to the top with water, add salt, and bring to the boil. Add the langoustines in batches, bring back to the boil, and cook for 1 minute only. Remove. The langoustines should feel firm – discard any soft ones. Put aside to cool. When cool, remove the shells. Toss the flesh with the chopped parsley and chilli, most of the lemon juice (save 1 tablespoon) and some extra virgin olive oil. Season with salt and pepper.

Heat the olive oil in a thick-bottomed saucepan, add the garlic, and cook until soft. Drain the beans and stir into the garlic. Toss the rocket with the remaining lemon juice and 3 tablespoons extra virgin olive oil. Stir into the beans, and serve with the langoustines on top.

roast ribollita
ribollita al forno

for 6
1.5 kg fresh borlotti beans, cooked (see page 244)
500 g summer Swiss chard, leaves only
Maldon salt and freshly ground black pepper
500 g borage or spinach leaves
1 kg ripe tomatoes, skinned (see page 253)
olive oil
500 g white summer onions or spring onions,
   green and white parts chopped
3 garlic cloves, peeled and finely chopped
2 tablespoons chopped fresh flat-leaf parsley
4 tablespoons fresh basil leaves
2 tablespoons fresh marjoram leaves
12 slices sourdough bread, 1.5 cm thick
extra virgin olive oil

Bring a large pan of salted water to the boil. Blanch the chard for 5 minutes, then remove, drain and chop. Blanch the borage or spinach in the same water, remove, drain and chop. Remove the hard centre core from the skinned tomatoes, then chop the flesh to a coarse pulp.

Heat 3 tablespoons olive oil in a large thick-bottomed saucepan, add the onion and fry until soft. Add the garlic, and half the herbs. Cook over a low heat just to combine. Add the tomato and 1 teaspoon salt. Simmer gently to a thickish sauce, about 30 minutes. Mash half the beans with a few tablespoons of their cooking liquid, and add with the whole drained beans to the sauce. Stir and cook for 5 minutes, then stir in the green vegetables. Season, add the remaining herbs, mix well and cool.

Preheat the oven to 220°C/425°F/Gas 7. Pour enough olive oil into a roasting tray to coat the bottom, and place on a flame. Place half the bread on the base and pour over the soup. Cover with the remaining bread, drizzle with olive oil, and bake in the oven for 15-20 minutes, until crisp and golden. Serve warm or cold, drizzled with extra virgin olive oil.

peaches

Peaches, almost more than any other fruit, should only be eaten when perfectly ripe. Unfortunately, their flesh bruises easily, so they don't travel well. As a result many of the peaches we buy here have been picked while still hard, and even when they do soften up, much of the flavour and perfume is lost. A ripe peach has a beautiful bloom and fragrance. When cut in half, the flesh comes easily away from the stone and exudes juice.

We buy white peaches from Italy whenever we can get them. Quite a few varieties arrive in July. A new, odd and particularly delicious variety, Saturna, is flatter with tiny stones, and an almondy perfume; it is very good to use when making sorbets and ice-creams. The white peach Perrigrin grows in Britain, and it is exquisite, as is the white nectarine Lord Napier. Yellow-fleshed peaches rarely taste so good, but Rochester, an English variety that grows well in warm, protected situations, is very good.

Vanilla sugar and lemon juice both bring out the flavour of duller peaches.

peaches marinated in moscadello
pesche al moscadello

for 6
1 kg ripe white peaches
1 bottle Moscadello, a sweet white wine
50 g caster sugar
3 vanilla pods, slit in half lengthways

In a large saucepan simmer the wine, sugar and vanilla pods for 5 minutes, stirring to dissolve the sugar.

Add the unpeeled peaches to the liquid, bring back to simmering point, then lower the heat and cook gently for 3 minutes. Remove the pan from the heat and allow the peaches to cool before skinning them.

Put the peaches in a bowl and pour over the liquid and vanilla pods. Serve at room temperature. If you wish, the stones may be removed after peeling, which makes the eating easier!

peach ice-cream
gelato alla pesca

For 10
2 kg ripe white peaches
1.75 litres double cream
450 ml milk
4 fresh vanilla pods, split lengthways
15 large, organic free-range egg yolks
caster sugar
juice of 1 lemon

In a large thick-bottomed saucepan, combine the cream and milk. Scrape the vanilla seeds out of the pods into the mixture, then add the pods. Heat until just below boiling point.

Beat the egg yolks and 350 g sugar together slowly for 10 minutes until pale and thick. Pour a little of the warm cream into the egg yolks and stir, then add the yolks slowly to the bulk of the cream mixture. Cook gently over a low heat, stirring constantly. It is important to concentrate, as the mixture will curdle if it gets to boiling point. Remove just before it reaches this stage. Allow to cool completely.

Skin the peaches, then cut in half and remove the stones. Smash the peaches with a fork into a thick purée and sprinkle with 1 tablespoon sugar and the lemon juice. Add the peaches to the cream, stir and pour into an ice-cream machine to churn, or freeze in a suitable container.

tomatoes

The first tomatoes of the summer are Italian. The English start only at the end of July. We buy most of our English tomatoes from two growers, who have experimented with thirty odd varieties. As we have so much choice, matching the kind of tomato to the recipe is part of the enjoyment.

The very large bulbous tomatoes, some weighing up to 500 g, are used raw in salads and with bruschetta because their skins are thin, with dense pulp, few seeds and juices, and a sweet flavour. Varieties include Japanese Oxheart, Brandy Wine, Dr Neal, Jubilee and the yellow Margold.

Plum tomatoes are good for making sauces, and the ripest make the sweetest sauce. They also have fewer seeds, more flesh and less juice. Their skins are usually thicker, which makes them easy to peel. Good plum varieties are Perini, Roma, Martino and San Marzano.

Cherry tomatoes have a strong sweet taste. They travel well and are best bought on the vine. Sweet One Hundred has a good taste if you wish to grow them yourself.

We store all tomatoes outside the restaurant, never in the fridge, to help the flavour develop.

When removing the skin, pierce the tomato with a pointed knife. Place in boiling water to the count of ten, then remove, place in cold water, and peel as soon as they are cool. Cut out any tough stalk core before chopping the flesh.

bruschetta of tomatoes and peppers
bruschetta con pomodori e peperoni

for 6
12 ripe medium tomatoes
3 large ripe red peppers, washed
Maldon salt and freshly ground black pepper
extra virgin olive oil
aged balsamic vinegar
6 garlic cloves, peeled
3 tablespoons fresh purple basil leaves, torn
6 slices sourdough bread, about 1.5 cm thick

Preheat the oven to 200°C/400°F/Gas 6.

Cut the peppers in half and then each half into thirds. Remove the seeds and any thick fibres from the inside. Place in an ovenproof dish, season generously with salt and pepper, then roast in the preheated oven for 15 minutes. Drizzle extra virgin olive oil over each piece, then dribble with balsamic vinegar. Return to the oven and roast for a further 15 minutes until the skin is crisp at the edges and the peppers are soft.

In a separate small roasting tray, place the tomatoes and 5 garlic cloves. Pour over a little extra virgin olive oil and 2 teaspoons balsamic vinegar. Roast in the oven until the flesh is soft and the skin has burst, about 10 minutes. Turn the tomatoes over in their juices. Mix the tomatoes, their juices and the garlic with the peppers and their juices, then add the basil and 1 further tablespoon of balsamic vinegar. Season with salt and pepper.

Toast the bread on both sides, then rub lightly on one side only with the remaining garlic. Drizzle with extra virgin olive oil and spoon on the tomato and pepper mixture.

fresh pasta pieces with tomato and olives

stracci al pomodoro e pecino

for 6

1.5 kg ripe cherry vine tomatoes, halved
  and seeded
250 g tinned peeled plum tomatoes
800 g Fresh Pasta (see page 454), made
  into stracci
3 tablespoons olive oil
3 garlic cloves, peeled and finely sliced
Maldon salt and freshly ground black pepper
3 tablespoons fresh basil leaves, torn into pieces
150 g black olives, stoned and cut in half
100 g Pecorino cheese, freshly grated
extra virgin olive oil

Heat the olive oil in a large, thick-bottomed pan. When hot, add the
garlic and allow to cook briefly until transparent and beginning to colour.
Add the tomato halves and some salt and push them around the pan,
keeping the heat high, until they become soft. Add the tinned tomatoes
and break them up to create the sauce. Stir to prevent sticking and cook
for about 5 minutes. Add the basil and olives. Check the seasoning,
adding black pepper.

Cook the pasta pieces in a generous amount of boiling salted water until
al dente. Drain and add to the tomato sauce in the pan and toss gently
together. Serve sprinkled with Pecorino and some extra virgin olive oil.

penne with tomato and nutmeg
penne con pomodoro e noce moscata

for 6

2.5 kg ripe cherry vine tomatoes, halved and
    seeded
1/2 nutmeg, freshly grated
400 g penne rigate
100 g unsalted butter
4 garlic cloves, peeled and finely chopped
Maldon salt and freshly ground black pepper
1 bunch of fresh basil, leaves picked from the
    stalks
120 g Pecorino Romano cheese, freshly grated

Use a thick-bottomed, low-sided saucepan. Melt half the butter in this, then add half the garlic and cook until the garlic begins to colour. Add the tomato and a teaspoon of salt and simmer over a medium heat for 15 minutes. Stir to break up the tomatoes. When it reduces to a sauce, grate in the nutmeg and add the remainder of the garlic. Cook for just a few more minutes to allow the flavours to combine. Test for seasoning, adding pepper, then stir in the basil leaves and remove from the heat.

Cook the penne in a large saucepan of boiling salted water until al dente, then drain. Add the remaining butter and half the Pecorino. Add the pasta to the tomato sauce, stir to coat with the sauce and serve with the remaining Pecorino.

grilled and marinated red and yellow tomatoes
pomodori rossi e gialli marinati

for 6
1 kg yellow tomatoes
1 kg red tomatoes
Maldon salt and freshly ground black pepper
2 tablespoons each of fresh thyme and marjoram
   leaves
3 garlic cloves, peeled and finely sliced
extra virgin olive oil

Remove the stalks and wash the tomatoes. Cut the tomatoes in half horizontally.

Preheat a griddle pan to very hot.

Put 2-3 tablespoons salt on a board. Place the cut side of the tomato into the salt and then place salt side down on to the hot griddle pan. Grill until the cut surface seals and is charred. Carefully turn the tomatoes over – they are very fragile – and grill briefly on the skin side. Remove to a large serving dish. Repeat.

Finely chop the marjoram, thyme and garlic together. Sprinkle over the tomatoes. Season with black pepper and drizzle with extra virgin olive oil. Serve as part of an antipasti with other grilled vegetables.

fresh pappa pomodoro
pappa al pomodoro fresco

for 6
2 kg very ripe, mixed tomatoes (plum, cherry vine,
    large yellow and red)
olive oil
4 garlic cloves, peeled and chopped
Maldon salt and freshly ground black pepper
3 ciabatta loaves, crusts discarded, cut into large
    pieces
1 large bunch of fresh basil, leaves torn
150 ml extra virgin olive oil

Preheat the oven to 150°C/300°F/Gas 2. Place the cherry vine tomatoes
in a baking tray, season with salt and pepper and drizzle with olive oil.
Bake in the preheated oven for 40 minutes. When ready, put through a
mouli into a bowl. Set aside.

Plunge the plum tomatoes in a large amount of boiling water for 1
minute, then remove and allow to cool in a large colander. Repeat with
the yellow tomatoes. When cool, skin the tomatoes, cut in half and
remove the seeds. Chop both the yellow and red tomatoes coarsely.

In a large, thick-bottomed saucepan, heat 2 tablespoons of olive oil and
gently fry the garlic until soft but not brown. Add the chopped red and
yellow tomatoes, season and cook over a medium heat for about 20
minutes, stirring occasionally. Add the puréed tomatoes and bring to a
boil. Add the bread to the tomatoes and turn off the heat.

Stir until the bread absorbs the liquid. If too dry add a small amount of
boiling liquid, but remember that the soup should be very thick. Add the
torn basil leaves, season with salt and pepper and combine with the
extra virgin olive oil. It is best to let the soup sit for at least half an hour,
as you should serve it lukewarm, never hot.

penne with capers and tomato
penne con pomodoro e capperi

This was served to us by Anna Tasca Lanza at her beautiful estate, Regaleali, in Sicily.

For 6
8 dry sun-dried tomatoes
1 kg ripe, organic yellow and red cherry tomatoes
4 tablespoons salted capers, prepared (see
   page 458)
400 g penne rigate
extra virgin olive oil
4 tablespoons fresh basil leaves
2 tablespoons olive oil
5 garlic cloves, peeled and finely sliced
Maldon salt and freshly ground black pepper
100 g ricotta salata, freshly grated

Put the sun-dried tomatoes in a bowl and cover with boiling water. Leave
to reconstitute for 30 minutes. Cut the fresh tomatoes in half and scoop
out the seeds and any hard core. Do this over a sieve in a bowl to collect
the juices. If the tomatoes are larger, cut them into quarters.

Put the drained sun-dried tomatoes, capers and 75-80 ml extra virgin
olive oil in a food processor and pulse-chop to a rough purée. Place this
purée in a large serving bowl and add half the tomato pieces, half the
basil and enough of the tomato juice to liquefy. Stir to combine.

Heat the olive oil in a frying pan and fry the garlic slices until soft and
lightly coloured. Season with salt and pepper, then add to the tomato
mixture. Leave for 30 minutes to allow the flavours to blend, then heat.

Bring a large saucepan of salted water to the boil, and cook the penne
until al dente. Drain, keeping 2 ladles of cooking water. Add the pasta to
the sauce, and stir in as much of the cooking water as necessary to
liquefy. Add the remaining tomatoes and basil, season and drizzle with
extra virgin olive oil. Serve with the grated cheese.

green beans stewed with yellow tomatoes
fagiolini e pomodori gialli in umido

In late July the purple, yellow and fine green beans are at their best. Beans picked and cooked the same day cook and taste far superior to the Kenyan green beans that are available the whole year through. This recipe combines fresh green beans with ripe yellow tomatoes such as Margold. This variety of tomato reduces to a sauce very quickly, retaining its fresh taste. Purple basil looks and tastes good in this recipe.

for 6
1 kg ripe yellow tomatoes
1.5 kg green beans, tailed
Maldon salt and freshly ground black pepper
3 garlic cloves, peeled
3 tablespoons fresh thyme leaves
3 tablespoons olive oil
2 small dried red chillies, crumbled
2 tablespoons fresh basil leaves
extra virgin olive oil

Prick the tomatoes with the pointed end of a knife and blanch for a count of ten in boiling water. Remove and cover with cold water. When cool, peel off the skin, remove the hard core and seeds, and roughly chop the flesh. Blanch the beans in boiling salted water for 10 minutes or until soft, not crunchy. Chop the garlic and thyme leaves together.

Heat the olive oil in a thick-bottomed saucepan and add the garlic, thyme and chilli. Cook for a minute until soft then add the tomato pieces and 1 teaspoon salt. Keeping the heat high, cook to reduce the tomato to a thick sauce, which should take about 10 minutes. Add the beans, stir to combine and season with black pepper. Add the basil leaves and serve drizzled with extra virgin oil.

zucchini

There are many different varieties of zucchini. We use the bright green ridged zucchini called Romanesco, which are crisp and have a strong flavour. The pale-green-skinned variety with small seeds and yellow flesh – a favourite of the Cypriots – are also delicious. Other varieties we like to cook are Black Beauty, Striato di Napoli, Yellow Straightneck and Goldrush.

In Italy in the summer, zucchini, like tomatoes, are in practically every dish you eat. There are so many ways of cooking zucchini that every time we go there we learn a new recipe.

Zucchini are best when still quite small, with glossy skins. Italians sell them with the flowers still attached, which indicates how recently they have been picked. The flavour and texture of zucchini deteriorate very quickly.

Soak the whole zucchini in cold water for 30 minutes then wash and prepare as directed. If you can only find large zucchini, those bigger than 15 cm in length, slice away any soft centre and large seeds and use just the flesh nearest the skin, as that is where the flavour is.

Young organically grown zucchini taste delicious raw, sliced thinly and drizzled with extra virgin olive oil.

zucchini and aubergine rigatoni
rigatoni con zucchini e melanzane

for 6
500 g yellow and green zucchini
2 large, firm and pale aubergines
400 g rigatoni
Maldon salt and freshly ground black pepper
2 tablespoons fresh flat-leaf parsley leaves
1 tablespoon each fresh mint and oregano leaves
juice of 1 organic lemon
extra virgin olive oil
120 ml olive oil
3 garlic cloves, peeled
1 ciabatta loaf, crusts removed, made into crumbs

Cut the aubergines into 1 cm thick discs. In a colander, scatter with salt
and let the juices run for 1 hour. Wash and dry. Place the zucchini in cold
water and leave for 30 minutes. Dry and cut lengthways into 5 mm slices.
Scatter with salt and leave for 30 minutes. Squeeze out the water and dry.

Preheat the griddle pan or barbecue to very hot. Grill the aubergine on
both sides until soft in the centre. Cut each slice into 5 mm ribbons. Grill
the zucchini on both sides until lightly charred. Cut into pieces the same
size as the aubergine. Chop the herbs together. Mix the aubergine and
zucchini in a bowl, then add the herbs, black pepper and salt if needed.
Mix the lemon juice with five times its volume of extra virgin olive oil and
add some salt. Pour over the vegetables and toss.

Heat the olive oil in a small, thick-bottomed saucepan. When hot, not
smoking, add the garlic cloves. Remove them as soon as they become
brown, then add the breadcrumbs and cook for 2-3 minutes until golden.
Drain on kitchen paper and season with salt. Cook the rigatoni in boiling
salted water for 10 minutes. Drain, keeping back 1 ladleful of the cooking
water. Put the pasta back in the saucepan with the water and add the
zucchini mixture. Toss together over the heat for 2-3 minutes. Serve with
the breadcrumbs on top.

zucchini, tomato and bread soup
pappa al pomodoro con zucchini

for 6
1.5 kg small, young and firm zucchini, trimmed
800 g ripe organic tomatoes
2 ciabatta loaves, crusts removed
3 tablespoons olive oil
2 garlic cloves, peeled and finely chopped
3 tablespoons chopped fresh flat-leaf parsley
Maldon salt and freshly ground black pepper
500 ml boiling water
2 tablespoons chopped fresh mint
extra virgin olive oil

Cut the zucchini lengthways into quarters then remove and discard the seeds. Cut into small dice. Place the tomatoes in boiling water and count to 10. Remove skin and tough stalks and centre bits, then chop the flesh roughly. Keep the juices.

Heat the olive oil in a thick-bottomed saucepan, add the garlic and half the parsley and cook for 5 minutes over a low heat. Add half the zucchini and stir to coat with the parsley and garlic. Season. Raise the heat to medium, and cook until the zucchini are brown.

Add half the boiling water, scraping up the caramelised bits of zucchini and cook for 10 minutes, stirring frequently, until the zucchini are a soft mush. Stir in the tomatoes and their juices, and cook for 5 minutes.

In a separate saucepan of boiling salted water, blanch the remaining zucchini for 1 minute, then drain and blend in a food processor. Add to the soup with the remaining chopped parsley and the mint.

Tear the ciabatta into pieces and place over the soup. Wet with the remaining hot water, then stir into the soup. It should be very thick. Check the seasoning and serve drizzled with extra virgin olive oil.

zucchini and prosciutto bruschetta
bruschetta con zucchini e prosciutto

for 6
1.5 kg small firm zucchini, trimmed
3 tablespoons fresh marjoram leaves
2 tablespoons fresh flat-leaf parsley leaves
1 tablespoon fresh mint leaves
1 thick-skinned lemon, washed
2 tablespoons olive oil
3 garlic cloves, peeled, 2 finely chopped
Maldon salt and freshly ground black pepper
6 slices sourdough bread
extra virgin olive oil
18 slices prosciutto di Parma

Cut the zucchini in half lengthways and then in half again. Slice across into rough dice. Chop the herbs together. Peel the lemon, remove any white pith, then finely chop the peel.

Heat the oil in a thick-bottomed saucepan with a tight-fitting lid. Add the chopped garlic and a few seconds later the zucchini. Stir to combine, keeping the heat up high. When the zucchini are beginning to brown, add half the herbs and salt. Put on the lid, lower the heat slightly, and cook for 5 minutes. Remove from the heat and leave for a further 10 minutes with the lid on.

Add the remaining herbs and half the lemon peel to the zucchini mixture. Season with salt and pepper.

Grill the bread on both sides, rub with the whole garlic clove on one side only and drizzle with extra virgin olive oil. Spoon over the zucchini, sprinkle with the remaining lemon peel and serve with the prosciutto.

august

cannellini beans [274] *soup* cannellini bean and pasta soup. cannellini bean and borage soup. *antipasto* cannellini beans, peppers and chard. **marjoram** [280] *pizza* focaccia stuffed with gorgonzola and marjoram. **sweet peppers** [286] *vegetable* peppers stewed with red wine. peppers stuffed with rocket and olives. *pasta* spaghetti with peppers and tomatoes. *antipasto* grilled and roasted vegetables. **raspberries** [294] *jam* roasted raspberry jam. *pudding* raspberry and lemon sorbet. **swiss chard** [298] *vegetable* braised swiss chard with chilli and garlic. swiss chard with lentils and herbs. **trompettes de mort and chanterelles** [302] *frittata* trompettes de mort and chanterelle frittata. *bruschetta* chanterelle and prosciutto bruschetta. *risotto* trompette and parsley risotto. *vegetable* braised potatoes and trompettes de mort.

cannellini beans

There is a special joy in getting hold of a box of fresh cannellini beans. Even in Florence, where these beans are so highly prized, there will only be a few market stalls selling them. We have been told that nearly all the crop is consumed by the growers and their families.

The original cannellini bean from Tuscany is a long, slender kidney shape, ivory white with a thin skin. They are very creamy when cooked and totally delicious eaten on their own simply with lots of extra virgin olive oil. A few varieties are grown, among them Toscanelli and Piattellini, each coming from a particular area around Tuscany. Other white fresh haricot beans are similar. These are usually a little fatter and rounder and are grown in Spain and the south of France. We buy these fresh and cook them the same way.

Look for firm pods that are still stiff, possibly browning at the edges, which indicates that the beans are ripe and fully developed. Cook them in unsalted water flavoured with parsley stalks, basil, garlic and tomato. Always serve with extra virgin olive oil.

Dried cannellini beans need to be soaked overnight and then cooked in the same way as fresh. They will take much longer.

cannellini bean and pasta soup
zuppa di cannellini con pasta

for 6
1.5 kg fresh cannellini beans in their pods
150 g orecchiette pasta
1 large, ripe tomato
1 small bunch of fresh flat-leaf parsley
1 whole bulb garlic, cut in half
2 tablespoons olive oil
3 garlic cloves, peeled and finely chopped
2 tablespoons chopped fresh flat-leaf parsley
1 litre chicken stock (see page 455)
Maldon salt and freshly ground black pepper
extra virgin olive oil

Pod the beans, then place the beans in a large, thick-bottomed saucepan. Cover with water and add the tomato, bunch of parsley and the garlic bulb. Bring to the boil, then simmer for 45 minutes, until the beans are very soft, but not mushy. Drain, reserving the liquid, and discard the tomato, parsley and garlic. Set the beans aside.

Return the empty saucepan to the heat and add the olive oil, the chopped garlic and parsley. Cook until soft but not brown. Add the cooked beans, stir and cook for 3 minutes. Add half the reserved cooking liquid from the beans and enough chicken stock to cover the beans. The soup should be thick, so you may not need to add all the stock. Bring to the boil and season with salt and pepper.

Remove about a third of the beans and pulse-chop to a purée in the food processor. Return to the pot and stir into the whole beans.

Cook the orecchiette in boiling salted water until al dente. Drain and stir into the beans. Check the seasoning, drizzle with extra virgin oil and serve.

cannellini bean and borage soup
zuppa di cannellini con borraggine

for 6

600 g fresh cannellini beans in their pods, cooked
   (see opposite), or 150 g dried beans, cooked
   (see page 376)
1.5 kg borage leaves and stalks, washed
Maldon salt and freshly ground black pepper
1.5 kg cherry vine tomatoes, washed
2 tablespoons olive oil
500 g spring onions, green and white parts,
   roughly chopped
10 garlic cloves, peeled and sliced
2 ciabatta loaves, tough bottom crusts removed
3 tablespoons chopped fresh flat-leaf parsley
2 tablespoons fresh marjoram leaves, chopped
extra virgin olive oil

Remove any tough stalks from the borage. Bring a large saucepan of water to the boil, add 2 tablespoons salt and blanch the borage for 5 minutes. Remove using a slotted spoon and drain. Chop finely. Keep 500 ml of the cooking water. Prick the tomatoes and place in the same boiling water for 30 seconds. Pick out with a slotted spoon (keeping the water again), drain and cool in cold water. When cool, peel off the skins.

Heat the olive oil in a large, thick-bottomed saucepan and add the onion. Fry gently until soft and translucent. Add the garlic and continue to cook over a low heat just to combine them. Add the tomatoes and a little salt. Simmer to break up and soften.

Tear the ciabatta up into thinnish pieces. Mash half the cannellini beans into their cooking juices, then add to the tomato saucepan, along with the whole beans, and stir briefly. Add the bread then wet with the 500 ml of borage cooking water. If too dry, add extra boiling water. Carefully fold in the borage and herbs. The soup should have just enough liquid for the bread to be plumped up. Serve with extra virgin olive oil drizzled over.

cannellini beans, peppers and chard
cannellini, pepperoni e bietola

for 6
1 kg fresh cannellini beans in their pods
3 large, ripe yellow peppers, washed
600 g Swiss chard, stalks removed, washed
1 large, ripe tomato
5 garlic cloves, peeled
3 sage leaves
extra virgin olive oil
Maldon salt and freshly ground black pepper
2 teaspoons dried wild oregano
3 tablespoons olive oil

Preheat the oven to 200°C/400°F/Gas 6. Place the cannellini beans in an ovenproof dish, cover with water and add the tomato, 2 garlic cloves and the sage leaves. Pour in 3 tablespoons extra virgin olive oil. Cover with foil as tightly as possible and pierce once with a pointed knife. Place in the oven and bake for 45 minutes or until the beans are cooked and most of the oil has been absorbed. Cool.

Remove and discard the sage, tomato skin and any hard core. Push half the beans, the garlic and tomato through a mouli, or pulse-chop in a food processor. Return to the whole beans and mix together. Season.

Cut the peppers in half lengthways, keeping the stalk on, and remove the seeds. Cut each half into three lengthways. Finely slice the remaining garlic and mix it with the oregano and the olive oil. Smear each piece of pepper with the mixture. Place the pepper slices skin side down on a large flat roasting tray. Season and bake in the preheated oven for 30 minutes or until the peppers are brown on the edges and cooked.

Cook the chard for 6-8 minutes in boiling, salted water, then drain and squeeze out all the water. Season then mix with 3-4 tablespoons of extra virgin olive oil. Serve all three vegetables together on individual plates.

marjoram

There are two major types of marjoram – sweet and pot. Sweet, the one we use in cooking, has fleshy, light green leaves and a delicate sweet flavour. Pot is much stronger and pungent and is much closer in flavour to oregano which, with its soft velvety leaves and purple flowers, is a closely related herb that grows wild. Both sweet and pot marjoram grow abundantly in the Mediterranean area, and also wild throughout this country.

We use large quantities of fresh marjoram in the summer, picking the leaves from the stems and using them with vegetables, fish and both mozzarella and ricotta cheese. One of the sauces that is always on the menu in this season is salmoriglio – marjoram crushed with sea salt and then combined with lemon juice and olive oil.

focaccia stuffed with gorgonzola and marjoram
focaccia con ricotta e maggiorana

for 6
focaccia dough
2 teaspoons granular dried yeast
225 ml warm water
400 g plain flour
Maldon salt and freshly ground black pepper
extra virgin olive oil
filling
3 tablespoons fresh marjoram leaves
500 g Gorgonzola cheese, crumbled
300 g mascarpone cheese

For the focaccia dough, mix the yeast with the warm water in a bowl, and allow to rest for about 5 minutes.

Put the flour and 1 teaspoon salt into the food processor. Add the yeast and 2 tablespoons of the olive oil. Pulse until a dough forms. If necessary add more flour. The dough should be smooth but not sticky. Transfer to a clean surface and knead the dough for a few minutes. Shape into a ball and place in a bowl greased with olive oil. Cover with a cloth and leave to rise in a warm place for about 45 minutes.

Punch the dough down with your fists to deflate it. Working in the bowl, knead the dough four or five times. Cover and allow to rise again in the warm place for a further half hour.

Preheat the oven to 225°C/425°F/Gas 7.

Transfer the dough to a clean surface and divide into six equal balls. On a lightly floured work surface, shape two of the dough balls with your hands into 25 cm rounds, about 1 cm thick. Place one round on top of the other and roll out to a circle 30 cm in diameter. Prick the surface with a fork, and place on a lightly oiled baking tray. Do the same with the remaining pieces of dough. Bake in the preheated oven for 8 minutes or until they are light brown.

Meanwhile, for the filling, stir the Gorgonzola into the mascarpone and add the marjoram. Season with black pepper.

Remove the pizzas from the oven and cut them in half horizontally using a large bread knife. Lift off the top layers and spread the middles with the cheese mixture. Replace the tops, brush with olive oil and sprinkle with salt. Return to the oven for 5 more minutes until brown and crisp. Cut into wedges and serve immediately.

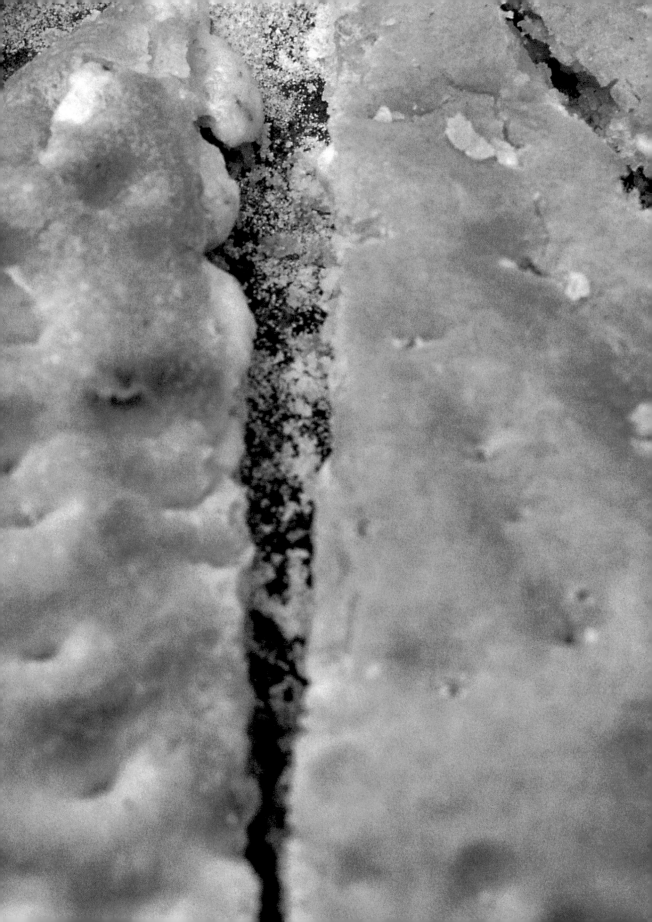

sweet peppers

One of the high points of summer occurs when the beautiful elongated Italian peppers arrive. There are so many delicious recipes for peppers spanning the regions, from the grilled and marinated peppers of Sicily to the Bagna Cauda of Piedmont.

We use only red and yellow peppers – green peppers do not have the same sweet flavour. It is really worth seeking out the irregularly shaped, thinner fleshed Italian peppers. The uniform peppers that are grown under glass with their thick flesh and skins have a completely different flavour. The best peppers are those which have ripened in the full heat of the sun.

When choosing peppers, look for a smooth, unblemished and glossy skin, with no soft parts. Any sign of green indicates that the pepper has not yet fully ripened and it may be less sweet. To ripen peppers yourself, leave in a sunny place for a few days. Yellow peppers are the sweetest of all. As peppers cook, they release light, syrupy juices which are delicious and distinctive.

It is essential that the white pith and seeds inside the peppers are removed before eating. If the peppers are being cut, then this is done before cooking. If the peppers are being grilled whole, then this process is done afterwards when the peppers are cool enough to handle. To skin peppers, see page 292.

peppers stewed with red wine
stufato di peperoni al vino rosso

for 6
5 large red Italian peppers
5 large yellow Italian peppers
500 ml Valpolicella (red wine)
6 tablespoons olive oil
6 garlic cloves, peeled and sliced
500 g tinned peeled plum tomatoes
Maldon salt and freshly ground black pepper
a handful of fresh basil leaves, torn
extra virgin olive oil

Heat half the oil in a thick-bottomed saucepan and add a third of the garlic. Cook until soft, then add the tomatoes and their juices and cook over a low heat, stirring frequently, for 45-60 minutes or until the sauce is very thick. Season to taste with salt and pepper.

Cut the peppers lengthways into quarters. Remove the white membranes and seeds, then cut each piece across in halves or thirds, depending on size.

Heat the remaining olive oil in a wide, thick-bottomed saucepan and add the remaining garlic and the peppers. Stir, coating the peppers with the oil and cook over a medium to low heat for about 30 minutes. They should go soft, but not black. Stir in the tomato sauce and then the wine gradually, letting one addition be absorbed by the peppers before pouring in the next. Add the basil and cook for a further 30 minutes, stirring frequently.

Remove from the heat, drizzle with extra virgin olive oil, and serve.

peppers stuffed with rocket and olives
peperoni ripieni di rucola

for 6
3 large red Italian peppers
3 large yellow Italian peppers
200 g rocket
150 g pitted Niçoise olives
1 tablespoon finely chopped fresh flat-leaf parsley
1 small red chilli, seeded and finely chopped
extra virgin olive oil
olive oil
4 garlic cloves, peeled and cut into slivers
Maldon salt and freshly ground black pepper
1 tablespoon red wine vinegar

Preheat the oven to 180°C/350°F/Gas 4.

Place the olives in a bowl and stir in the parsley, red chilli and
4 tablespoons extra virgin olive oil. Let marinate while you prepare
and cook the peppers.

Cut the peppers in half lengthways and remove and discard the white
membrane and seeds. Place the pepper halves cut side up in a lightly
oiled roasting tin. Place a few slivers of garlic into each half, season with
salt and pepper and lightly drizzle with olive oil. Pour about 200 ml of
water into the base of the roasting tin to prevent the peppers from
sticking. Cover tightly with foil and bake in the preheated oven for half
an hour. Remove from the oven, remove the foil and drizzle with a little
more olive oil. Reduce the oven temperature to 120°C/250°F/Gas 1/2 and
bake for a further 40 minutes or until the peppers are totally cooked.

Chop the rocket coarsely and dress with a mixture of the red wine
vinegar and 4 tablespoons extra virgin olive oil. Stuff each pepper half
with the rocket and spoon over the marinated olives.

spaghetti with peppers and tomatoes
spaghetti con peperoni e pomodori

for 6

4 peppers, red and/or yellow, grilled (see overleaf)
1 kg ripe tomatoes, skinned (see page 265) and
    hard cores discarded
400 g spaghetti
olive oil
6 garlic cloves, peeled, 3 finely chopped
6 salted anchovies, prepared (see page 458),
    roughly chopped
2 dried red chillies, crumbled
Maldon salt and freshly ground black pepper
50 g salted capers, prepared (see page 458)
3 tablespoons red wine vinegar
1 ciabatta loaf, bottom crust removed
3 tablespoons chopped fresh flat-leaf parsley

Heat 3 tablespoons of olive oil in a large, thick-bottomed saucepan, add the chopped garlic and cook briefly until light brown. Add the anchovies and chilli, stir to blend, then add the tomatoes and 1 large teaspoon of salt. Simmer, stirring occasionally, for 30 minutes. Add the capers. Peel the peppers, discard the skins and seeds and roughly chop the flesh. Add to the tomato sauce. Mix together and add the vinegar.

Tear the ciabatta into pieces and pulse-chop to coarse breadcrumbs in the food processor. Heat 100 ml olive oil in a small pan. When hot, not smoking, add the whole garlic, turn the heat down and cook until the garlic browns. Discard the garlic. Add the breadcrumbs to the flavoured oil, stir and cook for 2-3 minutes until crisp. Drain on kitchen paper.

Bring a large saucepan of salted water to the boil, add the spaghetti and cook until al dente. Drain and add to the sauce. Stir in the parsley, test for seasoning and serve sprinkled with the breadcrumbs.

grilled and roasted vegetables
verdura mista grigliata e al forno

for 6
2 red and 2 yellow peppers
2 yellow and 2 green zucchini, no thicker than a
    thumb
2 long and firm, deep purple aubergines
Maldon salt and freshly ground black pepper
olive oil
2 garlic cloves, peeled and squashed with
    1 teaspoon salt
4 tablespoons red wine vinegar
extra virgin olive oil
3 tablespoons fresh basil leaves

Preheat a griddle pan. Place the zucchini in a bowl of water and leave for 30 minutes. Cut the aubergines in half lengthways, then cut each half lengthways into three. Scatter salt over the pieces, place in a colander, and leave for 20 minutes. Wash and squeeze dry.

Grill the peppers on all sides until the skin is totally black. Put into a bowl, cover with clingfilm and leave to cool. Peel off the skin, remove seeds and stalks, and divide each pepper into eighths.

Preheat the oven to 200°C/400°F/Gas 6 and preheat the griddle pan again. Brush a large oven tray with a little oil. Put the aubergine slices on the tray, cut side up, and roast in the preheated oven for 15 minutes. Turn the slices over and roast for a further 5 minutes or until they are slightly crisp at the edges and soft in the centre. Drain and dry. Cut the zucchini in half lengthways, season with salt and pepper and place on the hot griddle, cut side down. Grill for 2-3 minutes or until the zucchini are brown. Turn over and grill the other side. Cool.

Put all the cooked vegetables into a large bowl. Mix the garlic with the vinegar and then add five times its volume of extra virgin olive oil. Add the basil and garlic dressing to the vegetables, season and toss together.

raspberries

Raspberries are native to cooler climates and some say that those grown in Scotland are the best in the world. They are not well known in the Mediterranean, except in the higher, rainier, mountainous regions such as Piedmont, Lombardy and the Tyrol. Although red raspberries are the most familiar, white, yellow and gold fruit can also be found. Some wild raspberries in Scotland are pale yellow.

In Italy, raspberries – lampone – are used in tarts and sorbets or, like strawberries, are served raw with lemon juice and sugar. They lose their unique and delicate flavour when cooked.

Raspberries are extremely perishable so always look at the bottom of the punnet for damp stains caused by rotting fruit. It is important to pick out any rotting raspberries for they contaminate the others. It is not necessary to wash raspberries as they grow high off the ground.

roasted raspberry jam
marmellata di lamponi al forno

Raspberries must be dry, so *do not* wash them.

makes about 5 kg
3 kg fresh, very ripe best-quality raspberries
2.7 kg caster sugar

Preheat the oven to 200°C/400°F/Gas 6.

Place the raspberries in a heatproof dish. Do the same with the sugar. Bake both in the preheated oven until very hot, about half an hour. The raspberries will sweat but will not totally collapse.

Combine the hot sugar and hot raspberries, and stir together. The raspberries will melt with the sugar and become instant jam! Put into clean jam jars and seal with wax paper.

raspberry and lemon sorbet
sorbetto ai lamponi e limone

for 6
800 g fresh ripe raspberries
1 whole thick-skinned lemon, washed
350-400 g caster sugar (depending on the
   sweetness of the raspberries)
juice of 1/2 lemon

Cut the whole lemon into 1 cm pieces and remove any pips. Put the pieces into a food processor with the caster sugar, and blend until the lemon and sugar have combined to a thick purée. Little pieces of the lemon skin should still be visible. Add the raspberries and continue to blend until combined. Add the lemon juice, then taste and add more juice if necessary. The lemon flavour should be intense, but it must not overpower the raspberries.

Pour into an ice-cream machine and churn for 20 minutes. Remove to the freezer and allow to get stiffer before serving. Alternatively, pour the mixture into flat freezing trays and freeze until solid, stirring to break up the crystals every half hour, about 1 1/2 hours.

swiss chard

Chard is a member of the beet family and is known in Italy as bietola. It is a beautiful vegetable with huge green leaves that taste like strong spinach and thick white stalks that are often cooked as a vegetable in their own right, or used as you do celery in the basic soffrittos for soups.

Colourful varieties of chard, known as Bright Lights or Rainbow, are easy to grow. The stems are slimmer and as they seem to be stringier, we do not use them in the same way as the white-stemmed chard. But the leaves are absolutely delicious and a favourite way to cook them is simply blanched in boiling salted water, drained, seasoned and tossed with extra virgin olive oil, to be served cold.

Choose chard that has fresh, crisp and strong leaves and stalks that are stiff, which means it has been recently cut. To prepare Swiss chard, cut the leaves from the stalks and keep separate. Use a small sharp knife to peel away the thick fibrous film that is on the outside and cut into centimetre strips.

braised swiss chard with chilli and garlic

bietole brasate con peperoncini e aglio

for 6
500 g Swiss chard
500 g ruby chard
500 g Bright Lights chard
Maldon salt and freshly ground black pepper
6 tablespoons extra virgin olive oil
6 garlic cloves, peeled and finely sliced
3 small dried red chillies, crumbled
2 tablespoons chopped fresh fennel herb
3 lemons, cut into wedges

Ruby chard and Bright Lights have tougher stalks than Swiss chard. Cut these off about 5 cm from the base of the leaf. Swiss chard in the summer has broader, more tender stalks and they are good to eat if they are white and crisp. If still green, cut them off as with the coloured chard. Cut the white stalks into 1 cm slices.

Bring a large saucepan of salted water to the boil. If you have them, cook the stalks first for 8 minutes. Remove with a slotted spoon. Cook the remaining leaves – you may have to do this in batches – for 5 minutes or until tender but still a little al dente. Drain and cool.

Heat the extra virgin olive oil in a very large, thick-bottomed frying pan. Add the garlic and cook briefly to soften it and flavour the oil, then add the crumbled chilli, fennel herb and the chard leaves and stalks. Stir them around in the pan to collect the flavours, then season generously. Serve with lemon wedges.

swiss chard with lentils and herbs
bietole e lenticchie con erbette

for 6
1.5 kg Swiss chard with stalks
250 g Castellucio or Puy lentils, rinsed
2 tablespoons each of chopped fresh marjoram
   and basil leaves
1 tablespoon each of chopped fresh fennel herb
   and mint leaves
Maldon salt and freshly ground black pepper
6 garlic cloves, peeled, 3 finely chopped
extra virgin olive oil
2 tablespoons olive oil

Cut the stalks from the leaves of the chard and cut them into 1 cm strips. Bring a large saucepan of salted water to the boil. Add the stalks and cook for 7-8 minutes until tender. Remove using a slotted spoon and put aside. Put the chard leaves into the same water, adding more salt if necessary, and cook for 4-5 minutes. Drain and roughly chop.

Put a separate, medium saucepan of water on the heat and add the lentils, the 3 whole cloves of garlic and the stalks from some of the herbs. Gently bring to the boil, turn the heat down and simmer, covered, for 30 minutes or until the lentils are al dente. Drain and pick out and discard the herb stalks and garlic. Pour in 3 tablespoons of extra virgin olive oil and season with salt and pepper.

Heat the olive oil in a large, thick-bottomed saucepan, add the chopped garlic and cook briefly to soften and colour. Add the chard stalks and let them cook in the garlic for 3-4 minutes, then add half of all the herbs. Stir to combine and fry briefly. Season with salt and pepper. Add the chard leaves to the mixture and stir only to incorporate the stalks with the leaves. Spoon in the lentils.

Serve with the remaining basil, mint and marjoram sprinkled over and a drizzle of extra virgin olive oil.

trompettes de mort and chanterelles

Chanterelles are golden yellow in colour, with a flattened undulating cap. They are one of the most fragrant and delicate of wild mushrooms, appearing in July and often lasting until the first frost, and can be found in woodland under pine, beech and birch trees.

To prepare chanterelles, cut off the root tips and clean with a soft brush. Most recipes for chanterelles begin with cooking them in a large frying pan with garlic and parsley in one layer over high heat in order to seal in the flavour.

Trompettes de mort are very dark brown to black in colour and have a strong hard texture. They are the most dramatic of wild mushrooms, appearing in late summer and autumn, beneath hazel and beech trees. They are rarely served on their own as they are so tough, but are perfect combined with chanterelles or other wild mushrooms. We make these traditional French mushrooms more Italian by putting them on bruschetta or in a risotto. See page 308 for how to clean.

trompettes de mort and chanterelle frittata
frittata di trombette di morto e cantarelli

for 2
500 g chanterelles, cleaned (see page 303)
200 g trompettes de mort or other summer
   mushrooms, cleaned (see page 308)
60 g unsalted butter
4 tablespoons olive oil
1 garlic clove, peeled and finely sliced
1 tablespoon fresh young sage leaves
1 tablespoon fresh oregano, leaves picked from
   the stalks
Maldon salt and freshly ground black pepper
juice of 1 lemon
4 large, organic free-range eggs, lightly beaten

Heat half the butter and half the oil in a large, thick-bottomed frying pan. Add the mushrooms and fry over a high heat for 3-4 minutes. Add the garlic and herbs, and cook for 3-4 minutes longer. Season generously with salt and pepper and squeeze in the lemon juice. Remove from the heat.

Preheat the oven to 230°C/450°F/Gas 8.

Heat the remaining butter and oil in an ovenproof frying pan. Stir half the mushrooms into the lightly beaten eggs, then pour into the frying pan. Lower the heat and cook until the frittata is beginning to set, loosening the egg at the sides. Cover with the remaining mushrooms, place in the preheated oven and bake for a minute or two. The frittata will have risen, but should be quite runny inside. Serve on warm plates.

chanterelle and prosciutto bruschetta

bruschetta con cantarelli e prosciutto

for 6
500 g chanterelles, cleaned (see page 303)
6 slices prosciutto di San Daniele
50 g unsalted butter
2 tablespoons olive oil
4 garlic cloves, peeled, 3 finely chopped
3 tablespoons chopped fresh flat-leaf parsley
Maldon salt and freshly ground black pepper
6 slices sourdough bread
extra virgin olive oil

Heat the butter and olive oil in a thick-bottomed saucepan. Add the chanterelles and fry over high heat for 3-4 minutes. Add the chopped garlic and parsley and cook for a further 4 minutes. If there is too much juice in the pan, pour it out and discard. Season the chanterelles generously with salt and pepper.

Grill the bread on both sides and rub on one side with the whole garlic clove. Drizzle over extra virgin olive oil. Spoon the mushrooms over each bruschetta, cover with the slice of prosciutto and drizzle over some more extra virgin olive oil.

trompette and parsley risotto
risotto alle trombette di morto

for 6
1 kg trompettes des morts
4 tablespoons chopped fresh flat-leaf parsley
1.5 litres chicken stock (see page 455)
Maldon salt and freshly ground black pepper
olive oil
3 garlic cloves, peeled and finely chopped
100 g unsalted butter
inner white heart of 1 head celery, chopped
1 red onion, peeled and roughly chopped
400 g carnaroli rice
freshly grated Parmesan

Heat the stock and test for seasoning. Cut off the base root stem of the mushrooms, and soak them in cold water, pushing them around to release leaves and stalks that may have got trapped in the trumpet. Dry. You can use a salad spinner.

Heat 3 tablespoons olive oil in a large thick-bottomed frying pan. When very hot, add half the mushrooms and fry, turning them over in the hot oil, for 2-3 minutes. Add half the garlic, season with salt and pepper and cook until the mushrooms have wilted and there is no liquid left in the pan. Repeat with the other half of the mushrooms.

Melt 50 g of the butter in a large thick-bottomed saucepan, add the celery and onion and cook to soften over a medium heat until beginning to colour. Add the rice and stir to coat each grain with the buttery vegetables. Start to add the stock ladle by ladle, stirring all the time, allowing each ladleful to be absorbed before adding the next. The rice will take 15 minutes to become al dente.

Stir in the mushrooms and cook for 2-3 minutes to combine them into the risotto. Finally stir in the parsley and the remaining butter. Test for seasoning. Serve with freshly grated Parmesan.

braised potatoes and trompettes de mort
trombette di morto e patate in padella

for 6
500 g trompettes de mort
1.5 kg potatoes (Linska or Roseval)
2 tablespoons olive oil
5 garlic cloves, peeled and finely chopped
3 tablespoons chopped fresh flat-leaf parsley
Maldon salt and freshly ground black pepper
extra virgin olive oil

Prepare and wash the mushrooms (see opposite).

Heat the olive oil in a large thick-bottomed saucepan, add the garlic and then the mushrooms, stirring to coat the mushrooms with oil. Continue cooking and stirring for about 5 minutes, then add 2 tablespoons of the parsley, and season with salt and pepper. Stir to combine, and set aside.

Peel the potatoes and cut into 2 cm cubes. Bring a large pot of salted water to the boil and cook the potato until tender. Drain, and season with salt and pepper.

Add the potatoes to the mushrooms, stir together, and cook over a low heat for 5 minutes to combine the flavours. Drizzle with extra virgin olive oil, sprinkle with the remaining parsley and serve hot.

september

aubergines [312] *antipasto* aubergine caponata. *vegetable* braised aubergines with potatoes. *salad* baked aubergines with oregano.

chillies [318] *antipasto* baked buffalo ricotta with chilli. *sauce* green chilli sauce. *antipasto* tuna carpaccio with chilli. **puffballs** [324] *bruschetta* bruschetta of puffball and field mushrooms with tomato and thyme. *antipasto* grilled marinated puffball. **figs** [330] *salad* figs, buffalo mozzarella and basil. *antipasto* marinated figs with balsamic vinegar. *pudding* figs baked with crème fraîche. **summer squash** [336] *vegetable* wood-roasted summer squash. braised summer squash. *risotto* summer squash risotto. **verbena** [342] *drink* verbena tea

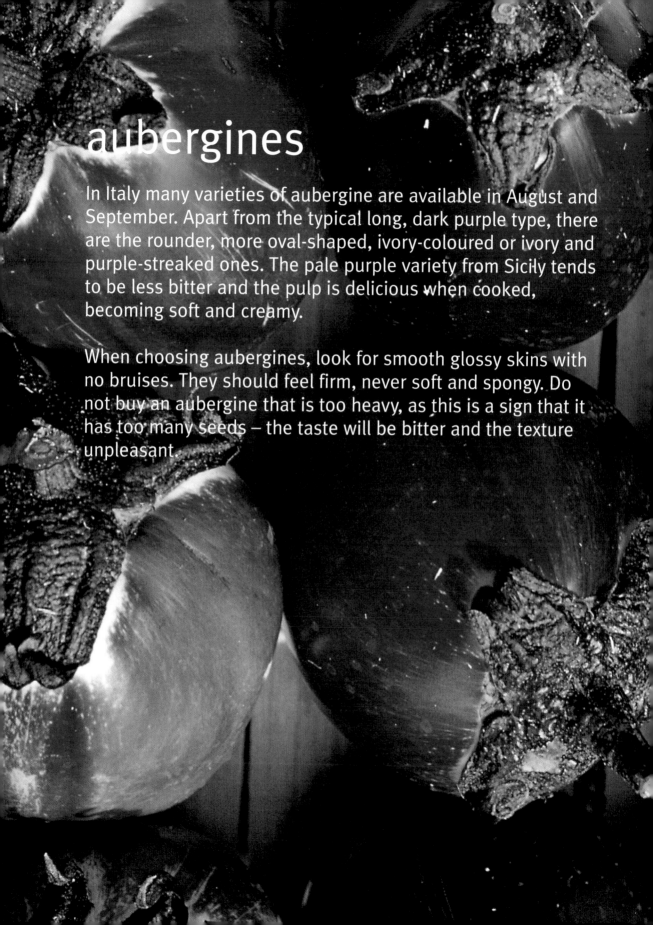

aubergines

In Italy many varieties of aubergine are available in August and September. Apart from the typical long, dark purple type, there are the rounder, more oval-shaped, ivory-coloured or ivory and purple-streaked ones. The pale purple variety from Sicily tends to be less bitter and the pulp is delicious when cooked, becoming soft and creamy.

When choosing aubergines, look for smooth glossy skins with no bruises. They should feel firm, never soft and spongy. Do not buy an aubergine that is too heavy, as this is a sign that it has too many seeds – the taste will be bitter and the texture unpleasant.

aubergine caponata
caponata di melanzane

for 6
2 large, firm aubergines with white flesh
Maldon salt and freshly ground black pepper
1.5 kg large and fleshy, ripe tomatoes
olive oil
2 medium red onions, peeled and chopped
3 garlic cloves, peeled and finely chopped
inner white heart of 1 head celery, finely chopped
   (keep any good fresh leaves)
3 tablespoons red wine herb vinegar
60 g black olives, stoned
50 g salted capers, prepared (see page 458)
4 tablespoons chopped fresh flat-leaf parsley
4 hard-boiled eggs, yolks only, roughly chopped

Wash the aubergines, cut off the stalk and base and cut the flesh into 2.5 cm cubes. Place in a colander and add 3 tablespoons sea salt. Toss to cover all the cubes and leave for an hour to allow the bitter juices to seep out. Wash and press dry. Skin the tomatoes (see page 265), then cut out the hard centre and the seeds. Chop roughly into a pulp.

Heat 2 tablespoons of the oil in a large, thick-bottomed pan, add the onion and fry gently until soft. Add the garlic and cook for 5 minutes, then add the tomato and 1 tablespoon salt. Simmer over a medium heat for about 25 minutes. Add the celery and simmer for a further 10 minutes.

In a separate large flat thick-bottomed saucepan, heat 4 tablespoons of the olive oil. When very hot, place one layer of aubergines in to brown. Use tongs to turn the cubes over so that they brown on all sides. Remove and drain on kitchen paper. Repeat with the remaining aubergine cubes until all are fried. Sprinkle the aubergine with vinegar, salt and pepper. Season the tomato sauce, then stir in the aubergines, olives, capers and half the chopped celery leaves and parsley. Serve scattered with the remaining celery leaves and parsley and the chopped egg yolk.

braised aubergines with potatoes
cianfotta di melanzane

for 6
1 large, firm aubergine
Maldon salt and freshly ground black pepper
4 large ripe tomatoes
3 large potatoes (a waxy variety such as Roseval)
1 large ripe red pepper
olive oil
1 medium red onion, peeled and finely chopped
3 garlic cloves, peeled and finely chopped
2 small dried red chillies, crumbled
3 tablespoons red wine vinegar
3 tablespoons fresh marjoram leaves
extra virgin olive oil

Preheat the grill. Wash the aubergine, cut off the stalk and base, and cut the flesh into 3 cm cubes. Sprinkle with salt, place in a colander and leave for an hour to allow the bitter juices to run out. Wash, squeeze and pat dry. Skin the tomatoes (see page 265), discard any tough centre and chop. Peel and cut the potatoes into 2 cm cubes. Grill the pepper until the skin is black on all sides. Place in a plastic bag to cool. Remove the blackened skin, stalk and any seeds. Cut into 2 cm strips.

Heat 2 tablespoons of the olive oil in a large thick-bottomed saucepan, add the onion, and let it soften and colour. Add the garlic and chilli, and cook for 3-4 minutes. Add the tomato and a teaspoon of salt, and simmer gently for 35 minutes.

Boil the potato in a small saucepan of salted water until al dente. Drain. In a separate large saucepan heat 4 tablespoons of olive oil. When hot add the aubergine cubes and brown on all sides. Cook until tender. Remove and drain. In a separate bowl, combine the tomato sauce with the aubergine, potato and pepper. Sprinkle with the vinegar, salt and pepper, and stir together. Add the marjoram. Serve drizzled with extra virgin olive oil, warm or at room temperature.

baked aubergines with oregano
melanzane al forno con origano

for 6
4 large, round, firm aubergines
Maldon salt and freshly ground black pepper
olive oil
3 tablespoons dried oregano
1 tablespoon coriander seeds, roughly ground
3 garlic cloves, peeled and finely chopped
3 handfuls of rocket leaves
juice of 2 lemons
extra virgin olive oil

Wash the aubergines and cut off the stalks and base. Slice into 1.5 cm thick discs. Place the discs in a large colander and sprinkle with salt. Put a plate on top with a heavy weight to push down on the aubergine slices. Leave for an hour.

Preheat the oven to 200°C/400°F/Gas 6.

Wash off the salt and the bitter juices and pat the aubergine dry. Line a large flat baking tray with foil, then brush this with olive oil. Sprinkle the surface with salt and pepper and some of the oregano, coriander and garlic. Place the aubergine slices close together on the tray. Brush the tops of the slices with olive oil and sprinkle with the remaining oregano, coriander and garlic. Bake in the preheated oven for 15-20 minutes. Turn the slices over when lightly brown, return to the oven and continue cooking for a few more minutes.

Wash and dry the rocket. Place a little rocket on each plate. Season with salt and pepper. Tear the baked aubergine slices in half and place over the rocket. Drizzle with the lemon juice and some extra virgin olive oil.

chillies

Peperoncini, the common Italian name for dried red chillies, are grown predominantly in the south of Italy. The hotter the climate, the more pungent the chilli. We use these small chillies, dried, in many of our sauces and soups. They are an essential part of the Italian larder.

In Abruzzo, little dried red chillies are cooked whole without being broken into the dish. It is the seeds that make the food really hot. They are called 'diavolicchio' and are used in many dishes.

The fresh, larger and thicker-fleshed red chillies, to be found in most supermarkets, have a milder taste. It is easy to remove their seeds to ensure that the flavour is sweet and spicy, not hot. Do so by halving the chilli lengthways and scraping out the seeds, then chop or slice. Mix chopped red chilli with extra virgin olive oil for a simple sauce.

Fully ripe green chillies have a fresher, less sweet flavour. They can often be quite mild, so are suitable for mixing with herbs, to enhance the flavour, and lemon juice before adding extra virgin olive oil.

An Italian way of flavouring vegetables is to add them to a pan in which you have softened garlic and dried chilli. Toss for a few moments and serve at room temperature.

baked buffalo ricotta with chilli
ricotta di bufala con peperoncini al forno

Serve warm with bruschetta and sliced ripe tomatoes.

for 6
6 small dried red chillies, crumbled
2 large fresh red chillies
2 whole x 250 g buffalo ricotta cheeses
olive oil
2 tablespoons dried wild oregano
Maldon salt and freshly ground black pepper
2 tablespoons fresh marjoram leaves
extra virgin olive oil

Preheat the oven to 220°C/425°F/Gas 7. Lightly brush with olive oil an ovenproof dish that will hold the whole ricotta.

Place the cheese in the dish. Generously scatter over the dried chilli, dried oregano, salt and pepper and drizzle with olive oil. Place in the hot oven and bake until the ricotta is lightly brown and feels solid when touched, about 10-15 minutes.

Split the fresh chillies in half and scoop out and discard the seeds. Finely chop the flesh, place in a small bowl and season. Separately chop the marjoram leaves. Add to the chilli, then cover with extra virgin olive oil.

Serve the warm baked ricottas with the chilli sauce spooned over.

green chilli sauce
salsa di peperoncini verdi

for 6
250 g green chillies, jalapeño or other thick-
   skinned variety
3 lemons, washed
2 garlic cloves, peeled
2 tablespoons chopped fresh flat-leaf parsley
Maldon salt and freshly ground black pepper
150 ml extra virgin olive oil

Wash the chillies. Cut each in half lengthways and scoop out the seeds.
Finely chop, using a mezzaluna if you have one.

Remove the peel from the lemons, carefully cut away any white pith and
chop the peel finely. Finely chop the garlic and mix together with the
lemon peel, parsley and chilli.

Season with salt and pepper and cover with the extra virgin olive oil.
Leave for a while to allow the flavours to blend.

tuna carpaccio with chilli
carpaccio di tonno al peperoncino

Ask your fishmonger for the top loin, tail end of bluefin tuna.

for 6
4 fresh red chillies, washed
1.5 kg tuna loin, trimmed of skin and sinew
Maldon salt and freshly ground black pepper
juice of 3 lemons
200 g wild rocket leaves, washed
extra virgin olive oil
2 lemons, cut into wedges

Preheat a griddle pan to very hot.

Cover a board with a mixture of sea salt and ground black pepper. Roll the tuna loin in this to crust the surfaces with a thick layer. Place the loin on the hot grill and seal briefly on all sides. The salt and pepper should cook into the surface, making a coat. The flesh should remain raw. Leave to cool completely.

Cut the chillies in half lengthways. Scoop out the seeds and then slice across as finely as possible.

Using a large, sharp thick-bladed knife, kept damp with a wet cloth, cut very thin whole slices from the tuna loin. Wet the knife each time you make a slice.

Arrange enough slices of tuna to completely cover each of the serving plates in one layer. Sprinkle over the chilli, squeeze on plenty of lemon juice and season generously with salt and pepper. Place a few rocket leaves on to each plate of carpaccio. Drizzle with extra virgin olive oil and serve with a wedge of lemon.

puffballs

Puffballs grow wild in grassy fields and near hedgerows. They can be enormous in size, resembling a white football. The larger puffballs have a thick, slightly rubbery skin which may be peeled off.

To check whether a puffball is good, slice it in half. It should be white all the way through and the flesh should be dense and firm.

The dense texture of puffballs makes them ideal for grilling, roasting or deep-frying. We sometimes stud the slices with garlic and rosemary.

bruschetta of puffball and field mushrooms with tomato and thyme
bruschetta con vesce, pomodori e timo

for 6
1.5 kg firm puffballs
1.5 kg firm, flat field mushrooms
1 kg large ripe beef tomatoes
1 large bunch of fresh thyme, leaves picked from
  the stalks
120 ml olive oil
6 garlic cloves, peeled, 5 finely sliced
2 small dried red chillies, crumbled
Maldon salt and freshly ground black pepper
6 salted anchovies, prepared (see page 458),
  roughly chopped
6 slices sourdough bread
extra virgin olive oil
2 lemons

Peel the puffballs and cut into pieces of about 3 x 1.5 cm. Peel the flat field mushrooms and slice across into 1 cm slices. Skin the tomatoes (see page 265), then remove the hard centre part and roughly chop the flesh.

Heat 3 tablespoons of the oil in a large, thick-bottomed saucepan. When hot, add half the sliced garlic and all the chilli, and fry until the garlic colours. Add the tomato and 1 teaspoon salt, and simmer briefly until the tomato pieces break up into a sauce. Add the anchovies and stir to combine.

In a separate large frying pan heat another 3 tablespoons of oil until very hot. Add half the puffball pieces in one layer and turn them over immediately in the hot oil. They will brown very quickly. Add a third of the thyme leaves, a third of the remaining sliced garlic and some salt and pepper. Turn over just to combine and slightly colour the garlic.

Remove and put aside. Repeat with the remainder of the puffballs, using half of the remaining thyme and garlic.

Wipe the pan clean and heat the remaining oil. Add the field mushroom slices and fry quickly, adding the remaining garlic and thyme, plus some salt and pepper. After about 5 minutes, combine the two types of mushroom and stir in the tomato sauce.

Meanwhile, grill the bread on both sides. Rub one side of each lightly with the whole garlic clove and drizzle with extra virgin olive oil. Spoon the warm mushroom mixture on to the bruschetta and serve as an antipasta with a piece of lemon.

grilled marinated puffball
vesce marinate

for 6
1.5 kg large firm puffballs
olive oil
Maldon salt and freshly ground black pepper
1 large bunch of fresh thyme, leaves picked from
   the stalks
4 garlic cloves, peeled and sliced
4 tablespoons extra virgin olive oil
juice of 2 lemons

Preheat the char-grill or cast-iron griddle pan.

Peel the puffball – the skin comes off very easily – cut into 1.5 cm thick slices and brush lightly with olive oil. Working in batches, place the slices on the grill and season with salt and pepper. When lightly brown, turn over, season again and grill as before. Repeat with the remaining puffball slices.

Finely chop the thyme with the garlic, using a mezzaluna. Put in a bowl, add the extra virgin olive oil and lemon juice and mix to combine.

Place the puffball slices on a large flat plate and cover with the marinade.

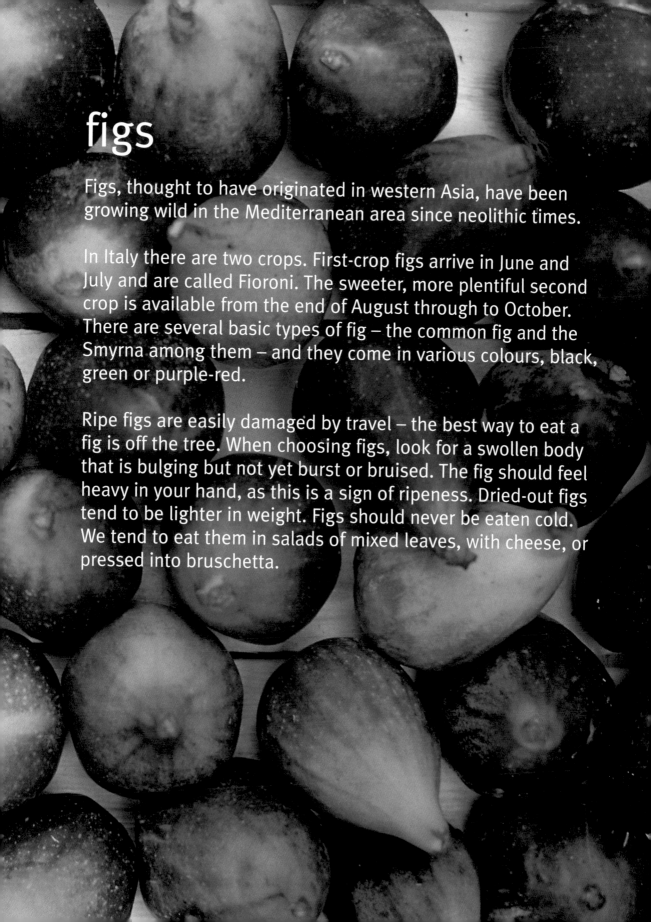

figs

Figs, thought to have originated in western Asia, have been growing wild in the Mediterranean area since neolithic times.

In Italy there are two crops. First-crop figs arrive in June and July and are called Fioroni. The sweeter, more plentiful second crop is available from the end of August through to October. There are several basic types of fig – the common fig and the Smyrna among them – and they come in various colours, black, green or purple-red.

Ripe figs are easily damaged by travel – the best way to eat a fig is off the tree. When choosing figs, look for a swollen body that is bulging but not yet burst or bruised. The fig should feel heavy in your hand, as this is a sign of ripeness. Dried-out figs tend to be lighter in weight. Figs should never be eaten cold. We tend to eat them in salads of mixed leaves, with cheese, or pressed into bruschetta.

figs, buffalo mozzarella and basil
fichi, mozzarella di bufala e basilico

for 6
12 fresh, ripe purple or green figs
1 bunch of fresh green basil
1 bunch of fresh purple basil
6 buffalo mozzarellas
Maldon salt and freshly ground black pepper
juice of 2 lemons
extra virgin olive oil

Wash the figs and cut off the top of the stem. Cut each fig through its stem in half and then into quarters. Pick the basil leaves from their stalks, discarding any that are wilted or damaged. Wash and spin dry. Tear the mozzarella into halves and then quarters.

Place the figs and mozzarella pieces on to individual serving plates. Scatter the basil leaves over, then season with salt and pepper.

Mix the lemon juice with three times its volume of extra virgin olive oil. Season. Pour over each plate and serve immediately.

marinated figs with balsamic vinegar
fichi marinati in aceto balsamico

for 6
18 fresh, ripe purple figs
2 tablespoons fresh thyme leaves and flowers,
    washed
2 tablespoons fresh marjoram leaves, washed
Maldon salt and freshly ground black pepper
juice of 2 small lemons
80 ml extra virgin olive oil
3 teaspoons aged balsamic vinegar

Cut off the top stem and base of each fig and then cut into 1 cm slices.
Finely chop three-quarters of the thyme and marjoram.

Place the fig slices on a large flat platter. Scatter over the chopped
herbs. Season generously with salt and black pepper and toss. Drizzle
over the lemon juice and extra virgin olive oil. Spoon the balsamic
vinegar carefully over the figs. Scatter a few whole herb leaves and
flowers over the top. Keep in a cool place for an hour before serving.

figs baked with crème fraîche
fichi al forno con crème fraîche

for 6
18 fresh, ripe purple figs
250 ml crème fraîche
90 ml thick honey
2 tablespoons water
120 ml grappa

Preheat the oven to 220°C/425°F/Gas 7.

Cut off the top stems of each fig and cut them horizontally in half.
Choose a large ovenproof china dish in which the figs will fit snugly side
by side, cut side up. Wet the bottom of the dish with the water, just to
form a film, no more. Place the figs in as close together as possible.
Drizzle a few drops of grappa over each. Spoon half a teaspoon of honey
over each piece of fig and on top of that a teaspoon of crème fraîche.

Place the dish high up in the very hot oven for 5 minutes, or until the
cream is slightly brown and the juices are running from the figs. Serve
immediately.

summer squash

In September boxes full of summer squash arrive in the River Cafe, in different sizes, colours, shapes and textures. The freshness of a summer squash is indicated by its skin. Newly picked, they have a slightly furry texture, rather like a peach – pickers sometimes get rashes from this – but if the squash sit in a box for days, this will disappear and their skins will be shiny and tough. The following are the varieties we use.

• Patty pan squash, also known as scalloped summer squash, can be white or yellow in colour, with scalloped edges. They are very juicy and sweet, with a fresh flavour that almost explodes in your mouth. They should not be larger than a golf ball.

• Crookneck squash are yellow-skinned with creamy white flesh and a curved neck. Their taste is slightly denser, more nutty, and they are less juicy. They are ideal for grilling or roasting when sliced. Italian crookneck come earlier in the season and have a more earthy flavour.

• Rotondo di Nizza is a thin-skinned, yellow-fleshed variety with a slightly sharper flavour.

wood-roasted summer squash
zucchine gialle e verdi al forno

for 6
2.5 kg mixed summer squash
1 kg mixed small zucchini
4 garlic cloves, peeled and finely chopped
3 tablespoons fresh marjoram, finely chopped
Maldon salt and freshly ground black pepper
100 ml olive oil
juice of 1 lemon
extra virgin olive oil

Put the squash and zucchini in a large bowl of cold water for an hour. Dry and cut into halves lengthways.

Preheat the oven to 200°C/400°F/Gas 6.

Mix together the garlic and marjoram, add plenty of salt and pepper and stir in the olive oil. Place the squash and zucchini in a large bowl, pour in the herb oil mixture and toss to coat each piece.

Place the squash and zucchini, cut side up, on to large flat trays and roast in the preheated oven for 15-20 minutes or until the tops are light brown. Squeeze lemon juice over and drizzle with extra virgin olive oil.

braised summer squash
zucchine gialle e verdi trifolate

For 6
350 g patty pan squash
350 g crookneck squash
500 g mixed yellow and green zucchini
Maldon salt and freshly ground black pepper
4 tablespoons olive oil
3 garlic cloves, peeled and finely chopped
3 dried red chillies, crumbled
3 tablespoons chopped fresh flat-leaf parsley
finely grated zest of 2 washed lemons
3 tablespoons fresh marjoram leaves
extra virgin olive oil

Wash the zucchini and place them in a bowl of cold water for an hour.
Dry and cut into 2 cm slices.

Wash the patty pans, cut off the stems, cut in half and then into
quarters. Wash the crookneck, cut in half lengthways then cut into 3 cm
lengths. Put the crookneck pieces in a colander, sprinkle with salt, and
leave for at least half an hour. Wash and squeeze dry thoroughly.

Heat the olive oil in a large thick-bottomed saucepan, add the squash
and fry quickly, browning on all sides. Add the zucchini and fry, stirring,
for 5 minutes. Stir in the garlic, chilli and half the parsley and season
with salt and pepper. Turn the heat down, cover the saucepan with a lid
and cook for 10 minutes. Remove from the stove and add the remaining
parsley, the lemon zest and marjoram. Test for seasoning. Drizzle with
extra virgin olive oil and serve hot or at room temperature.

summer squash risotto
risotto alle zucchine gialle e verdi

for 6
500 g crookneck and/or patty pan squash
500 g green and/or yellow zucchini
1 litre chicken stock (see page 455)
Maldon salt and freshly ground black pepper
125 g unsalted butter
1 red onion, peeled and finely chopped
inner white heart of 1 head celery, finely chopped
400 g carnaroli rice
150 ml extra dry vermouth
finely grated zest of 2 large washed lemons
2 tablespoons fresh thyme leaves
150 ml double cream
100 g Parmesan, freshly grated

Prepare the squash and zucchini as in the recipe opposite, then finely chop.

Heat the chicken stock and test for seasoning.

In a large thick-bottomed saucepan, melt the butter and cook the onion and celery on a low heat until completely soft. Add the rice and stir to coat each grain with butter. Add the vermouth and about a quarter of the chopped squash and zucchini. Allow the rice to absorb the vermouth, then start to add the hot stock ladle by ladle, allowing the last one to be absorbed by the rice before adding the next. After the first 15 minutes, add the rest of the chopped squash and zucchini. Cook, stirring continuously and adding stock, until the rice is al dente, about another 5 minutes.

Stir in the lemon zest, thyme, double cream and half the Parmesan and stir vigorously. Serve with the remaining Parmesan.

verbena

Verbena has a delicate lemony taste. The leaves are very aromatic and are ideal for making a tea, said to have a calming effect. Verbena grows wild all over Italy and can be grown here very successfully in sheltered gardens and pots. It has a wonderful fragrance when crushed in your hand. In the winter when the leaves have fallen off, cut back the branches and they will grow fuller the next season.

verbena tea
tè alla verbena

for 2

Pick a small handful of young
verbena leaves from the tips of
the plant. Wash them thoroughly.

Pour a small amount of boiling
water into the teapot to heat it.
Drain. Place the leaves in the
pot, cover with boiling water and
leave to brew for a very brief
time. Serve in heatproof glasses.

october

chestnuts ^{348} *soup* chestnut and celeriac soup. *pasta* gnocchi

with chestnut and sausage. pears ^{354} *pudding* pear, honey and

polenta cake. polenta ^{358} *polenta* polenta with hot olive sauce.

polenta with borlotti beans and rocket. pumpkin ^{362} *pasta*

pumpkin pansoti. pumpkin gnocchi. *risotto* pumpkin and cinnamon risotto.

fresh porcini mushrooms ^{370} *pasta* raw porcini

tagliarini. *soup* porcini and potato soup. *vegetable* porcini baked over

potatoes. porcini and bean stew. *antipasto* porcini baked in foil with mint.

white truffles ^{378} *pasta* gnocchi alla romana with white

truffles. *risotto* white truffle risotto

chestnuts

Throughout history chestnuts have been one of the most important ingredients in many of the regions of Italy and the Mediterranean. In Liguria, it was said that villages without 'l'albero del pane', the bread tree, could not survive.

The sweet chestnut season begins in mid October. In the Apennines the semi-wild trees produce the small rounded 'castagne', which are dried and ground into flour. This is used for making bread, gnocchi, castagnaccio and batter for fried pastries. The most prized variety of chestnut is the 'marroni', produced from grafted trees, which bear much larger nuts.

Fresh chestnuts feel firm and solid. To remove the skins, place the chestnuts flat side down and make a shallow cut with a sharp small knife across the curved part. Either roast in a hot oven at 200°C/400°F/Gas 6 until just soft and the skin opens up, or boil in water for 15 minutes. Do not let the chestnuts cool too much as it makes them harder to peel. For some recipes we boil them in milk, which preserves their natural sweetness.

Dried chestnuts – 'secchielli' – are available in Italy. These need to be soaked for 24 hours in water, then cooked in milk. Recently, frozen peeled chestnuts have become available. They have excellent flavour.

Chestnut flour is very perishable and if kept for more than 3 months turns sourly acidic.

chestnut and celeriac soup
zuppa di sedanorapa e castagne

for 6
500 g cooked and peeled chestnuts (see page 349)
4 small celeriac, peeled and cubed
60 g unsalted butter
150 g pancetta, finely sliced then cut into 5mm
    pieces
inner white heart of 2 heads celery, trimmed and
    roughly chopped
3 garlic cloves, peeled and finely chopped
chicken stock to cover, barely 1 litre (see page 455)
5 juniper berries, crushed
4 fresh bay leaves, centre spine removed, leaf part
    finely chopped
Maldon salt and freshly ground black pepper
150 ml double cream
100 g Parmesan, freshly grated
extra virgin olive oil

In a large, thick-bottomed saucepan, melt the butter, add the pancetta
and slowly cook until transparent. Add the celeriac and celery and stir to
combine the flavours for a few minutes. In a separate saucepan heat the
chicken stock. Add the whole peeled chestnuts and the chopped garlic
to the celeriac and celery. Cook on a low flame, stirring, then add the
juniper berries and bay leaves. Test the hot stock for seasoning, then
pour in enough to just cover the vegetables. Bring to the boil and
simmer for 15-20 minutes, or until the celeriac is soft.

Using a potato masher or wire whisk, break up the vegetables in the
saucepan to achieve a rough, thick soup. Alternatively pulse-chop half
the soup in a food processor, then return to the saucepan and combine.

Finally stir in the cream. Heat through and serve with grated Parmesan
and a drizzle of extra virgin olive oil.

gnocchi with chestnut and sausage
gnocchi con castagne e salsiccia

for 6
Potato Gnocchi (see page 455)
sauce
500 g cooked and peeled chestnuts (see page 349)
80 g butter
6 spiced Italian sausages, skinned
2 red onions, peeled and chopped
2 garlic cloves, peeled and sliced
3 dried red chillies, crumbled
2 tablespoons chopped fresh sage leaves
150 ml red wine
1 x 400 g tin peeled plum tomatoes
freshly grated nutmeg
Maldon salt and freshly grated black pepper
to serve
12 whole fresh sage leaves
2 tablespoons olive oil
100 g Parmesan, freshly grated

For the sauce, melt the butter in a medium, thick-bottomed frying pan and fry the sausage meat, stirring and breaking it up over a medium heat to allow the juices to evaporate and the meat to begin to brown. Add the onion, garlic, chilli and chopped sage. Cook gently for 30 minutes until the onions are soft. Pour in the wine and increase the heat until the wine evaporates. Add the tomatoes with half of their juices and the whole chestnuts, lower the heat and cook for about 30 minutes. Season with salt, pepper and nutmeg.

Fry the sage leaves until crisp in the olive oil. Cook the gnocchi in batches in a generous amount of boiling salted water. They are ready when they bob up to the surface of the simmering water. Serve with the sauce and Parmesan, topped with the sage leaves.

pears

As the summer ends and the strawberries and raspberries disappear, we look forward to the arrival of pears in early October.

Although delicious raw – and in Italy often eaten with Parmesan or Pecorino – pears are equally good when cooked. With their firm texture, they retain their identity even when cooked for a long time. Their taste is intensified by slow cooking with wine and enhanced by other flavours such as almonds, honey, vanilla and lemon. The cake here is our way of combining the ingredients we love most with pears.

Comice is the variety we generally use as the pears have a sweet buttery taste, are smooth in texture and full of juice. It is best to buy pears when firm and to allow them to ripen in a warm place. A ripe pear will give slightly around the stem and just yield when pressed around the neck. Pears deteriorate very quickly.

pear, honey and polenta cake
torta di polenta con pere e miele

This cake requires long cooking in a slow oven.

for 10
1 kg pears
130 g polenta flour
50 g runny honey
350 g unsalted butter, plus extra for the tin
250 g caster sugar
4 large, organic free-range eggs
130 g whole blanched almonds, ground coarsely
40 g plain flour
1 teaspoon baking powder
zest of 2 washed lemons

Preheat the oven to 150°C/300°F/Gas 2. Line the base of a rectangular bread tin, about 30 cm long, with parchment paper, and butter this and the tin generously.

Peel the pears, cut out the cores and roughly dice the pears into 2 cm pieces. Melt 80 g of the butter in a non-stick saucepan, add the honey and caramelise briefly. Add the pears and just turn them over to coat and flavour.

Beat the remaining butter and the sugar together in an electric mixer until light and fluffy. Beat in the eggs, one by one. Mix the ground almonds with the flours and the baking powder and add to the butter and egg mixture. Carefully fold in the warm pears and honey, along with the lemon zest. Gently spoon the mixture into the prepared cake tin and bake in the preheated oven for 1-1¹/₄ hours. The cake will be quite dark on top.

polenta

Polenta is the staple ingredient of the northernmost regions of Italy – Piedmont, Lombardy, Trentino and the Veneto. It was traditionally cooked daily in deep, unlined copper pots over the fire.

The maize is grown in the summer and harvested in October, after which it is dried and milled. This is when the polenta 'season' begins, and it lasts until March, after which the flour becomes stale and loses its intense taste of corn.

There are various types of polenta. We always use bramata, which is a blend made from five different varieties of corn, with a coarse texture which goes well with meat and game. In Venice you will find a white polenta served with fish, which has a smoother texture and a less distinctive flavour.

We would never use instant polenta, as it bears no resemblance to what we recognise as polenta. If you don't have the time to make polenta, it is better not to make it at all.

polenta with hot olive sauce
polenta con salsa calda di olive

for 6

polenta
350 g bramata polenta
1.75-2 litres water
Maldon salt and freshly ground black pepper
175 g unsalted butter
200 g Parmesan, freshly grated
hot olive sauce
300 g Ligurian black and green olives preserved in
   brine, pitted and rinsed
250 ml olive oil
5 salted anchovies, prepared (see page 458),
   chopped
3 tablespoons salted capers, prepared (see page
   458), chopped
3 garlic cloves, peeled and finely chopped
150 ml double cream

To make the polenta, bring the water to the boil in a large thick-bottomed saucepan and add 1 tablespoon salt. Pour in the polenta in a continuous stream, whisking all the time to prevent lumps forming, until the mixture is well blended and creamy. Reduce the heat and cook, stirring from time to time to prevent a skin forming and to ensure the polenta cooks evenly, for 45 minutes. The polenta is ready when it falls away from the sides of the pan. Test for seasoning.

Make the sauce. Heat the olive oil in a small saucepan until very hot. Add the olives, anchovies, capers and garlic. Stir and cook for 4-5 minutes, then remove from the heat. Add the cream immediately and stir until the sauce thickens. Stir the butter and two-thirds of the Parmesan into the hot polenta. To serve, divide the polenta between the plates. Spoon over the hot olive sauce and sprinkle with the remaining Parmesan.

polenta with borlotti beans and rocket

polenta con borlotti e rucola

for 6
800 g fresh rocket, washed and roughly chopped
300 g dried borlotti beans (di Lamon are the best)
1 tablespoon bicarbonate of soda
1 bunch of fresh sage
$1/2$ head fresh garlic
2 garlic cloves, peeled and chopped
a handful of fresh flat-leaf parsley, chopped
2 tablespoons olive oil
Maldon salt and freshly ground black pepper
1 dried red chilli, crumbled
extra virgin olive oil
to serve
Polenta (see opposite)
175 g unsalted butter
120 g Parmesan, freshly grated

Soak the beans overnight in plenty of water with the bicarbonate of soda. Drain and rinse, then place in a large saucepan and cover with fresh cold water. Bring to the boil, skim the froth off the top and add the sage and the garlic bulb. Lower the heat and simmer for up to $1^{1}/2$ hours, until the beans are tender. Drain, reserving the liquid.

In a separate saucepan, fry the chopped garlic and parsley in the olive oil. Add the beans and 2 tablespoons of their cooking water and stir just to combine. Add the rocket and possibly a little more of the cooking liquid and cook for a minute or so to wilt the rocket. Season with salt and pepper and the crumbled chilli.

Cook the polenta and stir in the butter and Parmesan. Put a portion of polenta on each plate. Spoon over the borlotti beans and some of their juices and drizzle with extra virgin olive oil.

pumpkin

Pumpkins, of which there are many varieties, are usually classified as winter squash. They grow vigorously throughout the summer, often trailing on long-stemmed running vines, with huge broad leaves, bearing male and female flowers. The male flowers are picked when open and used in fritto misto; the female flowers produce the fruits that ripen on the vine. We like to grow pumpkins outside the restaurant every summer, mainly for the male flowers but also for the tips of the trailing vines which can be cooked like greens. The actual pumpkins rarely get big enough because of a lack of space for the rich soil that is necessary.

The varieties we have grown for us are Golden Hubbard, Crown Prince, Onion Squash, Butternut and Little Gem. Most of these are varieties that have deep orange flesh with a dense texture, and thick skins.

When ripe and ready to cook, pumpkins should have hollow centres and well developed seeds. The harvest is in October, but as they store well, the pumpkin season can last until January. When buying pumpkins, they should have unblemished skins and should be heavy, indicating ripeness.

We usually roast pumpkins cut into 2 cm slices and well seasoned, which concentrates the flavour, before using in soups, risottos and pastas.

pumpkin pansoti
pansoti di zucca

for 6
Ligurian Basic Pasta (see page 454)
semolina flour and Tipo 'oo' pasta flour for dusting
freshly grated Parmesan
filling
1 kg onion squash or orange-fleshed pumpkin,
  washed
Maldon salt and freshly ground black pepper
3 tablespoons fresh marjoram leaves
2 garlic cloves, peeled and finely chopped
80 g fresh breadcrumbs
100 g Parmesan, freshly grated
100 g fresh ricotta cheese, lightly beaten
3 large, organic free-range eggs, lightly beaten
sage butter
1 large bunch of fresh sage leaves
180 g unsalted butter
Maldon salt and freshly ground black pepper

Preheat the oven to 200°C/400°F/Gas 6.

Cut the pumpkin in half, scoop out the seeds, then cut into 3 cm thick slices. Season each slice with salt and pepper, place in a roasting tin and dry-roast for 30 minutes or until the pumpkin is soft. Cool. Push the roast pumpkin, skin and all, through a mouli. Strain off any liquid, though there should not be much.

Chop the marjoram leaves together with the garlic and add to the pumpkin. Add the breadcrumbs, Parmesan and ricotta. Test for seasoning. Stir all together, then fold in the beaten eggs.

Sprinkle a mixture of semolina flour and Tipo 'oo' pasta flour on your work surface. Roll the pasta dough in the machine as outlined on page 454, or by hand. You want long strips the width of the machine. Cut these into manageable lengths and place on the floured work surface. Put tablespoons of the pumpkin filling at 10 cm intervals down the middle of each strip. Fold the pasta lengthways over the filling and gently press around the filling with your finger. Then, using a serrated-edged 5 cm cutter, cut around each mound, across the folds, to make semi-circles. You can re-roll and re-use the remaining pasta. You need to have about six pansoti per portion. Leave to dry slightly on a tray dusted with flour. See the photographs overleaf.

Make the sage butter. Gently melt 80 g of the butter over a medium heat. When hot, add the sage, and fry until beginning to crisp. Remove with a slotted spoon on to paper towel and discard the butter. Separately just soften up the remaining butter and mix with the sage leaves.

To cook the pasta, bring a large saucepan of water to the boil and add 2 tablespoons of salt. Put the pansoti into the water in batches and cook uncovered for about 5 minutes. Remove very carefully with a slotted spoon. Serve with freshly grated Parmesan and the sage butter.

pumpkin gnocchi
gnocchi alla zucca

for 6
1 kg ripe onion squash, skin washed
Maldon salt and freshly ground black pepper
2 small dried red chillies, crumbled
2 teaspoons dried oregano
olive oil
750 g Desirée potatoes, scrubbed
3 large, organic free-range eggs, beaten
100 g semolina flour
$1/2$ nutmeg, freshly grated
100 g plain flour and polenta flour for dusting
to serve
Sage Butter (see page 364)
freshly grated Parmesan

Preheat the oven to 190°C/375°F/Gas 5. Cut the squash in half, scoop out the seeds, then cut into 2 cm thick slices. Season each slice with salt, black pepper, chilli and a little oregano and drizzle with a little olive oil. Bake in the preheated oven for 35-40 minutes or until soft and beginning to crisp around the edges.

Boil the potatoes in salted water until soft, then drain, peel and cool. Put the potatoes and pumpkin through a mouli and cool. Add the eggs, stir to mix, then sieve in the semolina flour. Gently fold together. Season, grate in the nutmeg and beat to form a stiffish dough.

Dust a surface with a mixture of the dusting flours. Divide the dough into four. Roll out each piece into a sausage 2 cm thick and cut at 3 cm lengths. Form into gnocchi by rolling each piece over the back of a fork.

Bring a large saucepan of water to the boil, add 1 tablespoon salt and cook the gnocchi in batches in simmering water. The gnocchi will come to the surface after 2-3 minutes, but allow them to cook on for a further 2-3 minutes. Drain and serve with the sage butter and Parmesan.

pumpkin and cinnamon risotto
risotto alla zucca e cannella

for 6
1.5 kg pumpkin or onion squash, washed
1 cinnamon stick 5 cm long, crushed
1.5 litres chicken stock (see page 455)
Maldon salt and freshly ground black pepper
1 tablespoon dried oregano
olive oil
inner white heart of 1 head celery, finely chopped
2 small red onions, peeled and chopped
200 g pancetta, finely sliced, cut into matchsticks
3 garlic cloves, peeled and finely chopped
3 small dried red chillies, crumbled
400 g carnaroli rice
450 g tinned peeled plum tomatoes, drained and
　　put through a mouli
extra virgin olive oil
150 g Pecorino staginata cheese, freshly grated

Preheat the oven to 220°C/425°F/Gas 7. Heat the stock. Cut the pumpkin in half, scoop out the seeds, then cut each half into four or six pieces, depending on size. Season with salt, pepper and half the oregano, then place on an oiled oven tray and bake until browned and cooked, about 35-40 minutes. Push the pumpkin with its skin through a mouli.

Heat 3 tablespoons of olive oil in a large thick-bottomed saucepan, add the celery and onion, and soften for 5-6 minutes. Add the pancetta and garlic, then the chilli, remaining oregano and cinnamon. Fry together briefly, then add the rice. Stir to coat each grain with the oil and allow it to become opaque, about 2-3 minutes. Add the tomato pulp, allow to reduce, then start to add the hot stock, ladle by ladle, stirring continuously, not adding more until the previous ladleful has been absorbed. Continue until the rice becomes al dente, about 15 minutes. Stir the pumpkin into the risotto. Test for seasoning. Serve drizzled with extra virgin olive oil and Pecorino.

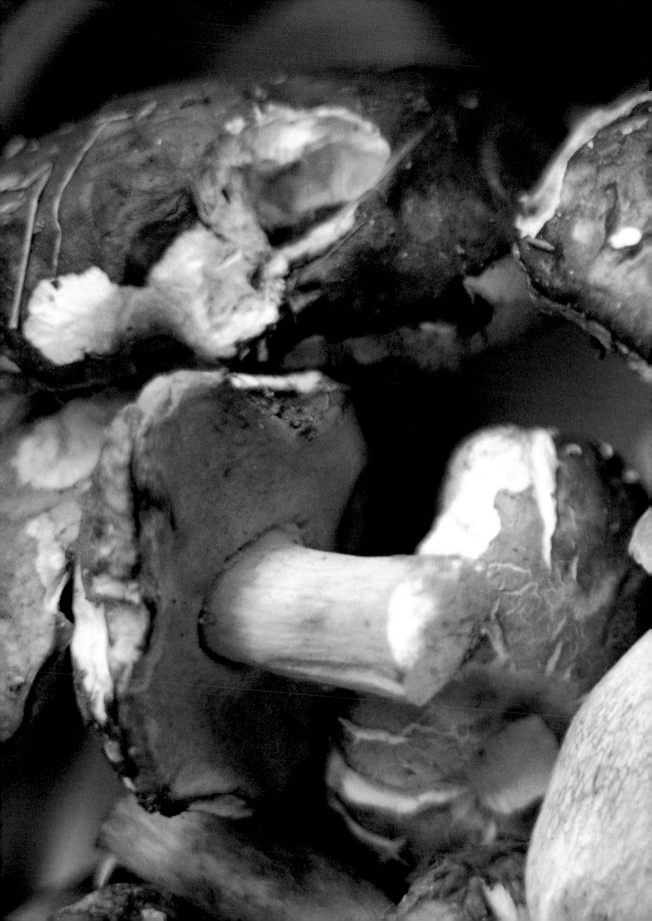

fresh porcini mushrooms

Porcini mushrooms are the most prized mushrooms in Italian cooking. The start of the season varies depending on the summer – often the first porcini appear around the beginning of September but if the weather has been very hot and dry it will be later. October is the main month and the season ends with the first frost.

The porcini you pick yourself will always be the freshest and most firm. Look for them in wooded areas. A strong smell indicates strong flavour. Use the porcini as soon as you find or buy them, as they deteriorate quickly. Porcini have never been successfully cultivated.

Varieties we use in our recipes include Penny Bun, Bay Boletus, Orange Birch Boletus and Slippery Jack. Porcini stems are as delicious as the caps. Choose porcini with open cups and plump round stems, not soft and spongy. They are equally delicious eaten raw in a salad or cooked.

To clean, wash the stalks, trimming away any earthy bits with a sharp paring knife. Use a damp cloth to brush and clean the top of the caps. Try to keep the spongy underside dry. Trim away any rotten pieces with a knife.

If you have large quantities of good firm porcini, it is well worth slicing and drying them.

raw porcini tagliarini
tagliarini con porcini crudi

for 6
1.25 kg fresh porcini, carefully cleaned
600 g Rich Egg Pasta (see page 454), cut into
    tagliarini
50 g butter
2 tablespoons olive oil
3 garlic cloves, peeled and finely chopped
1 medium bunch of fresh flat-leaf parsley, leaves
    picked from the stalks, finely chopped
Maldon salt and freshly ground black pepper
4 tablespoons double cream
100 g Parmesan, freshly grated

Separate the porcini stalks from the caps. Finely chop the stalks and
then finely slice the caps. Keep them separate.

Heat a large thick-bottomed frying pan and melt the butter with
2 tablespoons of the olive oil. When beginning to foam, add the
chopped porcini stalks, garlic and parsley and stir-fry briefly for 4-5
minutes until soft but not brown. Season with salt and pepper.

Cook the tagliarini in a large saucepan of boiling salted water until al
dente, then drain, keeping a cupful of the pasta water. Add the tagliarini
to the stalk mixture, and stir together. Add the cream and a few
tablespoons of the pasta water if dry. Cook for 1-2 minutes, then serve
on to individual plates. Cover each serving with the finely sliced porcini
caps. Sprinkle with salt and pepper, drizzle with extra virgin olive oil and
serve the grated Parmesan separately.

porcini and potato soup
zuppa di porcini e patate

for 6
1.5 kg fresh porcini, carefully cleaned
2 kg Roseval, Linska or Desirée potatoes, peeled
    and cut into even pieces
Maldon salt and freshly ground black pepper
5 garlic cloves, peeled
100 ml double cream
1 ciabatta loaf, cut into 6 slices at an angle
extra virgin olive oil

Simmer the potatoes in 1^1/$_2$ times their volume of salted water until they begin to break up, about 25 minutes. Meanwhile, separate the porcini caps from the stalks and roughly chop the stalks and 4 of the garlic cloves together. Add to the cooked potatoes and their cooking water, and simmer together for 5 minutes. Using a potato masher or slotted spoon start to mash the potatoes into a pulp. Continue until potato and water have become a thick soup.

Slice across the porcini caps as finely as you can, then add to the soup. Stir in the cream and season with salt and pepper. Stir together for 2-3 minutes, allowing the porcini slices to infuse their flavours into the potatoes, but retain a little texture, being barely cooked.

Toast the crostini and rub with the remaining halved clove of garlic. Put a crostini in each serving bowl and spoon in the soup. Drizzle with extra virgin olive oil and serve.

porcini baked over potatoes

patate al forno con porcini

for 6-8

1.5 kg fresh porcini mushrooms, carefully cleaned
1.5 kg Roseval potatoes, peeled
3 tablespoons chopped fresh flat-leaf parsley (or
   basil, torn)
Maldon salt and freshly ground black pepper
8 garlic cloves, peeled and chopped
5 tablespoons olive oil

Preheat the oven to 200°C/400°F/Gas 6.

Cut the potatoes lengthways into 5 mm slices. Place in a bowl of water.
Trim the end of the porcini stalks, keeping cap and stalk attached. Cut
the porcini caps and stalks lengthways into slices the same thickness as
the potato.

Dry the potatoes thoroughly and place in a large bowl. Season with salt,
pepper and garlic and toss together. Layer the potatoes in a baking tin
large enough so that you have no more than two or three layers. Place
the porcini over the top, covering the potatoes entirely, then cover with
the parsley. Pour the olive oil over the top of everything, letting it seep
through. Cover with foil, sealing very tightly, and bake in the preheated
oven for 45 minutes.

porcini and bean stew
stufato di porcini e fagioli

for 6
500 g fresh porcini, carefully cleaned and thickly
   sliced (keep small ones whole)
2 tablespoons olive oil
2 garlic cloves, peeled and finely chopped
1 teaspoon dried oregano
2 large ripe tomatoes, roughly chopped, or 200 g
   tinned peeled plum tomatoes, drained of their
   juices
Maldon salt and freshly ground black pepper
beans
750 g fresh cannellini beans in their pods
   (or 200 g dried, soaked overnight)
1 large tomato
a handful of parsley stalks
2 garlic cloves, peeled

Cook the fresh beans in a large saucepan with the tomato, parsley stalks
and garlic for 45 minutes. The dried soaked beans will take longer, up to
1½ hours. Leave the cooked beans in their liquid, removing the
flavourings. Season with salt and pepper.

Heat the olive oil in a thick-bottomed saucepan, add the crushed garlic
and oregano and allow to colour for a few minutes. Add the porcini slices
and the tomato, plus a few ladles of the bean cooking water. Stir and
simmer for about 15-20 minutes, then stir in the drained beans. Heat to
bring the beans up to the same temperature, then remove from the heat.
Season with salt and pepper, then leave to 'thicken' in a warm place for
about 10-15 minutes. The dish is best warm, served with bruschetta or
roast meats.

porcini baked in foil with mint
porcini al cartoccio con nepitella

for 6
2.5 kg fresh porcini, carefully cleaned
extra virgin olive oil
10 garlic cloves, peeled and sliced
Maldon salt and freshly ground black pepper
10 sprigs of fresh nepitella (see page 111), mint or
    oregano

Preheat the oven to 220°C/425°F/Gas 7. Tear six pieces of foil of about 25 cm in length and lightly oil the bottom half of each piece.

Slice the porcini into 1 cm slices. Layer the mushrooms lightly on the oiled halves of the pieces of foil, overlapping them with equal amounts of sliced garlic. Season with salt and pepper and sprinkle with the herbs and some extra virgin olive oil. Fold the top half of the foil over and seal the edges very tightly.

Place the packets flat on a baking sheet in the preheated oven and bake for 15 minutes. Open the foil packages at the table, and eat hot.

white truffles

White truffles are found in the foothills of the Apennines – the most famous area is around Alba in Piedmont. They grow between 5 cm and 30 cm underground, in association with oak, elm, poplar and lime trees. The season lasts until hard frosts and snow cover the ground.

White truffles are smooth, irregularly shaped and creamy coloured on the outside. When sliced, the colour inside varies from white to pinkish beige to brown. Truffles are unique amongst wild fungi as their pungent aroma is more overwhelming than their taste.

Only choose firm truffles that smell really powerful. Keep wrapped in damp paper in a sealed box in the fridge. Use as soon as possible as the perfume fades fast and they become less dense.

Clean truffles using a wet toothbrush to rub away clay and dirt. Only clean your truffle just before using it. Slice very finely with a truffle slicer.

gnocchi alla romana with white truffles

gnocchi alla romana con tartufo bianco

for 6
80-100 g white truffle
1 litre milk
200 g semolina flour
3 large, organic free-range egg yolks
120 g Parmesan, freshly grated
120 g unsalted butter, softened
1/4 nutmeg, freshly grated
Maldon salt and freshly ground black pepper

Preheat the oven to 200°C/400°F/Gas 6.

Bring the milk to a boil. Lower the heat to a simmer and slowly whisk in the semolina flour. Cook for 15 minutes, stirring constantly. It is essential to cook for this length of time or the gnocchi will fall apart later when baked. Remove from the heat and stir in the egg yolks, one by one, then 100 g each of the Parmesan and butter, the nutmeg, salt and pepper.

Moisten a tray with cold water and turn the gnocchi mixture on to it. Spread it to an even thickness of about 1 cm. With a glass or biscuit cutter dipped in cold water, cut out rounds of about 4 cm in diameter. Leave the gnocchi in the fridge to become firm for half an hour before baking.

Coat a baking dish with some of the remaining butter and arrange the gnocchi in it, overlapping slightly. Sprinkle with the rest of the butter and Parmesan.

Bake in the preheated oven for 15 minutes or until the gnocchi puff up and a light crust has formed on top. Serve hot with shavings of white truffle.

white truffle risotto
risotto al tartufo bianco

for 6
80-100 g white truffle
1.5 litres chicken stock (see page 455)
Maldon salt and freshly ground black pepper
150 g unsalted butter
inner white hearts of 2 heads celery, finely
    chopped
1 white onion, peeled and finely chopped
5 medium potatoes, peeled and cut into 1 cm dice
1 garlic clove, peeled and finely chopped
400 g carnaroli rice
1/2 bottle Gavi di Gavi (a white wine from
    Piedmont)
100 g Parmesan, freshly grated

Put the stock on to simmer and test for seasoning.

In a large, thick-bottomed saucepan melt half the butter, then add the
celery and onion. Allow to soften and begin to colour, then add the
potatoes and garlic to the pan. Cook for 2-3 minutes, just to colour the
potatoes. Add the rice and stir to coat each grain with the buttery
vegetables. Briefly cook, then add 120 ml of the wine. Allow to bubble
and reduce, then start to add the hot stock, ladle by ladle, stirring
continuously, not adding more stock until the previous ladle has been
absorbed. Continue until the rice is al dente, about 15 minutes.

Shave 20 g of truffle into the risotto, and stir in the remaining butter and
wine. Allow this to be absorbed, but the consistency must remain wet.
Serve with grated Parmesan and shaved truffle.

november

romanesco broccoli [386] *pasta* penne with romanesco broccoli. **celery** [390] *soup* celery acquacotta with poached egg. *risotto* celery and dried porcini risotto. *salad* celery and puntarelle roman style. **fennel** [396] *antipasta* grilled marinated fennel. *pasta* fennel and crab linguine. **olives** [400] *pasta* stringozzi with olives and mushrooms. *pizza* pizza with olives, radicchio and thyme. **pomegranates** [406] *salad* pomegranate and pheasant salad. *drink* pomegranate campari. **rosemary** [412] *risotto* rosemary and borlotti bean risotto. *bruschetta* rosemary bruschetta. **walnuts** [418] *pasta* ravioli with walnut and robiola pesto. *pudding* walnut and almond cake.

romanesco broccoli

Romanesco broccoli is an old Italian variety that has recently been revived, as it has an interesting flavour that is milder than calabrese broccoli. It is related to the cauliflower family and is sometimes called Minaret.

The heads, consisting of spiralling green, tightly packed florets, look more like cauliflowers. The centre thick stem, which is removed before cooking, has little flavour. Romanesco is harvested in the late autumn before the other broccolis. It has a very soft texture when cooked and easily reduces to a sauce. This is why the Italians traditionally mix it with the strong flavours of salted anchovies, brined olives, hot chillies and salty Pecorino.

To prepare Romanesco, cut away the thick stem at the base and any brown parts.

penne with romanesco broccoli
penne con broccoli romanesco

for 6
2 heads Romanesco broccoli, tough base stalk
  trimmed
400 g penne rigate
3 tablespoons olive oil
4 garlic cloves, peeled and finely sliced
3 small dried red chillies, crumbled
1 x 800 g tin peeled plum tomatoes, drained of
  their juices
Maldon salt and freshly ground black pepper
150 g Pecorino cheese, freshly grated
extra virgin olive oil

Heat the olive oil in a large, thick-bottomed saucepan with a tight-fitting lid. Add the garlic and fry gently until beginning to colour, then add the chilli and the broccoli. Cook just to combine the flavours. Spoon in the tomatoes around the broccoli, season with salt and pepper and cook for a further 5 minutes to allow the tomatoes to evaporate a little. Put on the lid, reduce the heat and slow-steam for 30-35 minutes or until the broccoli is soft and you can break it up into the tomato.

Bring a large saucepan of water to the boil and add plenty of salt. Cook the penne until al dente. Drain and add to the broccoli. Stir to combine the sauce with the pasta and check for seasoning. Add half the Pecorino and a drizzle of extra virgin olive oil. Serve with the remaining Pecorino.

celery

Celery is available throughout the year and is at its best from November onwards. In Italy celery is always sold with the leaves attached to the heads. This way, it is easy to see how fresh it is.

An Italian vegetable in origin, and used widely in Italian cooking, celery is a very important flavouring. It is part of the 'soffritto', the fried base of most of our risottos and soups.

We always buy celery heads with their leaves attached, as the pale leaves from the centre are excellent in mixed herb leaf salads. It is rather a wasteful vegetable as the outer green, stringy stems are only good for flavouring stocks. It is the inner pale and crisp hearts that we use in our cooking. These hearts are also used raw, sliced into winter salads with other stem vegetables such as fennel, sea kale and artichokes.

celery acquacotta with poached egg
acquacotta di montemerano

This soup comes from the Montemerano, an area near Grosetto, where they traditionally add poached eggs to their acquacottas.

for 6
inner white hearts of 3 heads celery, plus leaves
2 red onions, peeled and finely chopped
4 tablespoons fresh marjoram leaves
450 g tinned peeled plum tomatoes, drained and
    chopped
2 tablespoons olive oil
Maldon salt and freshly ground black pepper
3 dried red chillies, crumbled
6 large, organic free-range eggs
6 slices stale ciabatta bread
freshly grated Parmesan
extra virgin olive oil

Finely chop the celery hearts and half the leaves and put together with the chopped onion and 2 tablespoons of the marjoram in a thick-bottomed saucepan. Add the tomatoes, olive oil and enough water just to cover. Season with salt, pepper and dried chilli. Cook over a low heat, stirring from time to time, for 45 minutes. You may need to add small amounts of water as it cooks. There should be just enough always to cover.

Chop the remaining celery and marjoram leaves and stir into the soup.

Make six small wells in the soup and slightly increase the heat. Break an egg into each well, and spoon some of the soup gently over. Cook until the eggs are poached.

Place a slice of bread in each soup bowl. Cover each piece with grated Parmesan, then spoon over the soup. Sprinkle with more Parmesan and drizzle with extra virgin olive oil.

celery and dried porcini risotto
risotto al sedano e porcini secchi

for 6
inner white hearts of 3 heads celery, plus their
   leaves
1.5 litres chicken stock (see page 455)
Maldon salt and freshly ground black pepper
125 g unsalted butter
1 medium red onion, peeled and finely chopped
150 g dried porcini, soaked in 500 ml warm water
3 garlic cloves, peeled and chopped
400 g carnaroli rice
3 tablespoons finely chopped fresh flat-leaf
   parsley
120 g Parmesan, freshly grated

Put the stock on to simmer, and test for seasoning.

Melt half the butter in a large thick-bottomed saucepan, add the celery
and onion, and slowly allow to soften and begin to colour.

Drain the porcini, keeping the soaking liquid, then pass the liquid
through a piece of muslin. Rinse the porcini in a sieve to remove any
sand or grit, and roughly chop. Add to the risotto base with the garlic,
and stir to combine with the celery and onion. Cook for 5 minutes, then
season with salt and pepper. Now add the rice and stir to coat each grain
with the buttery vegetables. Briefly cook, then add a ladle of the porcini
liquid. Allow to reduce, then add the remainder, stirring continuously. As
soon as the liquid has been absorbed by the rice, start adding the hot
stock ladle by ladle, not adding another until the previous one has been
absorbed. Continue until the rice is al dente, about 15 minutes.

Stir in the remainder of the butter, the parsley and the finely chopped
celery leaves. Check for seasoning, and serve with freshly grated
Parmesan.

celery and puntarelle roman style
sedano e puntarelle alla romana

Puntarelle, part of the chicory family, is a unique vegetable. Grown for its large heads of hollow stems that are crowned with pointed bitter leaves. It is prized as a salad in Rome.

for 6
inner white hearts of 3 heads celery, plus their
   leaves
1 head puntarelle
8 salted anchovies, prepared (see page 458)
juice of 2 lemons
Maldon salt and freshly ground black pepper
3 dried red chillies, crumbled
extra virgin olive oil

Pick off the tender pale yellow leaves from the celery hearts. Slice across the hearts diagonally, about 5 cm thick. Place in a bowl of iced water for 30 minutes or more.

Break off the buds from the head of the puntarelle and finely slice each bud across, again at a diagonal, as finely as possible. Keep any of the fine green feathery young leaves and trim off any stringy parts. Place the puntarelle into iced water for 1 hour or more.

Cut the anchovy fillets in half, place on a flat dish, squeeze over half the lemon juice and season with black pepper and a little of the chilli. Pour over 2 tablespoons olive oil. Leave to marinate for 30 minutes.

Mix the remaining lemon juice with four times its volume of olive oil. Season with salt and pepper.

Take the puntarelle and celery from the iced water; they should be crisp. Spin dry. Toss together with the oil and lemon juice, then add the marinated anchovies and their juices. Sprinkle with the remaining chilli and the retained leaves.

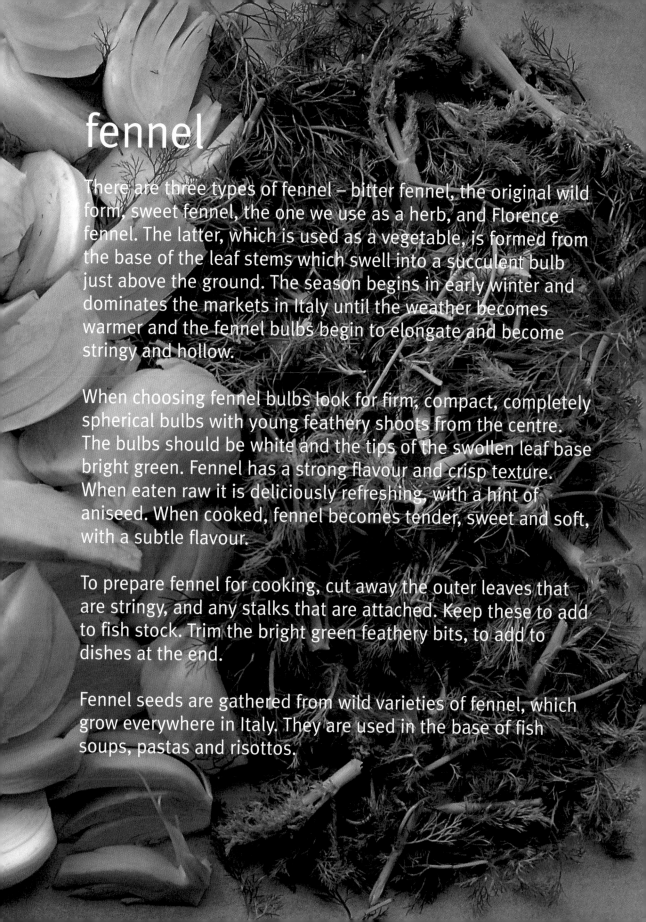

fennel

There are three types of fennel – bitter fennel, the original wild form, sweet fennel, the one we use as a herb, and Florence fennel. The latter, which is used as a vegetable, is formed from the base of the leaf stems which swell into a succulent bulb just above the ground. The season begins in early winter and dominates the markets in Italy until the weather becomes warmer and the fennel bulbs begin to elongate and become stringy and hollow.

When choosing fennel bulbs look for firm, compact, completely spherical bulbs with young feathery shoots from the centre. The bulbs should be white and the tips of the swollen leaf base bright green. Fennel has a strong flavour and crisp texture. When eaten raw it is deliciously refreshing, with a hint of aniseed. When cooked, fennel becomes tender, sweet and soft, with a subtle flavour.

To prepare fennel for cooking, cut away the outer leaves that are stringy, and any stalks that are attached. Keep these to add to fish stock. Trim the bright green feathery bits, to add to dishes at the end.

Fennel seeds are gathered from wild varieties of fennel, which grow everywhere in Italy. They are used in the base of fish soups, pastas and risottos.

grilled marinated fennel
finocchi marinati

for 6
6 bulbs fennel, with their green tops
Maldon salt and freshly ground black pepper
juice of 2 lemons
125 ml extra virgin olive oil
2 dried red chillies

Preheat the char-grill or griddle pan.

Cut off the tough outer parts of the fennel bulbs. Slice off the base root of each bulb. Keep the green parts of the fennel and finely chop. Cut the bulbs in 5 mm slices across to make thickish circles – these may fall apart a bit when you pick them up.

Carefully place the fennel slices on the grill and grill on both sides. Season with salt and pepper whilst grilling. They will take about 10 minutes.

Place the fennel slices on a warm plate. Pour over the lemon juice and drizzle with the extra virgin olive oil. Crumble over the dried chilli and scatter with the green fennel tops. Serve with bruschetta, olives and winter leaf salads.

fennel and crab linguine
linguine con finocchi e granchio

for 6
3 bulbs fennel, with leafy tops
2 large live male crabs, about 1.3-1.8 kg each
3 fresh red chillies, seeded and finely chopped
400 g linguine
Maldon salt and freshly ground black pepper
juice of 2 lemons
2 tablespoons chopped fresh flat-leaf parsley
4-6 tablespoons extra virgin olive oil

Place the crabs in a large saucepan with enough cold water to cover generously, add 3 tablespoons salt and slowly bring to the boil. Turn down the heat and simmer for a further 5 minutes. Remove the crabs from the pot and leave to cool.

Break the crabs open by pulling away the upper body shell. With a spoon remove the brown meat and put into a large bowl. Break the legs and claws from the bodies and pick out the white meat. Add this to the bowl of brown meat.

Remove and discard the tough outer leaves of the fennel bulbs and cut the bulbs lengthways into slices of about 1 cm. Remove the leaves from the fennel tops and chop coarsely. Add these chopped leaves to the crabmeat along with the chilli, lemon juice, parsley, salt and pepper. Slowly stir in the olive oil.

In a large saucepan, bring a generous amount of salted water to the boil. Add the sliced fennel, return to the boil and then add the pasta. Cook until the pasta is al dente, then drain. Return to the saucepan and stir in the crab mixture, adding more lemon juice or oil to taste.

olives

There are many varieties of Italian olives and according to taste
they are picked at different degrees of ripeness, which
determines both flavour and style. Green olives are picked
before they are ripe; purple when they are just ripe; and the
black at full maturity.

Most olives are cured in brine, which must be rinsed off before
using the olive. The flavour of the brine can be overpowering,
so always taste olives before buying. Olives, usually the ripe
black ones, can also be cured in oil, often combined with
herbs, garlic and chilli. It is quite often the case that these
additions, together with poor-quality oil, can obliterate the
fresh olive taste. You can marinate olives yourself at home –
use extra virgin olive oil and your own choice of herbs.

We choose to buy the small, oval, purplish olive from Liguria,
called Taggiasche. It is brined for a brief period and has a light
fruity taste with firm flesh. Niçoise olives are very similar.

Good preserved green olives, with that fresh olive taste and
texture, are harder to find. We tend to buy them when we are
in Italy. In the south, there is a fantastic choice.

stringozzi with olives and mushrooms
stringozzi con olive e funghi

Stringozzi is a hard wheat, string-like pasta, made with egg white.

for 6
pasta dough
200 g Tipo 'oo' pasta flour
250 g semolina flour, plus extra for dusting
1 large, organic free-range egg white
2 tablespoons olive oil
2 teaspoons Maldon salt
80 ml water
olive sauce
400 g black olives, pitted and roughly chopped
2 tablespoons olive oil
500 g flat field mushrooms, finely sliced
3 garlic cloves, peeled and chopped
2 dried red chillies, crumbled
Maldon salt and freshly ground black pepper
3 tablespoons finely chopped fresh flat-leaf
   parsley
80 ml double cream
to serve
100 g unsalted butter
2 large fresh red chillies, seeded and chopped
100 g Parmesan, freshly grated

To make the pasta, mix the two flours together and place in a food processor or mixer fitted with a dough hook. Add the egg white and olive oil, salt and water and knead until the pasta comes together to a firm dough, about 5 minutes. Wrap in clingfilm and put in the fridge for 45 minutes or longer.

To make the olive sauce, heat the olive oil in a medium thick-bottomed saucepan, then add the mushrooms. Fry, stirring over a high heat, until the mushrooms start to brown. Add the garlic, stir and season with the dried red chilli, salt and pepper. Remove from the heat. When the mushrooms are cool, put them into a food processor and pulse-chop roughly. Add the olives and parsley and pulse together very briefly.

To prepare the dough for cutting into 'strings', cover your surface with semolina flour. Use a pasta machine. Divide the dough into three. One piece at a time, put a piece of dough through the widest setting on the machine ten times, folding into three and turning the sheet each time to make a thick piece of dough. Keep the machine on this setting until the dough feels silky. Only then start to reduce the setting gradually down to 4 or 2.5 mm thick, ie a thick sheet. Put the thick sheet through the narrowest cutters to form strings. Alternatively cut by hand as narrowly as you can.

Bring a large saucepan of water to the boil, add 1 tablespoon salt and cook the pasta until al dente, about 3-4 minutes. Drain, keeping back a little of the pasta water. Return to the pan with the butter.

Heat the olive sauce gently and add the cream. Stir in the buttery stringozzi, turn over to coat evenly and serve with a little chopped fresh red chilli and freshly grated Parmesan.

pizza with olives, radicchio and thyme
pizza con olive, radicchio e timo

for 6, making 3 pizzas
about 450 g black olives, pitted
3 x Pizza Dough Bases, about 30 cm in diameter
    (see page 454)
3 heads radicchio
3 small bunches of fresh thyme
Maldon salt and freshly ground black pepper
extra virgin olive oil
juice of 2 lemons
3 buffalo mozzarella, finely sliced (approximately
    120 g each)

Preheat the oven to 220°C/425°F/Gas 7 for 30 minutes and put in a
pizza stone if you have one. Prepare the pizza base.

Put the olives in a bowl, season with salt, pepper and some thyme
leaves, add 1 tablespoon of olive oil, and leave to marinate for half an
hour.

Remove the outer leaves from the radicchio and cut the head in half,
then into shreds. Squeeze the lemon juice over the radicchio, add a
tablespoon of oil, season with salt and pepper and toss together.

Spread the radicchio over the pizza base and arrange the mozzarella on
top. Scatter over the olives and thyme, drizzle with olive oil and bake in
the preheated oven until the mozzarella melts and the pizza rim is crisp.

pomegranates

The pomegranate – or melagrana in Italian – is one of the most ancient cultivated fruits. There are references to it in the Bible and Homer's *Odyssey*. Although native to Persia, the small evergreen trees grow abundantly in southern Italy and Sicily.

When opened, pomegranates are full of seeds which, depending on the variety, range in colour from deep red to pale white pink. The seeds, bursting with juice, are in compartments separated by a white membrane. The latter contains tannin, and is totally inedible.

To choose a good pomegranate, look for skins without bruises, which have begun to dry out. This indicates that the seeds are at their best, with the right balance of sweetness and acidity. We use pomegranate seeds in salads, and make a drink with them.

To peel a pomegranate, score the skin from top to bottom with a small sharp knife, then gently break the fruit apart, separating the seeds from the membrane. Pay attention, as pomegranate juice stains are impossible to remove!

pomegranate and pheasant salad
insalata di melagrana e fagiano

for 6
2 large ripe pomegranates
1 well-roasted pheasant
Maldon salt and freshly ground black pepper
juice of 2 lemons
extra virgin olive oil
3 tablespoons aged balsamic vinegar
2 heads trevise
300 g prosciutto, cut into very thin slices
500 g cooked and peeled chestnuts (see
　　page 349)

Break open the pomegranates and pull out the fruit seeds. Place in a
bowl, season with salt and pepper and add a little of the lemon juice and
about 1 tablespoon of the olive oil.

Carefully take the breast meat off the pheasant and cut across into 2 cm
pieces. Pull away the leg meat, cutting off any tough bits, and chop
finely. Put the pheasant meat pieces into a separate bowl, season
and add 2 tablespoons lemon juice, the balsamic vinegar and about
4 tablespoons olive oil.

Cut off and discard the bottom white part of the trevise heads and
stalks, and chop the red leaves. Wash the leaves and spin dry. Combine
with the pomegranate seeds and immediately divide between the
serving plates, adding more lemon juice and oil as necessary. Arrange
slices of the prosciutto on top, then add some of the marinated pheasant
and 5 or 6 warm chestnuts broken in half. Drizzle with a little extra virgin
olive oil.

pomegranate campari
tintoretto

per person

2 ripe pomegranates

1 small orange, blood if possible

50 ml Campari

3-4 ice cubes

1 slice orange

Cut the pomegranates in half and squeeze using an orange juicer. Cut the orange in half and squeeze. Combine the two juices. Pour the Campari into the glass, add the ice cubes and pour over the juices. Place the slice of orange over the lip of the glass and serve.

rosemary

Rosemary is one of the most abundant wild herbs in the Mediterranean and is used in Italy all the year round.

As it has such a dominant flavour, rosemary is used very often to flavour winter tomato sauces when there is no basil. The fresh leaves are picked from the stalks and then chopped; they need to be used quickly as they are very oily and will soon go black.

We also use rosemary with anchovies. It is the primary flavour in the anchovy and rosemary sauce which has been on the River Cafe menu since we first started. We use branches of rosemary as skewers for spiedini of scallops. Rosemary is also pounded with sea salt and stuffed into every cut and crevice of porchetta – a whole roasted pig.

rosemary and borlotti bean risotto
risotto con borlotti e rosmarino

for 6

1 tablespoon fresh rosemary leaves, crushed with
   1 teaspoon Maldon salt
1.5 litres chicken stock (see page 455)
Maldon salt and freshly ground black pepper
80 g unsalted butter
100 g pancetta affumicata, finely sliced and cut
   into 1 cm pieces
inner white hearts of 2 heads celery, chopped
2 small red onions, peeled and chopped
3 garlic cloves, peeled and finely chopped
400 g carnaroli rice
120 g Parmesan, freshly grated

cooked dried borlotti beans

200 g dried borlotti beans, soaked overnight in a
   generous amount of water
1/2 head garlic
a few parsley stalks
2-3 celery stalks

rosemary butter

1 tablespoon fresh rosemary leaves
1 teaspoon Maldon salt
80 g unsalted butter, softened

To cook the borlotti beans, drain them then place in a large saucepan and cover with fresh water. Add the garlic, parsley and celery stalks and bring to the boil. Turn the heat down and simmer for 45-60 minutes or until the beans become soft and buttery in texture. Top up the water level if necessary and keep in the cooking liquid. Remove the celery, parsley and garlic and season with salt and pepper.

To make the rosemary butter, pound the rosemary leaves with the salt. When fine, add the butter and stir to combine.

Heat the stock to a simmer and check for seasoning.

Melt the butter in a thick-bottomed saucepan, add the pancetta and cook slowly just to allow the flavour to infuse with the butter. The pancetta must not brown. Add the celery and onion and continue to cook gently. When soft, add the garlic and smashed rosemary and stir together briefly. Add the rice, stir to coat each grain with the buttery vegetables and cook for 2-3 minutes. When the rice is opaque, start adding the hot stock ladle by ladle, adding the next only when the rice has absorbed the last. Stir continuously until the rice is al dente, about 15 minutes.

Remove the beans from their cooking liquid and purée half of them with a little stock, just enough to give a double cream consistency. Add the bean purée and the whole beans to the risotto, stir to combine, then add the rosemary butter and 2 tablespoons of the grated Parmesan. Serve with the remaining Parmesan.

rosemary bruschetta
bruschetta con rosmarino

for 6

1 branch fresh rosemary, leaves picked
   from the stalks, washed
6 slices sourdough loaf
3 garlic cloves, peeled
Maldon salt
new season extra virgin olive oil

Toast the bread on both sides,
and rub on one side only with
the rosemary. Lightly scrape the
same side with the garlic.
Sprinkle with salt and pour over
a generous amount of olive oil.

walnuts

Walnuts have great protein value. The trees grow all over the Mediterranean and are cultivated particularly on the Sorrento peninsula in Italy. Most Italian recipes using walnuts originate from Liguria.

Fresh walnuts, when their shells are still damp and the peel comes away from the kernel easily, are sweet, wet and juicy and excellent for pounding with sauces. Dry walnuts, usually those grown in the south of Italy and dried in ovens, are used for cakes, sweets, biscuits and chocolate.

Once shelled the kernels will become rancid quite quickly. Buy vacuum-packed shelled walnuts and use them soon after opening.

ravioli with walnut and robiola pesto
ravioli al pesto di noci e robiola

for 6
Rich Egg Pasta (see page 454)
Tipo '00' pasta flour for dusting
Maldon salt and freshly ground black pepper
1 tablespoon olive oil
Sage Butter (see page 364)
120 g Parmesan, freshly grated
walnut pesto
250 g fresh walnuts, shelled weight, grated
60 g unsalted butter
1 garlic clove, peeled and finely chopped
3 tablespoons chopped fresh marjoram leaves
1/2 nutmeg, freshly grated
600 g Robiola (a soft, fresh, melting cheese)
4 large, organic free-range egg yolks
2 tablespoons freshly grated Parmesan

For the filling, melt the butter in a frying pan, add the walnuts and garlic and push around just to colour the garlic and soften the walnuts. Add the marjoram, salt, pepper and nutmeg. Remove from the heat and leave to cool. Combine the mixture with the cheese, egg yolks and Parmesan.

Dust the work surface with flour. Roll the dough out as thin as you can into a long sheet. Spread three-quarters of the fairly wet walnut mixture, rather like butter, over the sheet lengthwise. Fold the sheet over to enclose the layer. Cut using a pasta cutter with a zig-zag wheel, which seals the two layers as it cuts, into ravioli 5 cm square. The ravioli will be very flat. Cook in batches in a saucepan of boiling salted water to which you have added the olive oil. Drain, keeping a little cooking water.

Stir 2 tablespoons of the hot cooking water into the remaining filling – you should have about 200 g. Place in a hot serving dish, add the ravioli and cover with the hot sage butter and remaining Parmesan.

walnut and almond cake
torta di noci e mandorle

for 8-10
200 g walnuts, shelled weight, finely chopped
380 g whole blanched almonds, finely ground
380 g unsalted butter, softened, plus extra
   for the tin
100 g plain flour, plus extra for the tin
380 g caster sugar
3 vanilla pods, very finely chopped
5 large, organic free-range eggs
1/2 teaspoon baking powder
125 ml Amaretto (apricot and almond liqueur)
icing
200 g bitter-sweet Callebaut chocolate, with a
   minimum of 70% cocoa solids
50 g unsalted butter

Preheat the oven to 160°C/325°F/Gas 3. Butter and flour a 25 cm cake tin.

Beat the butter and sugar together until pale and light. Stir in the ground almonds and vanilla pods. Beat in the eggs, one at a time. Fold in the walnuts, flour, baking powder and finally the Amaretto. Spoon into the prepared tin and bake in the preheated oven for $1^1/_4$ hours or until set. Allow to cool on a cake rack.

Melt the chocolate and butter in a bowl over simmering water until liquid. Use a hot wet knife to spread over the cake.

december

cavolo nero [424] *soup* cavolo nero and semolina soup. *polenta* cavolo nero polenta and sausages. celeriac [428] *soup* celeriac, chickpea and cabbage soup. *vegetable* smashed celeriac and potatoes. hazelnuts [432] *pasta* tagliatelle with hazelnut sauce. *pudding* hazelnut praline semifreddo. hazelnut meringue and chocolate cake. candied hazelnut and clementine cake. jerusalem artichokes [442] *salad* jerusalem artichokes with barolo bagna cauda. trevise/radicchio [446] *risotto* radicchio and bresaola risotto. *vegetable* braised radicchio and leeks. *soup* radicchio and broad bean soup. *soup* trevise and borlotti bean soup. *risotto* trevise and gorgonzola risotto.

cavolo nero

Cavolo nero is grown in most vegetable gardens in Tuscany and is one of the main ingredients in Ribollita, the famous soup of that region, made with beans, Tuscan bread, cavolo nero and extra virgin olive oil. Cavolo nero is now successfully grown here and is becoming widely available. If you want to grow it yourself, it is possible to buy seeds (see page 456).

The plants grow a metre high with plume-like leaves growing off the main stem, which means you can pick from the plant while it continues to grow – unusual for a member of the cabbage family. The dark blueish-green leaves should be tightly crinkled and stiff, just the tip bent over. The leaves have a tough texture and a fantastically strong, sweet flavour, unlike any other cabbage. The wonderful taste develops after the plants have had a few weeks of frost. Leaves picked too early taste bitter and stringy.

To prepare, remove the centre stem of each leaf. Keep whole the smaller leaves from the centre of the bunch. These tiny leaves are delicious eaten raw. We add them to winter salads.

cavolo nero and semolina soup
zuppa di cavolo nero e semolino

for 6
1 kg cavolo nero, tough stalks removed, washed
200 g coarse-grain semolina
1.5 litres chicken stock (see page 455)
Maldon salt and freshly ground black pepper
100 g unsalted butter
2 medium red onions, peeled and finely chopped
3 bay leaves, centre stem discarded, finely
    chopped
$1/2$ teaspoon freshly grated nutmeg
4 garlic cloves, peeled
150 g Parmesan, freshly grated
extra virgin olive oil

Heat the chicken stock and check for seasoning.

In a large, thick-bottomed saucepan melt the butter, then add the onion and gently fry until beginning to colour. Add the bay leaves, then the semolina and stir continuously over a low heat for 6-8 minutes. The semolina will become golden. Start to add the hot chicken stock, ladle by ladle, stirring all the time. The soup will become very thick and creamy. Grate in some nutmeg and season with salt and pepper. Simmer gently for 10-15 minutes.

Bring a saucepan of salted water to the boil, add the cavolo nero leaves and the whole garlic, and cook for 8-10 minutes. Drain, keeping back a little of the cooking water. Place the cavolo and garlic in a food processor with the retained liquid and pulse-chop to a coarse, thick purée.

Stir the cavolo purée into the semolina, just to combine in streaks rather than totally. Check for seasoning. Serve with freshly grated Parmesan and a drizzle of extra virgin olive oil on each plate.

cavolo nero polenta and sausages
polenta con cavolo nero e salsicce

for 6
2 kg cavolo nero, tough stalks and outer leaves
    removed, washed
Polenta (see page 360)
12 spiced fresh Italian sausages
4 bay leaves
Maldon salt and freshly ground black pepper
8 garlic cloves, peeled, 2 finely sliced
4 tablespoons extra virgin olive oil
1 teaspoon fennel seeds, crushed
120 g unsalted butter, melted
120 g Parmesan, freshly grated

Make the polenta. Put the sausages in a large frying pan, cover with water, add the bay leaves and bring to the boil. Turn the heat down and simmer gently until the water has evaporated, about 30 minutes. Then brown the sausages in the fat that has eased out during cooking.

Bring a large pan of salted water to the boil, add the cavolo nero and the 6 whole cloves of garlic and cook for 8-10 minutes or until the cavolo nero is tender. Drain, keeping the garlic and a little water. Place two-thirds of the cavolo nero and the boiled garlic in the food processor with 3-4 tablespoons of the water, and pulse-chop to a rough purée. Season with salt and pepper.

Heat the olive oil in a large, thick-bottomed frying pan, add the sliced garlic and fennel seeds and cook until soft. Add the remaining cavolo nero and fry for 3-4 minutes. Season generously and keep warm.

Mix the cavolo nero purée into the wet polenta, along with the butter, half the Parmesan, salt and pepper. Serve with a spoonful of the braised cavolo and the sausages on top. Sprinkle with the remaining Parmesan.

celeriac

Celeriac is a variety of celery cultivated for its large, thick, turnip-like root. The stalks and leaves, which look and smell like celery, are good for flavouring stocks. The celeriac flesh itself has a tough, fibrous texture, with a deliciously nutty celery flavour.

The season is very short for celeriac; it is only available in early winter, and frosts will damage the roots. Hard heavy roots indicate the celeriac is solid all the way through and has been freshly dug. The flavour is better from celeriac that has not been around too long.

To prepare, peel away the thick skin which is often gnarled with tiny roots. The insides are white and fresh, smelling like freshly cut celery hearts. Keep peeled, cut celeriac in acidulated water or it will oxidise and turn brown.

Celeriac is only found in recipes from the north of Italy, mostly used in soups.

celeriac, chickpea and cabbage soup
zuppa di sedanorapa, ceci e verza

for 6

800 g celeriac, peeled and cut into 2 cm cubes
200 g dried chickpeas, cooked (see page 23), or
    800 g tinned chickpeas, drained and rinsed
500 g Savoy cabbage, thick stalks discarded, finely
    shredded
4 tablespoons olive oil
150 g pancetta, cut into fine matchsticks
2 bay leaves
2 teaspoons fennel seeds, crushed
1 medium red onion, peeled and roughly chopped
1.25 litres chicken stock (see page 455)
Maldon salt and freshly ground black pepper
1 ciabatta loaf, cut on the diagonal into crostini
1 garlic clove, peeled
extra virgin olive oil
150 g Parmesan, freshly grated
2 tablespoons chopped fresh flat-leaf parsley

Heat the olive oil in a thick-bottomed saucepan, add the pancetta, bay leaves and fennel seeds and cook for a few minutes to allow the flavours to combine. Add the onion and celeriac, stir together and cook in the oil for 8-10 minutes. The onion should begin to colour and the celeriac soften. Now add the cabbage and the cooked chickpeas. Stir together and cook for a few minutes, then add enough hot stock just to cover. Season with salt and pepper and simmer gently for 30 minutes or until the celeriac is soft and the chickpeas have begun to break up.

Toast the crostini on both sides and rub lightly with the garlic. Place a slice in each soup bowl, drizzle with extra virgin olive oil and scatter with Parmesan. Ladle in the soup, sprinkle with parsley and generously pour over extra virgin olive oil to serve.

smashed celeriac and potatoes
purea di sedanorapa e patate

for 6
1.5 kg celeriac, peeled and cubed
2 kg potatoes, peeled and cubed
3 tablespoons olive oil
3 garlic cloves, peeled and finely chopped
1 tablespoon chopped fresh flat-leaf parsley
1 tablespoon chopped fresh sage
1 small red onion, peeled and finely chopped
700 ml chicken stock (see page 455)
Maldon salt and freshly ground black pepper
extra virgin olive oil

In a thick-bottomed saucepan heat the olive oil and gently cook the garlic, parsley, sage and onion for 10 minutes. Add the celeriac and potatoes and stir to combine.

Bring the chicken stock to the boil and add enough to the vegetables to cover them. Simmer, adding more stock as the liquid is absorbed, until the celeriac and potato are soft enough to be roughly mashed. Season with salt and pepper, and stir in plenty of extra virgin olive oil.

hazelnuts

Hazelnuts grow in abundance throughout Italy, in Liguria, Piedmont, Sicily and the Apennines. Although they are usually associated with cakes and biscotti, nougat and the well-known chocolate Gianduia, they are also used in regional recipes for sauces to accompany meat, pasta and fish.

We always roast shelled hazelnuts to intensify their flavour. The method varies depending on the recipe.

tagliatelle with hazelnut sauce
tagliatelle con salsa di nocciole

for 6
200 g shelled hazelnuts
500 g Fresh Pasta (see page 454) made into
    tagliatelle
2 garlic cloves, peeled
350 ml double cream
60 ml brandy
extra virgin olive oil
1 tablespoon 100% cocoa powder
freshly grated Parmesan
Maldon salt and freshly ground black pepper
1 dried red chilli, crumbled
1/2 nutmeg, freshly grated

Preheat the oven to 200°C/400°F/Gas 6.

Place the hazelnuts in a large cake tin and roast for 15 minutes. Place on a tea towel, fold it over the hot nuts and rub vigorously to loosen the skins. Shake the nuts in a coarse sieve to allow the skins to drop off.

Place the nuts and garlic in a food processor and pulse-chop until the nuts have broken up. Pour in the cream, brandy and 150 ml extra virgin olive oil. Add the cocoa powder and 100 g of the grated Parmesan and blend to a rough texture. Season with salt, pepper and the chilli. Grate in the nutmeg and stir.

Bring a large saucepan of salted water to the boil, add the tagliatelle and cook for 3-4 minutes or until the pasta is al dente. Drain, keeping back 2-3 tablespoons of pasta water. Mix the sauce with the tagliatelle, adding some of the cooking water if too thick. Serve with freshly grated Parmesan and a drizzle of extra virgin olive oil.

hazelnut praline semifreddo
semifreddo al croccante di nocciole

for 6
650 ml double cream
900 ml milk
8 large, organic free-range egg yolks
175 g caster sugar
120 ml Frangelico (hazelnut liqueur)
praline
300 g shelled hazelnuts with skins
225 g caster sugar

Preheat the oven to 200°C/400°F/Gas 6. Place the hazelnuts in a cake tray and roast for 5-6 minutes. Place on a cloth, cover and rub to loosen the skins. Shake off the skins in a sieve. Return the nuts to the tray and roast until chestnut brown, about 4-5 more minutes. Place on oiled paper. Dissolve the sugar in 150 ml water and bring to the boil, cooking until it turns dark caramel. Pour over the nuts and cool until solid. Break up the praline in a food processor as finely as possible.

To make the custard base, combine 300 ml of the cream and all the milk in a thick-bottomed saucepan and heat until just below boiling point. Remove from the heat. Whisk the egg yolks with the sugar until pale, about 5 minutes. Mix a cup of the hot cream mixture into the egg yolks, then transfer the whole lot back into the pan. Cook over a low flame, stirring constantly. Remove when the mixture has thickened and coats the back of a spoon. Pour into a bowl and allow to cool.

Stir the cooled praline powder into the cooled semifreddo mixture, then pour through a fine sieve. Put any bits of praline remaining in the sieve back into the pan with a ladle of semifreddo mix and cook, stirring, to loosen and gather final flavour. Sieve back into the semifreddo mixture. Put into an ice-cream machine and churn until softly frozen. Lightly beat the remaining double cream to the soft ribbon stage and fold in the Frangelico. Mix into the semifreddo and return to the freezer until set. Serve in bowls, as semifreddo is always softer than ice-cream.

hazelnut meringue and chocolate cake
meringa di nocciole e cioccolato

To achieve the best-textured mousse for this cake make it the day before.

for 10

meringue
150 g shelled hazelnuts, lightly roasted, skins
   rubbed off (see page 434)
olive oil and butter for greasing the trays
5 large, organic free-range egg whites
225 g caster sugar
110 g unsalted butter, melted
70 g plain flour
chocolate mousse
450 g bitter-sweet chocolate, at least 70% cocoa
   butter
2 tablespoons dry instant coffee dissolved in 80 ml
   boiling water
6 large, organic free-range eggs, separated
a pinch of Maldon salt
to serve
100 ml Vecchio Romagna brandy
200 g mascarpone, lightly whipped

For the chocolate mousse, melt the chocolate in a bowl with the coffee over a saucepan of simmering water. Do not let the water touch the bowl. Remove when the chocolate becomes liquid.

Beat the egg yolks at high speed in an electric mixer until pale, about 3-4 minutes. Reduce the speed and gradually add the melted chocolate mixture. Stop as soon as the two are amalgamated. Separately beat the egg whites with the pinch of salt to soft peaks.

Take a large spoonful of egg white and gently fold it into the chocolate mixture, then fold a further spoonful in and combine carefully. Finally fold the chocolate back into the remaining egg whites until no white shows. Cover with clingfilm and place in the fridge overnight.

To make the meringue, preheat the oven to 120°C/250°F/Gas ½. Rub olive oil over three flat oven trays. Line each tray with parchment paper. Liberally butter the parchment paper.

Put the hazelnuts into a food processor and pulse-chop to a medium fine flour. Using an electric mixer, beat the egg whites with half the sugar until stiff, then add the hazelnut flour and the remaining sugar. Beat briefly just to combine. Fold in the melted butter. Finally sieve the flour into the bowl and fold in carefully.

Spoon the mixture on to the three trays and spread it out flat, each the same shape and diameter, but as thin as you can. The layers should be 1 cm thick at most. Place in the preheated oven and bake for 50 minutes, or until set and almost crisp. Immediately peel off the paper whilst the meringues are still hot. Place on wire racks to cool.

To assemble the cake, choose a large flat cake plate. Divide the chocolate mousse mixture into two. Place the first meringue layer on the plate, shake over half of the brandy and let it soak in briefly. Cover with a thick layer of the chocolate mousse. Place the second meringue on top, sprinkle with the remaining brandy and spread with the remaining mousse mixture. Sit the last meringue on top, and cover with the mascarpone.

candied hazelnut and clementine cake

torta di nocciole e clementini

This is a traditional chocolate cake from Florence.

for 8-10

150 g shelled hazelnuts
500 g crystallised clementines
150 g unsalted butter, softened, plus extra for the
    tin
500 ml Vecchio Romagna brandy
100 g sultanas
600 g shelled whole blanched almonds
50 g caster sugar
100 g plain flour
3 large, organic free-range eggs
100 g soft dark brown sugar
150 g bitter-sweet chocolate, roughly chopped
peel of 2 lemons, pith removed, peel finely
    chopped
marzipan
250 g shelled whole blanched almonds
150 g caster sugar
150 ml Vecchio Romagna brandy

Preheat the oven to 150°C/300°F/Gas 2. Butter a 25 cm round cake tin and line the bottom with parchment paper.

Chop the clementines into 1 cm pieces and marinate in 400 ml of the brandy. In a separate bowl, marinate the sultanas in the remaining brandy.

Roast the hazelnuts for 6-8 minutes until the skin is loose and the nuts are brown. Remove the skins and chop the nuts. Roast 200 g of the almonds for 6-8 minutes, then pulse-chop in the food processor to coarse. Pulse-chop another 200 g of the almonds to coarse. Finely chop the remaining 200 g almonds to flour.

Cream the butter and caster sugar together in a food processor until pale. Sift in the plain flour and half the almond flour. Add the eggs one by one, beating all the time. Remove to a bowl. Stir in the brown sugar, the chopped nuts and remaining almond flour.

Drain the brandy from the clementines and the sultanas. Mix the brandy into the cake mixture to liquefy it and make it easier to combine. Finally stir in the clementines, chocolate, chopped peels and the sultanas. Spoon into the prepared cake tin and bake for 1¹/₂ hours or until cooked. Cool on a wire rack.

To make the marzipan, put the almonds into the food processor and process until finely ground. Add the sugar and brandy and pulse-chop to combine for 2-3 minutes. It should become a very thick, sticky paste. Spoon this on to the top of the cake in a layer about 1 cm thick. Rough up the surface with a fork. Place under a hot grill to brown.

jerusalem artichokes

Jerusalem artichokes are knobbly tubers that resemble potatoes, but taste more like a cross between a radish and a parsnip, with a hint of artichoke. They are not related to globe artichokes but are actually part of the sunflower family, and grow in a similar way. The plants are very tall with bright yellow, daisy-like flowers.

Jerusalem artichokes spread very easily and in Italy in the summer you see the plants everywhere in ditches and on banks by the roadside, as well as in most vegetable gardens. The tubers are ready to harvest after the frosts have killed off the tops.

A number of varieties are available, but it is most important to choose vegetables that are firm, freshly dug and preferably organic. Scrub or peel before using.

Jerusalem artichokes contain no starch and are delicious eaten raw, shaved thinly and tossed with lemon juice and extra virgin olive oil. They are equally good roasted and recently we have introduced them into fritto misto.

jerusalem artichokes with barolo bagna cauda

topinambur con bagna cauda al barolo

for 6
6 medium Jerusalem artichokes, peeled
4 medium carrots, peeled
2 fennel bulbs
inner white heart of 2 small heads celery
2 red peppers, grilled, seeded and skinned (see
    page 292)
Maldon salt and freshly ground black pepper
juice of 1 lemon
extra virgin olive oil
bagna cauda
400 ml Barolo or Nebbiola wine
2 whole heads garlic, cloves peeled and roughly
    cut up
10 salted anchovies, prepared (see page 458)
200 ml extra virgin olive oil
150 g unsalted butter

To prepare the bagna cauda, heat the wine in a small, thick-bottomed saucepan, then add the garlic and simmer for 4-5 minutes. Add the anchovies and the olive oil and continue to cook gently, stirring to break up the anchovies. Stir in the butter and on the lowest heat possible, cook for 45 minutes, until this dark red sauce is thick and creamy.

Cut the artichokes into fine slices. Cut the carrots lengthwise into quarters, then into quarters again. Discard the tough outer parts of the fennel and slice the bulb into eighths through the stem. Divide the celery hearts lengthwise into quarters or sixths, keeping the tender centre leaves attached. Divide the peppers into eighths lengthwise. Toss all the vegetables together in a large serving dish. Season with salt and pepper and drizzle with the lemon juice and some extra virgin olive oil. Serve with the hot bagna cauda poured over just before serving.

trevise / radicchio

Radicchio is the Italian name for many varieties of red-leafed chicory. We use three types in the restaurant.

• Radicchio rosso di Verona, commonly known as radicchio, is round and cabbage shaped. It is the least bitter and most widely available throughout the year. The leaves are thick and are very good deep-fried, grilled or roasted. Do not be tempted to use them in salads.

• Radicchio di Treviso rosso precoce Commonly known as trevise, this is the first to appear in the shops around Christmas; the season lasts until the end of March. The heads are elongated with thin, crisp red leaves and wide white ribs and stalks. The leaves are delicious in salads; use the white ribs and stalks in the base for risotto and soups.

• Radicchio di Treviso tardivo The most flavourful and prized, this comes last in the season. It is less common, even in Italy, as it is only grown in a small area around the town of Treviso. Identifiable by its large thick edible root and long, thin, pointed dark red leaves, it's delicious simply grilled or pan-fried and is equally good in salads.

Radicchio does grow in our climate. The growing period is throughout the summer, autumn and winter. For salads we pick the outer small green leaves in the early summer. Later on in the autumn we cut out the smallest centre leaves from the plants and use them in salads. The larger outer leaves eventually die off, which allows the plant to develop the second leaf crop that will be the familiar, crisp, dark red closed buds of the radicchio.

radicchio and bresaola risotto
risotto con radicchio e bresaola

for 6
2 large heads radicchio, trimmed and finely sliced
200 g bresaola, finely sliced, then cut into
   matchsticks
3 heads fennel, finely chopped, green parts kept
   separate
1.5 litres chicken stock (see page 455)
Maldon salt and freshly ground black pepper
100 g unsalted butter
1 red onion, peeled and finely chopped
$1/2$ teaspoon fennel seeds, crushed
3 garlic cloves, peeled and chopped
400 g carnaroli rice
100 ml Pinot Bianco (white wine)
100 g Parmesan, freshly grated

Heat the stock to a simmer and check for seasoning.

Melt 80 g of the butter in a large, thick-bottomed saucepan over a
medium heat and gently fry the onion and fennel until soft and
beginning to colour. Add the fennel seeds, garlic, 2 tablespoons of the
radicchio and the bresaola pieces. Stir and cook just to combine the
flavours. Add the rice, stir it into the vegetables and cook for 2 minutes.
Add the wine and let it bubble and reduce, then start to add the hot
stock ladle by ladle. Each time you add a ladle of stock add the
equivalent volume of radicchio. Stir together, allowing the rice to absorb
the stock and the radicchio to wilt. Continue to cook the risotto in this
way until the rice is al dente, about 20 minutes.

Keep back a little of the radicchio and chop it finely with the green of the
fennel. Stir this into the finished risotto with half the Parmesan. Serve
with the rest of the butter on top and the remaining Parmesan.

braised radicchio and leeks
radicchio e porri in padella

for 6
4 heads radicchio
1.2 kg leeks
3 tablespoons olive oil
Maldon salt and freshly ground black pepper
4 garlic cloves, peeled and chopped
juice of 1 lemon
extra virgin olive oil

Remove any damaged outer leaves from the radicchio. Cut each head in half through the stem and then into eighths. Peel the outer leaves from the leeks, cut off the tough green tops and trim the roots. Wash thoroughly and pat dry. Cut the leeks in half lengthwise, and then in half again. Cut these long pieces in half again.

In a large, thick-bottomed saucepan, heat the olive oil. Add the leek and push around to colour on all sides. Season with salt and pepper. Turn the heat to medium and cook for 15 minutes, stirring. Add the garlic and radicchio and fry together until the garlic is cooked and the radicchio has wilted and become brown. Test for seasoning and add the lemon juice and a little extra virgin olive oil.

radicchio and broad bean soup
zuppa di radicchio e fave bianche

for 6
1 kg radicchio, finely sliced, then roughly chopped
250 g dried skinless broad beans, soaked
    overnight
5 garlic cloves, peeled, 3 finely sliced
1 handful of flat-leaf parsley, leaves and stalks
2 fresh red chillies
4 tablespoons olive oil
Maldon salt and freshly ground black pepper
2 dried red chillies, crumbled
juice of 1 large lemon
extra virgin olive oil

Drain the beans. Place in a saucepan, cover with cold water and add the 2 whole garlic cloves, the parsley stalks and fresh red chillies. Bring slowly to the boil. Skim the surface, turn the heat down and gently simmer for an hour or until tender. Keep in their cooking liquid.

Heat the olive oil in a large, thick-bottomed frying pan. Fry the remaining sliced garlic gently, then add two-thirds of the radicchio. Stir and fry until the radicchio becomes limp and is starting to brown. Season with salt, pepper, dried chilli and half the lemon juice. Add the cooked beans and a couple of ladles of their cooking water, and cook together for a further 5 minutes, no longer. Place in a large saucepan.

Take half the soup, put into a food processor and pulse-chop briefly, just to break up the beans, not to purée them. Return this mixture to the saucepan with enough of the remaining cooking water to make the soup more liquid if necessary. The soup should be thick. Check for seasoning.

Chop the parsley leaves and mix with the remainder of the radicchio. Season with salt and pepper, then add the rest of the lemon juice and 4 tablespoons extra virgin olive oil. Serve, stirring the tossed raw radicchio and parsley into the soup. Drizzle with extra virgin olive oil.

trevise and borlotti bean soup
zuppa di trevisana e borlotti

for 6
5 heads trevise
300 g cooked dried borlotti beans (see page 414),
   with their cooking liquid
olive oil
2 small red onions, peeled and roughly chopped
inner white heart of 1 head celery, roughly
   chopped
3 garlic cloves, peeled and finely chopped
8 medium potatoes, peeled and cut into 1 cm
   cubes
1 x 400 g tin peeled plum tomatoes, drained
2 small dried red chillies, crushed
Maldon salt and freshly ground black pepper
3 tablespoons chopped fresh flat-leaf parsley
extra virgin olive oil

Cut the dark red tips of the trevise from the whole heads, about 5 cm,
and put aside. Roughly chop the remaining base of the leaves and the
tender part of the stems.

In a large thick-bottomed saucepan, heat 2 tablespoons olive oil, then
add the onion and celery heart, and gently fry until soft and beginning to
colour. Add all the trevise apart from the tips and the garlic and continue
to fry, stirring. When the trevise becomes limp, add the potato. Cook
gently for 5-6 minutes, then add the tomatoes, chilli and salt and
pepper. Add 4 tablespoonfuls of the cooked borlotti beans and enough
of their cooking liquid to cover. Simmer gently for half an hour.

Put half the remaining beans into a food processor with a few ladles of
the juice and pulse to a rough purée. Add to the soup. It should be very
thick, so add more beans if necessary. Season generously and add the
parsley. Ladle into individual soup bowls and cover with the red tips of
the trevise. Pour over each a generous amount of extra virgin olive oil.

trevise and gorgonzola risotto
risotto con trevisana e gorgonzola

for 6
4 medium heads trevise
3 medium leeks
1.5 litres chicken stock (see page 455)
Maldon salt and freshly ground black pepper
100 g unsalted butter
1/2 inner white heart of 1 head celery, finely chopped
1 medium red onion, peeled and finely chopped
1 garlic clove, peeled and finely chopped
400 g carnaroli rice
150 ml Pinot Grigio (white wine)
300 g Gorgonzola dolce, in small pieces
60 g Parmesan, freshly grated

Wash the vegetables well. Finely slice the stem – the white part of the trevise head – to about halfway up the head. Trim away the tough green parts of the leek and finely slice the white part. Separately, finely slice the pale green parts and the dark red tips of the trevise. Put the stock on to simmer on a medium to low heat. Season it well.

Heat half the butter in a large, thick-bottomed saucepan and add the celery and onion. Soften gently for 5-6 minutes. Add the white of the leek and the trevise stems, and stir for a minute. Add the garlic and rice and stir thoroughly. Cook for 2-3 minutes then pour in half the Pinot Grigio. Allow to bubble and reduce, then start to add the stock, ladle by ladle, stirring continuously, and not adding any more stock until the previous ladleful has been absorbed. Continue stirring and adding stock until the rice becomes al dente, about 15 minutes.

Meanwhile, melt the remaining butter over a medium heat. Add the trevise tips and the pale green part of the leeks, along with 1 teaspoon salt. Cover and leave on the heat for 2-3 minutes. Add to the risotto, with the remaining wine. Stir in the soft Gorgonzola bit by bit, keeping a few pieces to top each serving. Sprinkle with Parmesan.

Basics

Fresh Pasta

makes approximately 1 kg
500 g Tipo 'oo' pasta flour, plus extra for dusting
1 teaspoon Maldon salt
4 large, organic free-range eggs
6 large, organic free-range egg yolks
50 g fine semolina flour for dusting

Put the flour and salt in a processor, add the eggs and egg yolks, and pulse-blend until the pasta begins to come together into a loose ball of dough. Knead the pasta dough on a flat surface, lightly dusted with the semolina and a little extra flour, until the mixture is smooth, about 3 minutes. If the dough is very stiff and difficult to knead, you may have to put it back in the processor and blend in another whole egg. Cut the dough into eight equal-sized pieces and briefly knead them into individual balls. Wrap each ball in cling film and allow to rest in the fridge for at least 20 minutes (and up to 2 hours).

Prepare your pasta machine, setting it on the widest setting. Scatter the work surface with more flour, and push each piece of pasta dough through the rollers ten times, folding the sheet into three each time to return it to a short strip, then turn it by a quarter and push it through the rollers again. This process introduces air into the dough and stretches it to develop the texture. After ten such folds at this setting the pasta should feel silky. Only then reduce the setting gradually down to thin, as required. You should achieve long sheets; cut them in half if you find that they become too long to handle.

To cut **tagliatelle**, dust the sheets with flour and while still pliable fold each sheet loosely over and over again on itself until the whole sheet has been folded into a long, flat, rectangular roll 8 cm wide. Using a wide-bladed knife, cut the roll across into ribbons, 1 cm wide. Carefully unfold the ribbons, using both your hands with your fingers separated to lift and separate the ribbon rolls. Alternatively, if you have a cutter on your machine, put the pasta through the widest cutter. Make sure your surface is generously scattered with flour and separate the ribbons as they emerge from the pasta machine.

To cut **stracci**, cut the sheets into pieces 6-8 cm square.

Rich Egg Pasta

for 6
400 g Tipo 'oo' pasta flour, plus 100 g for dusting
20 large organic free-range egg yolks
1 tablespoon Maldon salt

Put the flour into the bowl of an electric mixer fitted with a dough hook, then add the egg yolks and salt. Mix slowly to knead to a dough, about 10 minutes. Remove from the mixer, wrap in cling film and leave to cool and rest for 1 hour.

Dust your work surface with the remaining flour. Divide the dough into four equal pieces. Pass the pieces through your pasta machine set on the widest setting at least ten times, folding the dough and turning it each time. The dough should feel silky. Then reduce the setting gradually until you have long sheets. Do not make your final sheet too thin – about 2-3 mm, or No l on your machine.

Fold the pasta sheets over three or four times back on themselves, then cut the pile as finely as you can into tagliarini, 2-3 mm wide. Toss the cut tagliarini to loosen and lightly coat with flour. Use as soon as possible.

Ligurian Basic Pasta

serves 6
500 g Tipo 'oo' pasta flour, plus extra for dusting
4 organic free-range eggs
50 ml white wine
2 tablespoons extra virgin olive oil
1 teaspoon Maldon salt

Sieve the flour into the bowl of an electric mixer fitted with a dough hook. Add the eggs, wine, olive oil and salt. Knead slowly, allowing the mixture to come together. Keep the mixer on low speed and knead for 10 minutes. The dough may be quite dry.

Dust your work surface with plenty of flour. Divide the dough into four pieces and work each piece by hand until completely smooth. Wrap each ball of dough in cling film and put in the fridge to chill for $1^{1}/_{2}$-2 hours.

To prepare the final stage of the dough, use a pasta machine. Put each ball of dough through the widest setting ten times, folding the thick sheet into three as it emerges, to form a short, very thick piece. Turn this around, and put it through the machine again. Keeping the machine on this setting, repeat this process until the pasta feels silky. Only then reduce the setting gradually down to a fine pasta sheet.

Cut as specified in individual recipes.

Pizza Dough
The dough quantity will serve six.

step 1
4 teaspoons granular dried yeast
125 ml warm water
150 g rye flour
step 2
250 ml warm water
2 tablespoons milk
4 tablespoons olive oil
1 tablespoon Maldon salt
500 g plain flour

Warm a bowl large enough to take the entire dough mixture.

For Step 1, mix the yeast with the warm water in the warm bowl. When 'melted', add the rye flour and stir well to combine. Leave in a warm place to form a sponge, at least 30 minutes.

When the mixture has formed a sponge, add the ingredients for Step 2. Put the mixture in a processor fitted with a dough hook and knead for 10-15 minutes. The dough will be quite wet and sticky (this texture will make a crisper crust). Place the dough in a bowl greased with extra olive oil and drizzle a little oil over the top. Cover with a cloth and leave to rise in a warm place for about 2 hours.

Knock the dough back and knead a couple of times, then return to the bowl and leave to rise for a further 40 minutes.

Preheat the oven as instructed in the individual recipe, and have ready a large flat baking tray or pizza stone (place the latter in the oven to preheat).

When the dough is ready, divide into three cricket-ball-sized pieces and individually form into balls. Roll out each ball on a floured surface with quick light motions as thinly as possible. A cricket ball of this dough should roll out to make a 30 cm pizza base, large enough for two people. Place on a baking sheet ready for the topping, then top and bake as advised in the individual recipe.

Potato Gnocchi

for 6
1 kg Desirée or other floury potatoes
Maldon salt and freshly ground black pepper
2 large, organic free-range egg yolks
150 g plain flour
100 g semolina

Cook the potatoes with their skins on in a large amount of boiling salted water. Drain and peel while hot. The potatoes must be very dry for successful gnocchi.

Put the potatoes through a mouli into a bowl, or mash with a potato masher. Lightly fold in the egg yolks, flour, semolina and salt, and work together quickly to obtain a dough.

Divide the dough into four. On a clean surface roll out each piece of dough into a long roll shape a little fatter than your index finger. Cut into 2 cm lengths. Roll each small piece over the back of a fork to make indentations which will catch a bit of the sauce.

Bring a large pan of salted water to the boil. Add the gnocchi and cook over a high heat until they rise to the surface. Remove with a slotted spoon, letting the spoon rest on a clean folded cloth to drain off any excess water.

Chicken Stock

In a perfect world – i.e. in Bologna for instance – the stock would include a veal bone, a beef shin and a piece of pancetta.

makes 2 litres
1 x 1.5-2 kg free-range chicken, all fatty parts removed
inner white heart of 1 head celery, white parts only, washed
2 large carrots, scrubbed
1 small red onion, peeled
2 tomatoes
1 head garlic, unpeeled
5 bay leaves
3 sprigs fresh thyme
1 teaspoon black peppercorns
3 litres cold water
Maldon salt

Put the chicken and the rest of the ingredients, apart from the salt, into a large saucepan, and gently bring to the boil. Turn the heat down and skim, then gently simmer for about 1 hour. Remove the chicken and strain out the vegetables and herbs. Season the broth.

Fish Stock

makes 1.5 litres
heads and bones of 1-2 large turbot
1 piece sea bass or head
a handful each of fennel and parsley stalks
1 whole head garlic
1/2 head celery with leaves
2 large plum tomatoes
1/2 tablespoon each of fennel seeds, coriander seeds and white peppercorns
1 large branch fresh bay leaves
2 dried red chillies
150 ml dry white wine
1.75 litres cold water
Maldon salt

Put all the ingredients, apart from the salt, into a large pan and bring to the boil, skimming off any scum if necessary. Lower the heat and simmer very gently for about 30 minutes. Strain and use immediately, seasoning to taste with salt.

Suppliers

London

General Ingredients

Baker & Spice
46 Walton Street, SW3 1RB
tel: 020 7589 4734
(Sourdough bread)

Bluebird Food Market
350 Kings Rd, SW3 5UU
tel: 020 7559 1153
(Speciality vegetables and Italian provisions)

I Camisa & Sons
61 Old Compton Street, W1V 5DN
tel: 020 7437 7610
(Italian provisions)

Clarke's
124 Kensington Church Street, W8
tel: 020 7221 9225
(River Cafe olive oil, some organic vegetables)

The Fifth Floor Food Market
Harvey Nichols, SW1X 7RJ
tel: 020 7235 5000
(Speciality vegetables, olive oil and other provisions)

La Fromagerie
30 Highbury Park, N5 2AA
tel: 020 7359 7440
(Italian vegetables and other provisions)

Jeroboams
96 Holland Park Avenue, W11 3AA
tel: 020 7727 9359
(Sourdough bread and parmesan)

Lina Stores
18 Brewer Street, W1R 3FS
tel: 020 7437 6482
(Italian provisions)

Luigi's
349 Fulham Road, SW10 9TW
tel: 020 7352 7739
(Italian provisions)

Michanicou Bros
2 Clarendon Rd, W11 3AA
tel: 020 7727 5191
(Unusual Italian vegetables, e.g. cavolo nero, trevise and cime di rapa)

Montes
23A Canonbury Lane, N1 2AS
tel: 020 7351 4335
(River Cafe olive oil, Italian vegetables)

Mortimer & Bennett
33 Turnham Green Terrace, W4 1RG
tel: 020 8995 4145
(River Cafe olive oil and Italian provisions)

Panzer Greengrocer & Market
13–19 Circus Rd, NW8 5PB
tel: 020 7722 8596
(Italian vegetables and provisions)

Planet Organic
42 Westbourne Grove, W2 5SH
tel: 020 7221 7171
(Organic supermarket selling vegetables, eggs, chickpeas etc)

Selfridges Food Hall
400 Oxford Street, W1A 1AB
tel: 020 7629 1234
(River Cafe olive oil, sourdough bread and a large selection of vegetables)

Villandry
170 Great Portland Street, W1N 5TB
tel: 020 7631 3131
(Seasonal Italian vegetables and provisions)

Wild Harvest
31 London Stone Estate, SW8 3QJ
tel: 020 7498 5391
(Vanilla pods, sea kale, asparagus, wild mushrooms, truffles)

Wild Oats Wholefoods
210 Westbourne Grove, W11 2RH
tel: 020 7229 1063
(Onion squash, sprouting broccoli, organic fruit and vegetables)

Specialist Suppliers

Blagdens Fishmongers
65-66 Paddington Street, W1M 3RR
tel: 020 7935 8321
(Samphire and gulls' eggs)

La Marée
76 Sloane Avenue, SW3 3DZ
tel: 020 7589 8067
(Gulls' eggs, clams, samphire)

M & C
35 Turnham Green Terrace, W4 1RG
tel: 020 8995 0140
www.comM+CFRUITANDVEG.co.uk
(Specialist in Italian vegetables)

Stefano Vallebona
Unit 29, 86–96 Garratt Lane, SW18 4DJ
tel: 020 8877 0903 www.lascorpacciata.com
(Bottarga, good tinned tomatoes and other Italian provisions; mail order)

Farmers' Markets

Borough Market
Borough High St, SE1
tel: 020 7407 1002
Saturdays 9am – 5pm. Many producers sell here on the 3rd Saturday of every month, including Guidetti Fine Foods (e-mail: guidetti@compuserve.com) who sell Italian larder products to the general public.

Islington Farmers' Market
Essex Road, N1
tel: 020 7704 9659
Sundays 10am – 2pm
(Organic vegetables)

Notting Hill Gate
Newcomb House car park,
Notting Hill Gate, W11
Saturdays 9am – 1pm
tel: 020 7704 9659
(Organic sourdough bread and vegetables)

Organic Food Market
Spitalfields Market,
Brushfield St, E1 6AA
tel: 020 7377 1496
Sundays 9am – 5pm.
(Organic flour, fruit and vegetables)

Swiss Cottage Farmers' Market
Market Square, NW3
Wednesdays 12pm – 4pm

Camden Lock Farmers' Market
Camden Lock, NW1
tel: 020 7704 9659
Fridays 11am – 3pm

For more information on organic farmers' markets in London, contact Wheatland Farmers' Markets
tel: 020 7704 9659
www.wheatlandfarmers.com

Outside London

Abingdon
Wells Stores
Peachcroft Farm
Abingdon OX14 2HP
tel: 01235 535978
(Martin Pitt eggs, asparagus in season, fruit and vegetables, bread, Neal's Yard cheeses)

Bath
Radford Mill Farm
Timsbury, Bath BA3 1QF
tel: 01761 472549
(Organic vegetables, herbs and fruit)

Brighton
Infinity Foods
25 North Road, Brighton BN1 2AA
tel: 01273 603563
(Organic fruit and vegetables)

Cambridge
Cambridge Cheese Company
All Saints Passage, Cambridge CB2 3LS
tel: 01223 3238672
(River Cafe olive oil, parmesan, mozzarella)

Cumbria
J & J Graham Ltd
Market Square
Penrith, Cumbria CA11 7BS
tel: 01768 862281
(Italian provisions)

Dorset
Trenchermans
The Old Dairy
Compton Park
Sherbourne, Dorset DT9 4QO
tel: 01935 432857
(Italian provisions and River Cafe olive oil)

East Sussex
Beckworth's Deli
67 High St
Lewes, E. Sussex BN7 1XG
tel: 01273 474502
(Italian provisions)

Seasons Forest Row Ltd
10 Hartfield Rd
Forest Row RH19 5DN
tel: 01342 824673
(Organic fruit and vegetables)

Edinburgh
Valvona & Crolla Ltd
19 Elm Row
Edinburgh EH7 4AA
tel: 0131 556 6066
www.valvonacrolla.co.uk (mail order)
(Italian provisions and vegetables – sea kale, asparagus, cavolo nero, tomatoes – and Scottish organic vegetables, River Cafe olive oil, Italian dry produce)

Glasgow
Mise-en-Place
122 Nithsdale Rd
Glasgow G11 5RB
tel: 0141 424 4600
(Italian provisions)

Peckhams
Clarence Drive
Glasgow G12
tel: 0141 334 2345
(Organic vegetables)

Roots & Fruits
Great Western Rd
Glasgow
tel: 0141 334 3530
(Seasonal fruit and vegetables)

Gloucestershire
The Fine Cheese Company (Cheltenham) Ltd
5 Regent St
Cheltenham GL50 1HE
tel: 01242 255022
(Italian provisions)

Greater Manchester
Chorlton Wholefoods
34 Beech Rd
Chorlton-Cum-Hardy M21 1EL
tel: 0161 881 6399
(Organic fruit and vegetables)

Herefordshire
Ceci Paolo Delicatessen & Caffe Bar
21 High Street, Ledbury, Herefordshire HR8 1DS
Tel: 01531 632 976 (e-mail:
patriciaharrison@compuserve.com)
(Italian provisions)

Hay Wholefoods & Deli
Lion St, Hay-on-Wye, Herefordshire HR3 5AA
tel: 01497 820708
(Organic vegetables and provisions)

Lancashire
Ramsbottom Victuallers
16–18 Market Place, Ramsbottom
tel: 01706 825070
(Buy once a week from Milan markets. Seasonal
vegetables, Italian olive oil, Parmesan, peppers,
fennel etc)

Leeds
Beano Wholefoods Workers Co-op
36 New Briggate, Leeds LS1 6NV
tel: 0113 2435737
www.beanowholefoods.co.uk
(Some Italian vegetables and seasonal English
broad beans and squashes)

Harvey Nichols Food Market
107–111 Briggate, Victoria Quarter
Leeds LS1 6AZ
tel: 0113 2048888
(Specialist vegetables, olive oil and provisions)

Liverpool
No 7 Delicatessen
15 Faulkner St, Liverpool 8
tel: 0151 709 9633
(Italian provisions)

Manchester
Atlas Delicatessen
345 Deansgate, Manchester M3
tel: 0161 834 2266
(Italian provisions)

Selfridges & Co. Food Hall
1 The Dome
The Trafford Centre
Manchester M17 8DA
tel: 0161 629 1234
(Specialist vegetables and provisions)

Norfolk
Patrick Kemp
Evergreen Farm, Church Lane
Gressenhall NR19 2QH

tel: 01362 860190
(Small organic grower of vegetables and fruit,
e.g. artichokes, redcurrants, Ratte potatoes,
baby broad beans)

North Yorkshire
Arcimboldos
146 Kings Rd
Harrogate, N. Yorkshire HG1 5HY
tel: 01423 508760
(Italian provisions)

M. Snowden
Wharfdale Grange. Harewood LS17 9LW
tel: 0113 2886320
(Pick your own vegetables, chicories and rocket)

Northern Ireland
John McCormick
Box scheme
Holywood, Co. Down
tel: 01232 423063
mobile: 028 90423063

Oxford
Fasta Pasta
121 The Covered Market, Oxford OX 3DZ
tel: 01865 241973
(Italian provisions. Organic bread and pasta)

Shrewsbury
Appleyards Deli
85 Wyle Cop, Shrewsbury SY1 1VT
tel: 01743 240180
(Italian provisions)

Southampton
Sunnyfields Organic Farm
Jacobs Gutter Lane
Totton, Southampton SO40 9FX
tel: 0118 9842392
(Organic farm with farm shop. Onion squash,
cavolo nero, zucchini, chard and other specialist
Italian vegetables)

Suffolk
Adnams
The Kitchen Store, Victoria St
Southwold IP18 6JW
tel: 01502 727222
(Italian provisions)

Tayside
Eassie Farm
By Glamis, Tayside DD8 1SG
Contact: Sandy Paltullo
tel: 01307 840303
(Sea kale and asparagus in season only – mail
order)

Yorkshire
Heber Wines
34 Swadford Street
Skipton, N. Yorkshire BD23 1RD
tel: 01756 795815
(River Cafe olive oil)

Ireland

Dublin
Denis Healy
Templebar Market
Saturday 9.30–5.30
mobile: 00353 87 2485826
(Unusual vegetables, fennel, rocket etc)

Guy Stuart
Food stall in George Arcade
(6 days a week)
mobile: 00353 87 2219954
(Some organic vegetables and fruit, dried
chickpeas)

Co. Leitrim
The Organic Centre
Rossinver
Co. Leitrim
(Box scheme)
tel: 00353 72 54338

Galway
The Saturday Market
Galway

Directories

Farmers' markets

National Association of Farmers' Markets
South Vault, Green Park Station
Green Park, Bath BA1 1JB
(For list of national farmers' markets, send SAE.
Many new farmers' markets are starting up all
over the UK)

The Soil Association
Bristol House
40 – 56 Victoria House
Bristol BS1 6BY
tel: 0117 929 0661
e-mail: info@soilassociation.org
(List of organic farmers' markets)

Just Organic
tel: 020 7704 2566

Organics Direct
(Box scheme)
www.organicsdirect.com

For information on organic retail outlets, box
schemes, pick your own farms and gate sales,
see *The Organic Directory – Your Guide to Buying
Organic Food*, ed. Clive Litchfield, Green Earth
Books 1996. tel: 020 7729 2828

Seed producers

Bavicchi
Via della Valtiera 293
06087 Ponte San Giovanni
tel: 0039 075 599243
e-mail: info@bavicchi.it
www.bavicchi.it

Ferme de Sainte Marthe
PO Box 358
Walton, Surrey KT12 4YX
tel: 01932 266630
e-mail: chaseorg@aol.com
(Rare vegetable varieties)

The Organic Gardening Catalogue
River Dene Estate, Molesey Road
Hersham, Surrey KT12 4RG
tel: 01932 253666

Seeds of Italy (Franchi Seeds)
260 West Hendon Broadway
London NW9 6BE
tel/fax: 020 8930 2516
e-mail: italseeds@tesco.net
(Italian herb, organic and flower seed price list
tel/fax: 020 89302516 mail order
www.seedsofitaly.sageweb.co.uk)

Suffolk Herbs – Organic Seed Catalogue
Monks Farm
Coggeshall Rd
Kelvedon, Essex CO5 9PG
tel: 01376 572456
fax: 01376 571189

Notes on ingredients

Organic Free-range Eggs Buy eggs laid by free-range chickens that have been fed organically, on a diet of vegetables and grass, and have a dated laying stamp, which ensures that they are fresh.

Extra Virgin Olive Oil It is now possible to buy extra virgin olive oil that comes from a named estate and shows the date of the year that it was pressed. Tuscan oil is famous for its dense green colour and spiciness; Ligurian oil for its softer, fruitier flavours; Puglian and Sicilian oils have a more pronounced olive flavour and a richer, nutty taste as the trees have grown in a warmer climate.

Extra virgin olive oil changes, in the bottle, throughout the year. In November to January, when it has first been pressed, there is definitely a strong peppery taste. As the oil ages, this becomes softer.

Farro Farro, known as 'spelt' in English, is a type of hard wheat grown in Tuscany and Umbria and used in the distinctive soups of those regions. It should be soaked for 1-2 hours before cooking, although if you buy it where it is grown it may not require soaking at all.

To serve 6, soak 150 g farro in cold water for 1-2 hours. Drain it, then put into a medium saucepan and cover with fresh cold water. Bring to the boil, then cover and simmer until the farro expands and is al dente, about 20 minutes. Season with Maldon salt and freshly ground black pepper.

Lemons Lemons sold with some of their stalk and leaves attached are usually the freshest and the leaves are a good indication of freshness – they should be glossy and green. Choose thick-skinned, firm lemons that have a strong perfume and oily zest. It is particularly important to buy organic lemons as non-organic ones have usually been treated or coated with wax.

Pecorino Staginata A small hard cheese made with sheeps' milk, this has a grainy texture with a flavour of grass and should be aged for at least six months. It comes from Tuscany, where it is made by Sardinians. It is often used to grate on pastas as an alternative to Parmesan.

Ricotta Salata This is a dry, salty cows' and sheeps' milk cheese, made in Puglia, Sardinia and Sicily. White in colour, it has no rind and its condensed hard texture makes it easy to grate.

Robiola Cheese This is a soft fresh mixed cows', goats' and sheeps' milk cheese from Piedmont. It is very rich and creamy but with a sharp tangy flavour.

Salted Anchovies Whole anchovies, which have been preserved in salt in large tins or barrels then sold by the gram, should be used immediately. Once removed from the tin they will begin to oxidise and the flavour will be spoilt. The best fish are the largest, and they should be red in colour (rather than brown), stiff and not at all wet. Tinned anchovies in oil are no substitute.

To prepare, rinse the whole anchovies under a slow-running cold tap to wash off residual salt. Carefully pull the two fillets off the central spine of each fish and discard the heads. Pat dry and use immediately – or cover with lemon juice and extra virgin olive oil.

Salted Capers We always use capers preserved in salt. The small ones have the best flavour.

To prepare, rinse the capers in a sieve under a running cold tap for at least one minute. Taste to check if they are still salty. Leave to soak in a bowl of cold water for half an hour. Rinse again and use immediately, or cover with red wine vinegar.

Salt Cod Choose fillets cut from a very fresh whole cod.

To salt 1 kg fresh cod fillet, you will need about 1 kg natural coarse sea salt. Place a flat board on a slant (with a saucer underneath one end) inside a tray. Cover the board with a layer of salt about 1 cm deep. Place the fish on this, skin side down. Cover the other side of the fish with about 1 cm salt. Put in the fridge for from 24 hours to 5 days. Remove the salt by rinsing the fish under a running cold tap for 5 minutes. Then place in a bath of water for 6 hours, changing the water as frequently as possible. Dry and use as instructed in individual recipes.

Tinned Italian Plum Tomatoes Peeled plum tomatoes vary enormously in quality. The best are those that have been picked when ripe and preserved in their own natural clear juice. Try to avoid tomatoes tinned in thick tomato pulp and choose organic ones wherever possible.

Index

The authors would like to thank: Design **David Eldridge** Editorial **Denise Bates**
Lucy Boyd Gary Evans Susan Fleming Stefan Marling Andrew Marr Laraine
Mestman Rosalba Napolitano Chefs **Peter Begg April Bloomfield Ben Hayes**
Perry Hill Yolanda van der Jagt Ben O'Donoghue Tommy Parsons Arthur
Potts–Dawson Theo Randall Amy Rosenblatt John Simeoni Alex Tidy
Garry Wilson Suppliers **Adrian Barran Renzo Bentsik Andreas Georghiou**
Patricia Michelson Ian Nelson Rushton Scranage Additional Photography
Caroline Gavazzi Max Jourdan Sandra Lousada Martyn Thompson and **Ossie**
Gray and all the staff of the River Cafe David Macilwaine and **Richard Rogers**

This edition published for The Book People, Hall Wood Avenue, Haydock, St Helens WA11 9UR
First published in 2000 1 3 5 7 9 10 8 6 4 2 Text copyright © Rose Gray and Ruth Rogers 2000
Photography copyright © Martin Gray 2000 All rights reserved. No part of this publication may be reproduced,
stored in a retrieval system, or transmitted in any form or by any means, electronic, mechanical,
photocopying, recording or otherwise without the prior permission of the copyright owners. Rose Gray and
Ruth Rogers have asserted their right to be identified as the authors of this work. First published in the
United Kingdom by Ebury Press, Random House, 20 Vauxhall Bridge Road, London SW1V 2SA Random House
Australia (Pty) Limited 20 Alfred Street, Milsons Point, Sydney, New South Wales 2061,
Australia Random House New Zealand Limited 18 Poland Road, Glenfield, Auckland 10, New Zealand Random
House South Africa (Pty) Limited Endulini, 5A Jubilee Road, Parktown 2193, South Africa The Random House
Group Limited Reg. No. 954009 www.randomhouse.co.uk A CIP catalogue record for this book is available
from the British Library. ISBN 0 09 186543 3 Printed in Germany by Appl, Wemding.